NĀ PULE KĀHIKO
Ancient Hawaiian Prayers

NĀ PULE KĀHIKO

Ancient Hawaiian Prayers

June Gutmanis

Drawings by Susanne Indich

An Editions Limited Book

Cover: From an etching of a kahuna by Jacques
Grasset de Saint Sauveur, Encyclopedie des
Voyages, Paris, 1796. Courtesy University of
Hawaii, Hawaiian Collection.

Half title: From a lost drawing of a priest's
house by Captain Cook's surgeon William Ellis,
1779. Courtesy Bishop Museum.

Library of Congress Number 83-082056

ISBN 0-9607938-6-0 (softcover)
ISBN 0-9607938-7-9 (special edition)

4th Printing

Published by Editions Limited
P.O. Box 10150
Honolulu, Hawaii 96816
EditionsLimited@hawaii.rr.com

Typesetting and layout by Jean Dodge

Cover design by David Rick

Printed in Hong Kong

PAPA KUHIKUHI
Table of Contents

'OLELO MUA
Preface

Hawaiian was an oral language when discovered by Westerners. From Captain Cook's coming upon these islands in 1778 until the arrival of the American Protestant missionaries in 1820, the language had not been transposed into orthography, hence one will find Hawaiian place and people names spelled in many, diverse ways. British explorers spelled the names of ports and valleys differently from French navigators who heard and spelled them differently again from American traders and merchantmen.

Orthography of the Hawaiian language was introduced in 1822 when the American missionaries set up the first printing press in Honolulu: on the first Monday of January that year, the first sheet of printed Hawaiian was struck off. The orthography established by the missionaries has stood the test of time —what they put down in 1822 basically has remained unchanged for over 160 years.

The Hawaiian language, once set to type, appeared to be standardized, even though the missionaries were not in total agreement on some aspects. For example, arguments arose whether to accept "r" for "l," "v" for "w," and "k" for "t." They heard and were aware of one sound in particular that had to be resolved; this was the glottal stop, which was used, but not consistently. In the Bible (*Baibala Hemolele*) glottal stops were used in the possessive case, singular number only. The missionaries also used the apostrophe to indicate a dropped letter. The practice of using both glottal stops and apostrophes can be seen in *Na Pule Kahiko*.

It is to Dr. Samuel H. Elbert that we turn today, as scholars, for help in reading, writing, speaking and understanding the Hawaiian language, for guidance in the use of diacritics, the glottal stop and the macron.

When one has access to printed Hawaiian documents, pamphlets, books and newspapers from 1822 through to the middle of this century, one notices that the diacritics were absent or used in a way inconsistent with usage recommended in the *Hawaiian Dictionary* by Mary Pukui and Samuel Elbert, University of Hawaii Press, Honolulu 1971. This is not to say that early writers were wrong. Rather, it behooves the scholar to read and research the meaning of the language at the time and in the context in which it was written, for a wealth of information is to be found there. It is through the unadulterated texts that the scholar will widen his knowledge of this seemingly simple language. Here he will discover a complex, intricate language of a people who willingly shared with non-Hawaiians their most personal prayers for their deepest desire to survive, thereby guaranteeing a continuum from their earliest ancestors on to their descendants.

The chants and prayers in this work have been untouched except for Theodore Kelsey's interpretations and translations. The compiler has not interfered by imposing diacritics. Preservation of the language as it appeared in its original form, in its first printing, is essential, for in this manner we acknowledge the value of the authors' perception of the language they encountered. Presenting the language in this form, making it available to the entire community, will greatly enhance our understanding of it and will contribute to a deeper communication with Hawaii's human and profound past.

Esther T. Mookini

HA'AWI'AI
Presentation

Praying seems to be an almost universal impulse of man. The methods, times, postures, and gods prayed to may vary, but the favors sought, whether with a demanding shout or a plaintive whimper, are nearly universal. This book contains a portion of the daily dialogue between the ancient gods of Hawai'i and the people who, past and present, worship those gods.

The prayers in this book follow the traditions that existed before the overthrow of the ancient *kapu* system. That system prescribed the rituals, prayers, obligations, restrictions, rights, privileges, power, and marks of respect for both the gods and man. The "overthrow" of the *kapu* was in October 1819, five months after the death of Kamehameha I, and six months before the arrival of the first Christian missionaries to Hawai'i. After the overthrow, which some consider to have been more political than religious, many Hawaiians continued to worship their ancient gods. They only slowly and reluctantly gave up what they considered to be family ties as they converted to Christianity. However, in some families, most frequently those of hula dancers, chanters, and medicinal practitioners. fragments of the old worship, rituals, and *kapu* continued to be part of their lives.

As overall changes in life styles, laws, and personal values took place, some of the old prayers such as those accompanying human sacrifice ceased to be used. Many other prayers were adapted to meet changing technology and modern patterns of living. Throughout this book, the grammatical tenses in the text reflect which prayers are no longer in use and which prayers are still used either as part of personal religious practices or for public ceremonial purposes.

The prayers presented in this book have been collected from many sources. The Hawaiian orthography, translations and family names are those found in the original source,

resulting in a variety of spellings and markings. It should be noted that Theodore Kelsy, who collected a number of these *pule*, and translated several others, normally uses the conventional macron, breve, accent, and glottal as well as a marking he calls a glide or *olali*. The exigencies of publishing have dictated that, of these markings, only the glottal will be used. The reader should also note that while the ancient Hawaiian culture was relatively homogeneous, there were and are many variations in the uses and meanings of individual words. These variations are reflected in the language of this collection. Also reflected in these prayers are regional, family, and what might be called denominational differences in the roles assigned the various gods and the manner of worshipping them. The translations also frequently reflect the personalities, beliefs, and prejudices of the translators as well as ongoing changes in the English language.

Throughout, for lack of a better term, the word *akua* is generally translated as god. However, it should be kept in mind that the Polynesian concept of god does not parallel that of the all-powerful, all-present divinity of Western religion. The Polynesian gods are the personal ancestors of the people who, with the passage of time, acquired so much *mana* that they could do supernatural works; the gods are called upon as family members.

Finally, the author would like to point out that this book is not intended to be an academic dissertation wherein the gods of Hawai'i, their origins, their histories, or their roles in religion and society are endlessly analysed, or compared with those of other religions, or speculated upon. Nor is it a catechism of the ancient religion with a listing of approved beliefs. It is a prayer book with appropriate expositions in each section. For those who choose to seek, there are other prayers that, like other knowledge, may be found in other *halau*.

Waianae, Hawaii
June 1983

June Gutmanis

Mai ho‘ohalahala ia kakou. E a‘o ia kakou ka mea kupono e ho‘ohuhu ‘ole ai makou.

Do not criticize us. Teach us what is proper that we may not offend.

Anonymous Hawaiian saying

I NĀ PULE
The Prayers

The exchange between man and his gods, called prayer, is an ancient acknowledgment by man of his relationship to the gods. Prayer may be a spontaneous outpouring of love, fear, or need, expressed wherever man may be. Or prayer may be highly formal with strictly prescribed rituals.

For the worshipers of the gods of old Hawaii who see manifestations of the gods wherever they look, prayer may be as frequent as conversations between close friends. Overwhelming in number, the gods are not kept at a distance by their perfection, but are direct ancestors of the chiefs who in their turn are the progenitors of the *maka'ainana*, or common people. The power of the gods comes from generations of accumulated *mana*.[1]

The potency of the prayers offered to these gods comes not only from the reminders of family ties but can also come from the sincerity of the person praying, from the power inherent in the words used, and from the *mana* the prayers have acquired through repeated and successful use. It can also come from the skill of the one who is offering the prayer.

Generally not propitiated, the gods of Hawaii are approached with just requests for help as members of a family. They may be ordered, bargained with, or threatened. If a particular god does not produce the desired results, the dissatisfied supplicant can denounce the failure, scold the unresponsive god, and seek help elsewhere.[2]

The following prayer, handed down from generation to generation in the family of the late David Malo Kupihea, illustrates the relationship between the gods and man.

O na Kumuakua apau i hanauia i ka Po i ka
    Lahiki ku;
Ea mai ke kai mai!
O na Kumualii apau i hanauia I ka Po i ka
    Lahiki ku.
Ea mai ke kai mai!
O na Lala alii apau i hanauia i ka Po i ka
    Lahiki ku.
Ea mai ke kai mai.
O na Welaualii apau i hanauia i ka Po i ka
    Lahiki ku.
Ea mai ke kai mai!
O na Pua alii apau, eku eola
A kau a kanikoo pala lau hala
Liau makaiole Kolopupu

Oh original gods born in remote antiquity where
    the sun rises,
Rise up out of the sea!
Oh original chiefs, born in remote antiquity in the
    sunrise,
Arise from the sea!
Oh relatives of all the chiefs born in remote antiquity in
    the sunrise,
Arise from the sea!
Oh distant kin of all the chiefs born in remote
    antiquity where the sun rises.
Arise from the sea!
Oh descendants of the chiefs
Stand up and live! Live to remote old age!
Stand until the support of a cane is needed![3]

NOTES:

1. *Mana* is a spiritual force that at times shows physical manifestations. It can be acquired as a gift of the gods, through ritual, prayer, the force of words, or through inheritance.
2. "A god had to get results to keep his worshipers satisfied, or they publicly and ceremoniously cast him off and adopted a new god, perhaps one of proved merit who was advancing the destinies of a neighboring island." (Luomala 1949, p. 140) This Polynesian tendency to reject gods who are inattentive or who have become weak may have accounted for the overthrow of the *kapu* and the ready acceptance of Christianity by many Hawaiians in the early 19th century.
3. Taylor, November 18, 1947.

II NĀ AKUA
The Gods

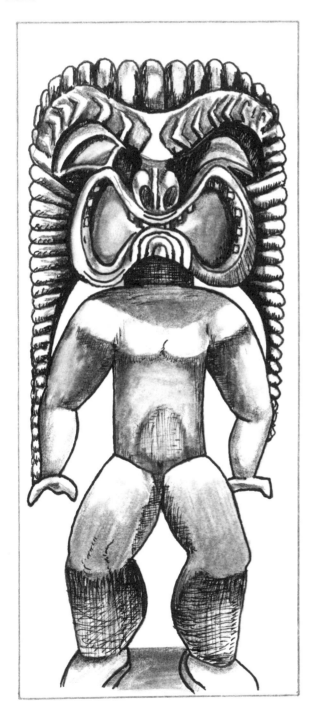

Many are the gods of Hawaii. So numerous are they that in ancient times they were called *na pu'a ali'i 'uhane* or "the chiefly flock of spirits." These gods are to be found not only in the heavens but also in the plants, birds, fish, rocks, and everything of nature, a god for every need of man. And like their descendants, man, this host of gods has a hierarchy of importance, some gods outranking others.

KA 'EKAHI, 'IO: THE ONE, 'IO

For some who worship the gods of Hawaii there is the one, the one above all others, the one from whom all others issue forth. For these, as with their Polynesian cousins, that one is 'Io—'Io, whose name is too sacred to speak in the open and is used only in silent prayer. For some this great name may be invoked only by certain chiefly and *kahuna* families. Some say 'Io and Uli are synonymous. Others do not believe in the importance of 'Io.

The following prayer to 'Io descended from the *kahuna* Ka-haku'i-ka-wai-ea to his daughter, Mary Jane Fayerweather Montano, and then to his granddaughter, Mrs. Emma Ahuena Taylor. It is a prayer for healing.

A'ai manu i none	Gnawing bird lazily poised
O ka pueo kani mai ana	'Tis the owl crying nearby
O kona luakini	From his sacrificial pit
Ina e ke kamali'i	Here is the boy-child (stricken)
Hiki lele na ohana e	Suddenly agitated are the relatives,
E ko, e ko, e ke kia	Let it come to pass, let (the sorcerer) be done to death
Pau, e Lono e, ua ola e.	Finished, oh Lono (god of healing) he lives![4]

KA HA: THE FOUR

Throughout Hawaii there are The Four: Ku, Kane, Kanaloa, and Lono. These are the *akua* to whom prayers are directed "from the place of the sun's rising to its resting place, from the north to the south, and from the highest heaven to the foundation of the earth below."[5] One by one these great gods came to Hawaii after moving through Polynesia where they had established traditions that are as familiar in those islands as they came to be in the Hawaiian Islands.

Ku

Ku, the first of the great gods, arrived in Hawaii with eyes bulging and tongue protruding, announced by the violence of nature. While the earth convulsed and shuddered, quake followed quake and violent whirlwinds tore across the ocean, whipping it into a frenzy. Along the shores of the islands of Hawaii trees were uprooted and plants flattened. Driving rains tore rocks from the mountainsides, sending them rushing down streams swollen to rivers.

Landing on the debris-strewn beach at Ku-moku, Lanai, Ku in his many forms established himself as the protector of all Hawaii, its various island kingdoms, and individual families.[6]

As protector of the individual kingdoms, Ku was also the war god of the ruling chiefs. In this role he was worshiped as Ku-nui-akea (Ku-the-supreme-one), Ku-ka-'ili-moku (Ku-snatcher-of-land), Ku-ke-olo'ewa (Ku-the-supporter), Ku-ho'one (Ku-pulling-together-the-earth), and Ku-ka-lani-'ehu-iki (Ku-the-heavens-sent-spray). In time Ku as the war god also became god of sorcery, known as Ku-waha-ilo (Ku-of-the-maggot-mouth), more fully known as Ku-waha-ilo-o-ka-puni.

As guardian of the welfare of both the nation and the individual family, Ku is intimately associated with farming. He is not only associated with the coconut and breadfruit but also worshiped as Ku-kulia (Ku-of-dry-farming) and Ku-keolowalu (Ku-of-wet-farming), as well as Ku-ka-'o 'o (Ku-of-the-digging-stick). He is also one of the gods of fishing and as such is known as Ku-'ula (Red-Ku) or Ku-'ula-kai (Ku-of-the-abundance-of-the-sea). Other forms of Ku are special to canoe makers, feather gatherers, medical practitioners, hula teachers, and others whose work takes them to the upper forests.

The following is one of the many prayers to Ku.

E Ku i ka lana mai nuu!	O god Ku, of the sacred altar!
E Ku i ka ohia lele!	O Ku of the scaffolding of *ohia* timber!
E Ku i ka ohia-lehua!	O Ku carved of the *ohia-lehua!*
E Ku i ka ohia-ha uli!	O Ku of the flourishing *ohia-ha!*
E Ku i ka ohia moewai!	O Ku of the water-seasoned *ohia* timber!
E Ku mai ka lani!	O Ku, come down from heaven!
Ku i ke ao!	O Ku, god of light!
E Ku i ka honua!	O Ku, ruler of the world!
E ka ohia ihi!	O magnificent *ohia* tree!
E Ku i ka lani-ka-ohia, ka haku-ohia!	O Ku of the *ohia* tree carved by a king, lord of *ohia* gods!
A ku, a lele, ua noa.	It lifts, it flies, it is gone.
A noa ia Ku.	The tabu is removed by Ku.

Ua uhi kapa mahana,	Robed are we in warm tapa,
Hoomahanahana heiau.	A warmth that relaxes the rigors of the *heiau.*
E noa! e noa!	Freedom! Freedom!
Amama wale! Ua noa!	The load is lifted! There is freedom![7]

Kane and Kanaloa

With the vigor and lustiness of young adventurers, Kane and Kanaloa came to Hawaii traveling on the surface of the ocean from Kahiki. Landing at Ke'ei, Maui, the pair flung themselves into the joys of exploring new lands and wherever they went they celebrated the pleasures of life with *'awa.* As they wandered around the islands they left behind them many springs which were brought into being when Kane struck an outcropping of rocks with his *kauila* staff. The water which gushed forth was used for mixing with the *'awa* which they carried with them. Before moving on they planted *'awa* around these new springs.

Although constant companions in their many adventures, Kane's name generally precedes that of Kanaloa in the stories about them as well as in the prayers to them.

In time, Kane became the patron of fresh water and Kanaloa of the ocean, especially the deep ocean. Both are associated with canoes; Kane as builder and Kanaloa as sailor. Kane as Kane-koa is associated with the increase of the *'o'opu* fish in streams while Kanaloa is the *'aumakua*[8] of the squid and octopus. To some extent both are also associated with medicine.

The east is spoken of as the "high road traveled by Kane" or the "red road of Kane." The west is called the "much traveled road of Kanaloa." The route of the northern limit of the sun is called the "glistening black road of Kane" and the southern limit of the celestial ecliptic is the "road of Kanaloa."[9]

Individually, Kane is associated with sunlight, bamboo, taro, sugarcane, *wauke, popolo,* and coral; Kanaloa is associated with the ocean winds and bananas. Both are associated with red roosters and black pigs. Kane, the fair one, has at least seventy aspects, epithets, or forms associated with him. In Hawaii, Kanaloa has no such known forms.[10]

This prayer to Kane-i-ka-wai (Kane-of-the-water) is a prayer used when making *'awa.*

Ka wai laahia, e Kane-i-ka-wai.	The sacred water, o Kane-of-the-water.
Ka wai la ia, e Kane.	It is the water of Kane.
Ka wai i ka hikina, e Kane.	The water in the east, o Kane.
Nou Ka Wai Koo-lihilihi.	Yours is the water that supports the petals,
Ka wai i ka olo la hua'ina.	The water in the long gourd gushing forth.
Kulia o lau mahu'e luna, o lau meha.	Position of leaves wide open above, lone leaves.
O na meha huli honua.	Lone leaves that face the earth.
Hoouka kai hoe, e Kane,	Put your paddle inside, o Kane,
A holo, e Kane, a kele, e Kane,	And go, o Kane, and sail away, o Kane,
He kaua ka lua kaala hoku,	A war is the pit for sling stone stars,
A hopu i ke aka, i ke aka o Kane.	And hold the reflection, the reflection of Kane.
A, kolo, i kolo a'e, kolo anuenue,	And move gently along, move the rainbow,
E ukuhi i ka wai	Pour out the water
Pakahi ka lau na'ena'e, ka lau 'ala o ka nahele.	One by one the leaves, the fragrant leaves of the woodland.
Kihikihi oo ia	Projecting at angles
Keekeehi iho no oe i ka hikina.	Tread firmly to the east.
Owai ia alii o ka hikina?	Who is the chief of the east?
O Kane alii oe la, o no Uli,	You are chief Kane, of the Uli line.
'Au'au i ka wai poni-hiwa, e Kane,	Bathe in the dark waters of Kane
He aka-ku kau i ka manawa,	A vision placed on the top of the head,
Ku mai a'e la ipu hele, e Kane	Caused the traveling gourd to land, o Kane
Ina ke oho o Mano ka hele ana, e Kane,	Here the hair of Mano is going, o Kane,

5

I ke ala kapua'i akua, kapau'i no Hina.

In the way of the footprint of deity, footprint of Hina.

Eia ka pule, eia ke kanaenae nou, e Kane ke akua.

Here is the prayer, here is the chant of eulogy for you, O Kane the deity.[11]

This prayer to Kanaloa is one used in treating a sick person. After putting the patient to bed without medicine, the treating *kahuna* recites the following over the sick person:

E Kanaloa, ke akua ka hee!
Eia kau mai o (inoa).
E ka hee o kai uli,
Ka hee o ka lua one,
Ka hee i ka papa,
Ka hee pio!
Eia ka oukou mai, o (inoa)
He mai hoomoe ia no ka hee palaha.

O Kanaloa, god of the squid!
Here is your patient, (name)
O squid of the deep blue sea,
Squid that inhabits the coral reef,
Squid that burrows in the sand,
Squid that squirts water from its sack!
Here is a sick man for you to heal, (name)
A patient put to bed for treatment by the squid that lies flat.

Towards morning a fisherman is sent out to catch a *hee mahola,* that is, an octopus which is lying on the sand, outside of its hole, with its legs extended on the ocean floor. While letting down his hook and lure the fisherman prays as follows:

Eia ka leho,
He leho ula no ka hee-hoopai.
Eia ka kao, he laau,
He lama no ka hee-mahola, no ka hee-palaha.
E Kanaloa i ke Ku,
Kulia ke papa,
Kulia i ka papa hee!
Kulia ka hee o kai uli!
E ala, e Kanaloa!
Hoeu! hoala! e ala ka hee!
E ala ka hee-palaha! E ala ka hee-mahola!

Here is the cowry,
A red cowry to attract the squid to his death.
Here is the spear, a mere stick,
A spear of *lama* wood for the squid that lies flat.
O Kanaloa of the tabu nights,
Stand upright on the solid floor!
Stand upon the floor where lies the squid!
Stand up to take the squid of the deep sea!
Rise up, O Kanaloa!
Stir up! agitate! let the squid awake!
Let the squid that lies flat awake, the squid that lies spread out.[12]

Lono

Lono, the messenger, with restless eyes and many formed cloud-bodies, came to Hawaii with the rushing of heavenly sound as a voice coming over the water.[13] Landing first on Maui, he brought with him the techniques of the farmer and became patron of the fertility of the land. As such he was represented in the men's eating house of each family by a gourd covered with wickerwork and hung by strings attached to a notched stick. Food, fish, and 'awa were kept inside the gourd.[14]

As the patron of agriculture, Lono is closely associated with sweet potatoes, pigs, gourds, rain clouds, and heavy rain. As Lono-puha, he is also the major patron of the *kahuna la'au lapa'au* or herbal doctor. In this form he is associated with many medical plants.

The following is a prayer to Lono said when offering food.

E Loni-i-ka-po,
E Lono-i-ke-ao.
E Lono-i-ke-ka'ina o mua
E Lono-nui-a-Hina
Mai 'aniha mai 'oe iau, e Lono.

O Lono in the night,
O Lono in the day.
O Lono of the leading forward
O great Lono given birth by Hina
Do not be unfriendly to me, o Lono.

6

E Lono maka hialele,
A lele 'oe i ke kai uli,
A lele 'oe i ke kai kea,[15]
I one huli la, i one 'ele,
I mahinahina,
I ke one i hanana
O pipipi, o unauna,
O 'alealea, o naka,
O hee, o kualakai,
O ka pakii moe one 'ula;
O ka 'ulac niho wakawaka 'oi;
O kama a 'opihi kau-pali
O kulele poo; o helele'i ke oho
O Waha-lau-alii; o Poli-hala;
O kahi i waiho ai o ka hua 'olelo
O Pii-ma-lana o 'Oheke;
O kama a Poepoe;
O ka wahine i ka ipu 'olelo;
E kama e i ke-ola nui;
Eia ka 'ai,
E Ku, e Lono, e Kane.
E Lono i ke ao uli e,
Eia ka 'ai.

O Lono of the restless sleepless eyes,
You fly to the dark sea,
You fly to the white sea,[15]
To the sand that seeks the sun, to the black sand
In the pale moonlight,
At the sand that was overflowed
Of small mollusks, hermit crabs,
Of *'alealea* shellfish, of *naka* fish,
Of octopus, of sea slug,
Of the *pakii* flounder that lies on red sand;
Of the lizard fish with serrated sharp teeth;
Of offspring of the limpet that rests on the cliffs
Of head that scatters, of scattered hair
Of Waha-lau-alii, of Poli-hala;
Of the place that the word is left
Of Pii-ma-lana, together with 'Oheke;
Of offspring by Poepoe;
Of the woman of the voice gourd;
O offspring of the great life;
Here is the food
O Ku, o Lono, o Kane.
O Lono in the firmament,
Here is the food.[16]

KE KANAHA: THE FORTY

For those who know the esoteric, the forty are male gods or aspects or forms of Kane. According to some traditions, the four major gods each have ten of these aspects associated with them.

The following prayer is one that may be said before the beginning of a *hula* performance. It lists some of the forms of Kane. It is uncertain if those forms referred to as "The Forty" are among those recited in this prayer.

E Kane Kanaloa!
E Kane-kauila-nui-makeha-i-ka-lani,
E Kane-i-ka-wawahi-lani,
E Kane-i-ke-poha(ku)-ka'a,
E Kane-i-ka-puahiohio,
E Kane-i-ke-anuenue,
E Kane-i-ke-pili,
E Kane-i-ka-ua,
E Kane-i-ke-ao-lani,
E Kane-i-ka-maka-o-ka-opua,
E Kane-i-ka-maka-o-ka-ao-lani,
E Kane-i-ke-ao-luna,
E Kane-i-ke-ao-lewa-lalo,
E Kane-i-ke-ao-pali-luna,
E Kane-i-ke-ao-pali-lalo,
E Kane-i-ka-hoku-lani,
E Kani-i-ke-ao,
E Kane-i-ka-opua,
E Kane-i-ka-punohu-ula,
E Kane-i-ka-makani-nui,
E Kane-i-ka-makani-iki,

O Kane-Kanaloa!
O Kane-of-the-great-lightning-flashes-in-the-heavens,
O Kane-the-render-of-heaven,
O Kane-the-rolling-stone,
O Kane-of-the-whirlwind,
O Kane-of-the-rainbow,
O Kane-of-the-atmosphere,
O Kane-of-the-rain,
O Kane-of-the-heavenly-cloud,
O Kane-standing-before-the-pointed-clouds,
O Kane-standing-before-the-heavenly-clouds,
O Kane-in-the-cloud-above,
O Kane-in-the-cloud-floating-low,
O Kane-in-the-cloud-resting-on-the-summit,
O Kane-in-the-cloud-over-the-low-hills,
O Kane-of-the-heavenly-star,
O Kane-of-the-dawn,
O Kane-of-the-clouds-on-the-horizon,
O Kane-of-the-red-rainbow,
O Kane-of-the-great-wind,
O Kane-of-the-little-wind,

E Kane-i-ke-aheahe-malie,	O Kane-of-the-zephyrs,
E Kane-i-ka-pa-kolonahe,	O Kane-of-the-peaceful-breeze,
E Kane-i-ka-pahu'a-nui,	O Kane-of-the-strong-thrust,
E Kane-i-ka-pahu-wai-nui,	O Kane-of-the-great-water-source,
E Kane-i-ka-pahu-wai-iki,	O Kane-of-the-little-water-source,
E Kane-i-ka-holoholo-uka,	O Kane-traveling-mountainward,
E Kane-i-ka-holoholo-kai,	O Kane-traveling-seaward,
E Kane-noho-uka,	O Kane-dwelling-in-the-mountain,
E Kane-noho-kai,	O Kane-dwelling-by-the-sea,
E Kane-noho-pali-luna,	O Kane-dwelling-by-the-upper-precipice,
E Kane-noho-pali-lalo,	O Kane-dwelling-by-the-lower-precipice,
E Kane-ha-lo-luna,	O Kane-gazing-upward,
E Kane-ha-lo-lalo,	O Kane-gazing-downward,
E Kane-ha-lo-lewa-luna,	O Kane-glancing-at-the-upper-spaces,
E Kane-ha-lo-lewa-lalo.	O Kane-glancing-at-the-lower-spaces,
Kane-moe,	Sleeping-Kane,
Kane-moe-awakea,	Kane-sleeping-in-the-great-light,
Kane-kokala,	Kane-of-the-coral,
Kane-kokala-loa,	Kane-of-the-long-coral,
Kane-kokala-lu-honua,	Kane-of-the-quaking-coral,
Kane-kokala-ku-honua,	Kane-of-the-steadfast-coral,
Kane-kokala-i-ke-kiu,	Kane-of-the-sharp-pointed-coral,
Kane-kokala-i-ke-ahe,	Kane-of-wafted-coral,
Kane-i-ka-holo-nui,	Kane-the-swift-runner,
Kane-i-ka-holo-iki,	Kane-the-slow-runner,
O Kane!	Kane!
O Kane! O Lono!	Kane! Lono!
E ola no au ia 'oukou a pau e o'u mau akua.	I will live through all of you my gods.[17]

KA LAU: THE FOUR HUNDRED

As the four great gods came to Hawaii one by one or in family groups, so did the lesser gods who are known as The Four Hundred. Many of them are now unknown, although once their names were common throughout the Hawaiian Islands.

Hina

Perhaps the first of these mighty, but lesser, gods to come to Hawaii was Hina. She was the traveling companion of Ku on his violent trip from Kahiki. In the ages that followed their landing in Hawaii, they became the special protectors of all the generations whose ancestors came from Kahiki.

As Ku is the expression of the male generative powers by which the race is made fertile, Hina is the expression of womanly fruitfulness with the powers of growth and reproduction. Paired in many activities, Ku and Hina are associated with the sun, which at its rising is referred to as *ku* and when "leaning down" at sunset is called *hina.* When gathering medicine, Hina is addressed while picking herbs with the left hand, and Ku is prayed to while picking with the right hand. Both are patrons of fishermen.

Hina is possibly the most widely known goddess or demi-goddess in all Polynesia. In Hawaii, besides her role as the mate of Ku, she became the woman-in-the-moon. In one form or another she is also known as the wife of Akalana and the mother of the adventurer Maui. In another aspect she is known as the mate of Kahiki-'ula and mother of Kama-pua'a. As the wife of Wakea she was the mother of the island of Molokai, which is celebrated in song as *Molokai Nui a Hina.* Some say that she and Wakea are also the parents of the island of Ka-ho'olawe, while others say she and Kanaloa

8

were the parents of that island.

The following prayer to Hina is one that is used by fishermen.

O Hina hoi, Hina ukiuki,
O Hina hoi, Hina we'awe'a,
O Hina waianoa, la'i e i ka polikua kane,
Kani ae la Hina ha'ihala,
He akua kona i ka Nonomea.
O Ka wai e auau ai Hinakua,
Kani holo Hina i ke alanui,
He kaua huna na Peapea,
A i ole i hiki ka maia o ka wai e,
E ka wai e auau ai Hina makua!
Iho mai Hina mai ka lani,
Kona alanui o ka anuenue,
Kulukulu ka ua, ka pakapaka,
Ke ala a Hina i pii ai,
Kaukini Hina i ka hele one,
Kani ae Hina i ke ahua,
He manini ka i'a e ai Hina,
Ua loaa e.

O Hina, Hina the tantalizer,
O Hina, Hina the procurer,
O Hina unrestrained resting on the husband's breast.
Hina proclaims the wrong doing
She has a god at Nonomea.
The water assigned Hinakua for bathing,
Hina revealed through the streets,
The secret delayed by Peapea,
Else the juice of the banana was the water,
The water that elder Hina bathed in!
Hina came down from heaven,
Her way was by the rainbow.
The rain sprinkled, heavy rain fell,
The way by which Hina ascended.
Hina noted for sand walking,
Hina proclaimed from a high place,
The manini as Hina's fish food,
Found indeed.

Kaumaha ia, kaumaha ia,
Ka papa i kai, ke koa panoa,
Ka halelo, ka hee ku kohola, ka pe'ape'a,
Ka aalaihi, ka palani,
Kaa i ka onini he i'a paoa nui,
Na Hina ia i'a.
Kai-na mai i uka,[18] unuhia mai i kaa walu
Ka i'a Hina makua kala
Ai Hina i ka i'a makamaka maikai
Au e Hina e! Na Hina ka hoi ua i'a.

Sacrifice, sacrifice,
The seaward flat, the bared coral rock,
The halelo, the squid of the reef, the pe'ape'a,
The aalaihi, the palani,
Hold the onini, the unlucky fish,
It is Hina's fish.
Pull[18] from shoreward, drive into the net,
The kala is elder Hina's fish.
Hina eats the good fresh fish
It is yours O Hina! For Hina indeed is the fish.

Kaumaha ia, kaumaha ia,
Ka papa i kai ka haku moana
Ka lua kupua ka wai lua ono,
Kahakai o Hina, makai na 'ku ana,
Nana ia 'ku o Palaiuli, o Palaikea.
O Hina malailena, o Hina ai kanaka,
O ka Hina ia nona ka i'a,
Hanaua[19] mai he i'a e Hina e!
Na Hina ka hoi ua i'a.

Sacrifice, sacrifice,
The shore reef is the ocean guard;
The wizard's pit affords fresh (twin) water.
The beach of Hina beyond is guarding,
Watch for Palaiuli, for Palaikea.
O vengeful Hina, Hina the man-eater,
That is the Hina who owns the fish,
Give birth[19] to fish, O Hina!
It is Hina's own fish.

Kaumaha ia, kaumaha ia,
Hookelekele ana Hina i kana i'a;
Maunu i ka makaau o Hina makua kahi,
Pa i ka ilikai o Hina makua lua,
Ai mai ka i'a a ke kupua, o Hina makua kolu,
Ka'ika'ina iluna o Hina makua ha,
Hoouka i ka waa o Hina makua lima.
Kuukuu ka alae[20] na Hina,
Kuu aku i lalo i manawai,
I ka wai puna, i ka wai kahe,
I ka wai auau no Hina,

Sacrifice, sacrifice,
Hina boasts of her fish;
Bait the hook, O parent-Hina one,
Touch the surface of the sea, O parent-Hina two,
Bite the fish of the wizard, parent-Hina three,
Lift it above to parent-Hina four,
Put in the canoe of parent-Hina five,
The mudhen[20] came down for Hina,
Came down below to the water-source,
To the spring, to the flowing water,
To the bathing pool of Hina.

Hamo ana i ka ili, nana i ka ula	By rubbing the skin, producing redness
I ka maikai, hoopau Hina i ona kino,	To cleanliness, Hina absolved her several body forms,
Ua lele a manu, ua kau a lupe,	They flew as a bird, suspended like a kite,
Pau ma koaʻe, o Kane ka imua	Past the difficult places, Kane leading.
O Hina ka i ka hope	Hina followed at a distance
O Hakiololo ka i muli mai ou e Hina.	Hakiololo came behind you O Hina,
Kau ka lupe, kolo ka alae a Hina la.	As the kite rose the mudhen crawled to Hina.[21]

Haumea

The pleasure-seeking, *ʻawa*-drinking pair, Kane and Kanaloa, had a sister, Haumea, who was also the mate of Kanaloa. Her home was in Nuʻu-mea-lani and it is said that she "made" the first man as well as the all-important first sail mat.

A unique being, Haumea's children were not born naturally but from different parts of her body. Of her children, Pele is said to have been born from her thighs;[22] Halulu-i-ke-kihi-o-ka-moku, a bird god, from her shoulder; Na-maka-o-kahaʻi and all the Hiʻiaka sisters excepting the youngest, Hiʻiaka-i-ka-poli-o-Pele, from her breast. The younger Hiʻiaka sister was born as an egg from Haumea's mouth.

Despite the unnaturalness of her own deliveries, Haumea became the patron of childbirth and, when asked, can transfer birth pains from a mother in labor to another person. She is also a patron of fertility in both humans and the upper forests.

The following prayer is to increase the race and/or the productivity of the land.

Kupuʻeu hou na moku, ʻeu Hau-mea.	The islands have a new heroine, Hau-mea is a heroine.
Nuu akahi lawe pololei i na moku a pau	One placed in highest royalty takes all the islands
Kupu ʻeu hono uli ka lani	The wonder one unites the heavens of dark blue royalty
Pahakea honua i lau puni na moku	Uncultivated be the earth that the islands be many all around
Hawaii kua uli. Ola ka ʻaina.	Hawaii with verdant back. The land lives.
Hoomaha ka leo o ka wahine.	The voice of the Woman (Pele) rests.
Kiʻeikiʻe ka mauna; haahaa ka honua[23]	High is the mountain; low is the earth.[23]
E Hau-mea paʻi ku ka lani, ʻopiʻopi ka honua[24]	O Hau-mea, who slaps the heavens defiantly, who rolls up the earth.[24]
Ke kupuʻau o na moku ehiku	The heroine of the seven islands.
Kahiki-ku ia o Hawaii.	Hawaii is Ka-hiki-ku
Hoʻike mai i ke aloha nui-puni ka ʻaina	Show the great love all round the land.
O Hawaii o Ke-awe, Maui a Kama, Molo-kaʻi nui a Hina	Hawaii of Ke-awe, Maui of Kama, Offspring of Eight Branches (of genealogy), Great Molo-kaʻi of Hina
Oʻahu o Ka-kuhihewa, Kauai o Mano-ka-lani-po	Oʻahu of Ka-kuhihewa, Kauai of Mano-ka-lani-po
Nii-hau ka palena o na moku	Nii-hau, the end of the islands
Ka-ʻula Ku-hai-moana	Ka-ʻula of Ku-hai-moana
Hoʻike i ka nani o ka ʻaina	Show the beauty of the land.
He palena o Ka-ʻula no Hawaii,	Ka-ʻula is a boundry of Hawaii,
Nihoa kuhikuhi puu one	Nihoa of sand hill divination.
A laa, a noho, a paa, a mau loa Hawaii.	Make sacred and stay; make firm and long continue Hawaii.
ʻAmama, ua noa, a lele waele.	Amama. It is free of tabu. It has all flown away.[25]

Nu'a-kea

At the time that Lono came to Hawaii there also came the goddess Nu'a-kea, sometimes called Kea-kea or Kea-kea-lani. She was said to be a "part" of Haumea, one of the *kumu 'aumakua* or source gods. In Hawaii she became the patron of nursing mothers and is prayed to when an increase or decrease in the flow of milk is desired. When a boy-child was to be sent from the women's eating house to that of the men, Nu'a-kea was prayed to in the ritual of separation. At that time she was asked to give the child prosperity and to guard against the malice of sorcery.

The following prayer to Nu'a-kea is one that is said when a nursing mother is ready to wean her child.

E Lono, e Kane, e Nua-kea, ka wahine iaia ka poli-waiu o ke keiki.	O Lono, O Kane, O Nua-kea, the woman with breast of milk for the child.
Eia ke ukuhi nei o (inoa).	We are about to wean (name).
E lawe aku oe i ka waiu o ka makuahine.	Staunch the flow of milk in his mother.
Ia oe e ka la, ke mahina, ka hoku;	Yours are the sun, the moon, the stars;
E lawe oe a kukulu o Kahiki!	Carry away to the pillars of Kahiki
Haalele aku i ka omimo, ka uwe wale o (inoa)	And there leave the emaciation, peevishness and wailing of the child.
A e hanai oe i ka ia kapu a Kane,	Feed him with the sacred fish of Kane,
Oia ka hili, ka noho malie,	That is repose and quiet,
Ke ola ia oe, Kane!	This is your blessing, O Kane!
Amama. Ua noa.	Amama. The prayer is ended.[26]

Pele

A late arriving family was that of the volcano goddess Pele. The family was split when Pele had a love affair with the husband of Na-maka-o-ka-ha'i, her *kaikua'ana* (older sister or female cousin). The family left their ancient homeland and came to Hawaii in two groups. Pele's father and several brothers and sisters traveled with her as they searched for a new home. The other group traveled with the outraged Na-maka-o-ka-ha'i, following Pele as she moved down the island chain. From Kauai to Hawaii they destroyed each site at which Pele attempted to establish a home until she finally found safety at Hale-ma'uma'u. The following prayer to Pele is an *'awa* offering prayer.

O Pele la ko'u akua	Pele is my deity
Miha ka lani, miha ka honua,	Silent the heavens, silent the earth,
Awa iku, awa lani	Ceremoniously dug 'awa, heavenly 'awa
Kai 'awa'awa, ka 'awa nui a Hii-aka[27]	The large 'awa of Hii-aka was bitter[27]
I ku i Mauli-ola e, i Mauli-ola,	That stood at Mauli-ola,
He 'awa kaulu ola e na wahine	'Awa on the ledge of life by the woman
E kapu, e kapu kai ka 'awa e Pele-honua-mea,	Make ceremonially tabu, ceremonially tabu by sea bath,
O ka la'e ka Hau-mea	The clearing up of the breath of Hau-mea
O ka wahine nana i ai a hohonu ka lua.	The woman who ate the pit till deep.
O wau wahine a Maka-lii	I am a wife of Maka-lii
O lua wahine o ka lani	Two women of the heavens
O Kuku-'ena, o na wahine i ka inu hana 'awa	Kuku-'ena of the women who drink 'awa while making it
Kanaenae a'u a he kua malihini[28]	My chant is of supplication and eulogy, a chant of mine by a foreign deity[28]
Hele ho'i ke ala mauka o Ka'u	The road goes upland of Ka'u,
Hele ho'i ke ala makai o Puna.	The road goes seaward of Puna.
I Ka-maamaama la i Ka-pua-lei	In the brightness of the sun Ka-pua-lei

11

Loaa ka 'awa la i 'Apua,
Ka piina i Ku-ka-la-'ula.
Hoopuka aku ka i Puu-lena
'Aina a ke kua i noho ai
Kanaenae a'u a ke kua malihini a.

Got the *'awa* at 'Apua,
The rise at Ku-ka-la-'ula.
Come forth at Puu-lena
Land in which the deity lived.
I chant my *kanaenae* by the foreign deity.[29]

Hi'iaka-i-ka-poli-o-Pele

Pele has several sisters named Hi'iaka. Of these, Hi'iaka-i-ka-poli-o-Pele was born as an egg from the mouth of their mother Haumea. The egg was carried under Pele's bosom until the child matured. This Hi'iaka, best known for her trip to Kauai to bring Pele's lover Lohi'au to Hawaii, is a patron of the *hula* and of healing. The following prayer is to Hi'iaka-i-ka-poli-o-Pele.

E hii e, hii e, hulia ka moku Hawaii-nui-o-Ke-awe
Manomano ka nani, maika'i ka 'aina.
He kupu'eu hii ka wahine nona ka honua.

O Embracer, o embracer
Great is the beauty, fine is the land.
An embracing rascal is the woman of whom is the earth.

Ka lapa uila o na moku, 'olapalapa na moku.

The lightning flash of the island, repeated flashing of the island.

Ka pae 'aina o Ke-awe Nui Hanau Moku.

The group of islands of great Ke-awe, giver of birth to islands.

Hii ka lani, hii ka honua, hii ka mauna,

Embracer of the heavens, embracer of the earth, embracer of the mountain,

Hii 'Olapa-ka-lani, na pae Moku o Ke-awe Nui Hanau Moku.
He pua hii ka lani a puni
Paepae na moku o Hawaii Kua Uli

Embracer flashing in the heavens, the island groups of great Ke-awe giver of birth to islands.
A flower that embraces all around the heavens
Sustain the islands of Hawaii of the darkly verdant back.

Huli honua, huli ka moana, huli ka 'aina

Overturn the earth, overturn the ocean, overturn the land.

O Ke-awe ke lii mai Ka-hiki-ku a Ka-hiki-moe

Ke-awe is the chief from Upper Ka-hiki to Lower Ka-hiki.

Moe ke alaula a Kana-loa.

Lie upon the land the light of early dawn and sunset glow of Kana-loa.

Paepae Ke-awe no na moku.
Lihi-lani, lihi honua, lihi moana, lihi mauna

Ke-awe is the sustainer of the islands.
Edge of the heavens, edge of the earth, edge of the ocean, edge of the mountain

'E Ku e, eia ka nani, ka maika'i o Hawaii Kua Uli Nui a Ke-awe.
Paopao o Ke-awe ka wahine o ka lani
He kupu, he 'eu, he loa ke ala 'e hiki ai
Pau luna, pau lalo, pau kai, pau uka.

O god Ku, here is the beauty, the fineness of Hawaii of the great Uli line of Ke-awe.
Paopao-o-Ke-awe, the woman of the heavens,
An upstart, a mischief, long is the road to attainment.
Ended above, ended below, ended in the sea, ended in the upland.

O ka la ua paa; ka mahina ua paa, na hoku helele'i

The sun is held fast; the moon is held fast; the stars fall scattered.

Ao akahi, ao 'alua, ao 'akolu, ao 'aha, a pau e, a pauloa.
Amama, ua noa, lele wale.

First daylight period, second, third, fourth, then ended, entirely ended.
Amana. The tabu is lifted, It has simply flown away.[30]

Na Akua E: Other Gods

Many other gods came to Hawaii. Among these were a number of *mo'o* or lizard gods, the most famous of which is Kiha-wahine. Some say she was a Maui chiefess who at death became a *mo'o*.

The matriarch of all *mo'o* gods and goddesses is Mo'o-i-nanea. Other *mo'o* are Waka, Kiha-nui-lulu-moku, Hauwahine, and Kaikapu, a cannibalistic *mo'o*.

Sharks are also a god form and perhaps the best known is Ka-moho-ali'i, an older and favorite brother of Pele who accompanied her to Hawaii from Kahiki. Another brother of Pele who has a shark form is Ku-hai-moana who lives at Kaula islet. Other shark gods are Kua, an ancestor of many people of Ka'u, Ke-ali'i-kau-o-Ka'u, another shark god of Ka'u, Ka-'ahu-pahau, the chiefess of the shark gods of Pu'u-loa (Pearl Harbor), and Ka-'ahu-iki-mano-o-Pu'u-loa.

The wind has a number of patron gods. Among these are Hokeo, who assisted Lono in bringing the winds to Hawaii. Another is Makani-ke-oe who, with Hokeo, is associated with sorcery.

Still others of the great multitude are Niolo-pua, the god of sleep; Kalai-pahoa, a Molokai god of sorcery; Ma'i-ola, a god of healing; Lima-loa, a god of mirages; Ka-'onohi-o-ka-la, who escorts the souls of dead chiefs; and Makua-'aihue, a god worshiped by thieves. Whatever his needs, man has an ancestor-god to whom he can appeal for help.[31]

KE KINI AKUA: THE GREAT MULTITUDE OF GODS

Wherever man walks, there too the gods can be found. Not just the four great gods or the four hundred mighty gods but also the four thousand and the four hundred thousand, who all together are called the *kini akua*. As the names of many of these gods are sometimes forgotten, and to avoid offending a god that might have an interest in one's affairs, even if unknown, prayers and offerings are directed to the *kini akua*. The following prayer is for all the gods.

E kini o ke 'kua,	Ye forty thousand gods,
E ka lehu o ke 'kua	Ye four hundred thousand gods,
E ka lalani o ke 'kua,	Ye rows of gods,
E ka pukui akua,	Ye collection of gods,
E ka mano o ke 'kua,	Ye four thousand gods,
E kaikuaana o ke 'kua,	Ye older brothers of the gods,
E ke 'kua muki,	Ye gods that smack your lips,
E ke 'kua hawanawana,	Ye gods that whisper,
E ke 'kua kiai o ka po,	Ye gods that watch by night,
E ke 'kua alaalawa o ke aumoe,	Ye gods that show your gleaming eyes by night,
E iho, e ala, e oni, e eu,	Come down, awake, make a move, stir yourselves,
Eia ka mea ai a oukou la, he hale.	Here is your food, a house.[32]

NA 'UNIHIPILI: THE SPIRITS

Among the great multitude of gods are the *'unihipili* who are also called *'uhinipili*. They are the spirits of deceased persons that have been wooed into staying in a "bundle." The bundle, wrapped in tapa, contains bones and hair that had been removed from the body at the time it was being prepared for burial. Prayers and offerings were also made to court the spirit.[33]

The person who performs this ritual has the obligation of constantly attending the *'unihipili*. If not regularly cared for, it will turn against its guardian and become a renegade. Properly kept, the spirit will take on the good or evil character of its caretaker and will go on whatever mission it may be sent. Part of the care of such a spirit is the regular serving of *'awa* and food.

The following is a prayer to be said before feeding such a spirit.

E Puhi, e ho'i mai,	Return, O Puhi,
Eia kou ai,	Here is thy food,
Eia kou i'a,	Here is thy fish,
Eia kou kapa,	Here is thy kapa,

13

Eia kou 'awa,
Eia kou malo,
E ho'i mai a 'ai a ma'ona,
A hele a pa'ani a lelele,
Amama, ua noa.

Here is thy 'awa,
Here is thy malo,
Come and eat thy fill,
Then go, play, leap about,
Amama, it is freed.[34]

NA 'AUMAKUA: THE GUARDIANS

Among the great multitude of gods are also found the 'aumakua, the personal guardians of each individual and their family; the ancient source gods from whom the people of old were descended.[35] The form of an 'aumakua varies from family to family. Among the more common forms are those of sharks, owls, and lizards, as well as various fish and birds. Whatever its form, the 'aumakua is one specific shark, owl, etc. However, all members of the species are treated with the respect of family members.[36]

Since the 'aumakua are intimate members of the human family, spiritual relationships with them are especially close and their presence is sought for feast and festivity as well as in time of crisis. They act as healers and advisors, counteracting troubles and punishing faults.

The following are two prayers to 'aumakua.

Na 'aumakua a ka po, na 'aumakua o ke ao,

Ia Ku, e Kane, e Kana-loa,
Na 'aumakua i a Olo-olo i Honua-mea
Ke kani mai nei ka hoe
Hoe ma'o, i o Kanaka-o-kai.
'Ai wale i ka i'a, kou kohu ia e ke kua
A noho, a ulu
E Kila e, e Kila,
O Kila iuka, O Kila i kai
O Kila pa wahine, o Ho'oipo i ka malanai
He kama au na Luu-kia i hanau, he kupua
'Ano 'ai, ma'ane'i mai
Heaha ka hua?
He hua ka'u na Lei-makani, na Hina,
Na ka wahine kupua e noho ana i ka pali o Pu'u-kilea
    nei la e.
Pa mai, pa mai ka makani nui o Hilo a
O Hilo ia, ka aina a ke kupua i noho ai.

He kupua ka la; he kupua ka ua;
Mai hi'ikua, mai hi'ialo.
Ina ilaila ke kanaka 'ili pakakea
Ua paka kahu, ua paka lua, ua paka kolu,
Ua paka ha, ua paka lima
Alima kupua o Ka-hiki e Lono e
Ka ulia ke ola i He-lani-ku a
'Ano'ai a.

The family gods of the night, the family gods of the day,
To Ku, to Kane, to Kana-loa,
The gods long and narrow in Honua-mea.
The paddle sounds
Paddle yonder, to yonder Man-of-the-sea.
Only eat of the fish. You have the choice o deity.
Stay, and grow
O Kila, o Kila
Kila in the upland, Kila by the sea.
Kila, the last born of the woman Ho'oipo-i-ka-malanai
Your child by Luu-kia,
Greetings, come.
What is the thought in the heart?
A fruit (offering) is mine by Lei-makani, by Hina,
By the supernatural woman dwelling at the cliff of
    Pu'u-kilea.
Blow, blow, big wind of Hilo.
It is Hilo, the land where the supernatural woman
    lived.
A supernatural being is the sun, is the rain
From carried on the back, from carried in the arms.
There goes the man with a skin of white rain drops
Single rain drops, double rain drops, triple rain drops,
Four rain drops, five rain drops.
Five demigods of Ka-hiki, o Lono
The sudden coming, the life in He-lani-ku
Greeting.[37]

14

E na 'aumakua mai ka pa'a iluna ka pa'a ilalo

Ka hooku'i a me ka halawai
E ka 'ai, he 'awa
'E 'ike ia'u ia (inoa) ka 'oukou pulapula
O ke ola mau loa no ko'u a kau i ka pua'aneane
A kanikoo, a pala lauhala
Kolopupu, a haumaka 'iole
O ke ola ia a 'oukou, e na 'aumakua
'Amama, ua noa, lele wale.

O guardians from the solid above to the solid below[38]
From the zenith to the horizon.
Here is the food and the *'awa.*
Take notice of me, your offspring
Let my life continue till I reach extreme old age
Until the cane sounds (and I am)
Bent with age, and blurred eyes of a rat.
It is life by you, O 'aumakua
'Amama, free of tabu, flown away.[39]

Some prayers are not said in the form of direct appeals or statements but in the form of allusions to previous happenings within the family, to famous events, or to traditional stories. The following *pule mano* is such a prayer.

Akahi ka mano, puka mai ka mano
'Alua ka mano, 'ea mai ka mano.
'Akolu ka mano, puka mai ka mano.
'Aha ka mano, 'ea mai ka mano.
Lima ka mano; puka mai ka mano.
Ono ka mano; 'ea mai ka mano
Hiku ka mano; puka mai ka mano.
Walu ka mano; 'ea mai ka mano
'Aiwa ka mano, puka mai ka mano
O lele-hauli, o ka i'a kele 'au moku

O ka hauli o ka i'a Kele'ahana[40]
O Kane ma laua o Kana-loa.
Ea Ku-hai-moana,[41] ka i'a i ke ale,
Puka Ku i'a me ka i'a papani moku,

Ea mai Lua'ehu, ka i'a kanaka mea,
Kapa'i[42] a Ku, kapa'i a Lono,
Ea kini o ke kua, ka mano o ke kua,
No laua ka mauli lele iluna
No ke kino mano la i hookanaka.
He mano Kua, he 'a'a no ka moku.
He hiluhilu no ka moku o ke lii
He 'a'e moku mai Kahiki a Hawaii[43]
Holo mai O'ahu a Maui.
E'e mai Ke-e'e-wahine, ka mano alii
I ke kaohi i ke kuala o ka 'i'a
O ke alanui no ia i hiki ai
I ke kua kapu o ke kaikunane.
O Kua o Wa-kea, o Ka-hole-a-Kane.
O na i'a i kapekupeku ke kuala
I ala ka mahamaha kuku o ka i'a
O Ke-kau-i-ke-aweawe-'ula
Kaikunane o ka makuahine o Ka-welo
O Ka-welo i ka welowelo la.
Ea mai Kua, ka 'ai ka hohonu
Ka mano niho 'ooi, niho wawaka.
Lua'i po'i ke a luna me ke a lalo.

One shark, the shark comes forth.
Two sharks, the sharks appear.
The third shark, the third shark comes forth.
The fourth shark, the sharks appear.
The fifth shark, the fifth shark comes forth.
The sixth shark, the sharks appear.
The seventh shark, the seventh shark comes forth.
The eighth shark, the sharks appear.
The ninth shark, the ninth shark comes forth.
Greatly stirred is the fish that swims all around the island.
The spirit of the fish Kele'ahana[40] that swims
Kane and Kana-loa.
Arose Ku-hai-moana,[41] the fish in the ocean waves,
That came with schools, that hid from view the island
Arose Lua'ehu the fish like a man with reddish skin.
Kapa'i[42] of Ku, of Lono
Arose the 40,000 of the deity, the 4,000 of the deity.
Of the two was the spirit that flew upward,
Of the shark body that turned human.
There was a shark Kua, a daring one of the island.
A beautiful one of the island of the chief
A mounter of islands from Kahiki to Hawaii.[43]
They swam from O'ahu to Maui.
Mounted Ke-e'e-wahine, the shark chiefess.
With the holding down of the dorsal fin of the fish.
That is the road that made it possible
On the tabu back of your brother.
Kua-o-Wa-kea, Ka-hole-a-Kane.
The fish that splash with the dorsal fin
Rose up the sharp gills of the fish
Ke-kau-i-ke-aweawe-'ula
The brother of the mother of Ka-welo
Ka-welo in the streaming of the sun.
Kua-deity appeared, the fish in the deep
The shark with sharp teeth, flashing teeth.
Expelled fiercely the upper and lower jaws.

15

I kupu ke koʻa ʻula, koʻa kea i ka lae,[44]	Red coral and white coral grew on the forehead,[44]
I ulu mai ke kalaku, ke kala i aoa	Grew the bristling, the barking proclamation
O ke oho ia o Kua, o ka mano alii.	The outcry of Kua, the shark chief.
O ka iʻa ʻula, manoa pepeekue	The red fish of solid thickness
I kakau i paniʻoniʻo o pahaʻohaʻo kona ʻili	Marked with streaks that make its skin a wonder
Oia ia nei, o ka mano hele honua	That is him here, the shark that goes over the earth
He inoa.[45]	He inoa.[45] [46]

E LOAA ANA HE ʻAUMAKUA: **FINDING AN ʻAUMAKUA**

If for some reason one loses contact with their *ʻaumakua* they can call on a deceased parent or grandparent to reestablish their ancient family ties. The parent or grandparent in turn will call out to all the *ʻamakua* and find among them their rightful place as relatives.

There are two sets of prayers for contacting an *ʻamakua;* one set is to the male line and one to the female line. The following is the prayer to the male line.

E kulou mai e na lani	Bend down, O heavens,
E hoʻolohe mai e ka honua,	Listen, O earth
E haliu mai hoʻi e na kukulu,	Harken, O pillars [of heaven],
Na ʻaumakua i ka hikina a ka la a i kaulana,	[O] ʻaumakua at the rising and the resting places of the sun,
A mai kela peʻa kapu a keia peʻa kapu;	From that sacred border to this;
Eia ka alana a me ka mohai,	Here are the offerings and sacrifices,
He mohai pilikia i ke Akua.	A sacrifice to the gods for our trouble [our lack of an ʻaumakua].

At this point, the petitioner makes his offerings, calling the gods' attention to each one. He then prays as follows.

Ia Kanenuiakea,	To Kane-nui-akea,
Ia Kane o Kanaloa,	To Kane and Kanaloa
Ia Kanehekili,	To Kane-hekili,
Ia Kanewawahilani o Nakoloilani,	To Kane-wawahi-lani and Nakoloilani,
Ia Kauilanuimakehaikalani,	To Kauila-nui-makeha-i-ka-lani,
Ia Kamohoaliʻi,	To Kamoho-aliʻi,
Ia Kanakaokai,	To Kanaka-o-kai,
Ia Kahoʻaliʻi,	To Ka-hoʻaliʻi,
Ia Lonomakua,	To Lono-makua,
Ia Kanehunamoku,	To Kane-huna-moku,
Ia Kaneikauhanaʻula,	To Kane-i-kauhana-ʻula,
Ia Kahuilaokalani,	To Ka-huila-o-ka-lani,
Ia Kekumakaha,	To Ke-ku-makaha,
Ia Kapoiauʻena,	To Ka-po-i-Auʻena,
Ia Ola,	To Ola,
Ia Kikiaola,	To Kiki-a-Ola,
Ia Kaʻilihonu,	To Kaʻili-honu,
Ia Kahoʻowahaakananuha,	To Ka-hoʻowaha-a-Kananuha,
Ia Kaʻonohi,	To Ka-ʻonohi,
Ia Kuhemu,	To Ku-hemu,
Ia Kapakanaka,	To Ka-pa-kanaka,
Ia Kauhiahiwa,	To Kauhi-a-Hiwa,
Ia Kapohakahiaku,	To Kapoha-ka-hi-aku,

Ia Kalani'aukai.
I na 'aumakua kane a pau loa,
Ia 'oukou pale ka po, pale ka make, pale ka pilikia.

Owau nei o Kiha ka pua keia i ke ao;

Homai i mana.

To Ka-lani-'au-kai.
To all the male 'aumakua.
It is yours [the mana] to brush aside darkness, brush
   aside death, brush aside trouble.

This is I, Kiha, your descendant in this world of the
   living;

Give me mana.

The following is the prayer said to contact a female 'aumakua.

O na 'aumakua wahine me na kupuna wahine ali'i,	O female 'aumakua and ancestral chiefesses,
Na 'aumakua wahine i ka hikina, a i kaulana a ka la,	Female 'aumakua at the rising and setting places of the sun,
Na wahine i ka lewa lani, i ka lewa nu'u,	Female [spirits] in the firmaments of the heavens and of the clouds;
O Walinu'u,	Walinu'u,
O Walimanoanoa,	Walimanoanoa,
O Kaneikawaiaola,	Kane-i-ka-wai-a-ola,
O Kahinaaola,	Kahina-a-ola,
O Haumea wahine,	Haumea,
O Kanikawi, O Kanikawa,	Kanikawi, Kanikawa,
O Kuho'one'enu'u;	Kuho'one'enu'u;
O Pelehonuamea,	Pele-honua-mea,
O Kalamainu'u,	Ka-la-mai-nu'u,
O Kamohailani,	Ka-mohai-lani,
O Nu'a,	Nu'a,
O Nu'akea,	Nu'akea,
O Hulikapa'uianu'akea,	Huli-ka-pa'u-ia-Nu'akea,
O Uliwahine;	Uliwahine;
Ia Kahawali,	To Kahawali,
Ia Kaneluhonua,	To Kane-lu-honua,
Ia Kukalaniho'one'enu'u,	To Ku-ka-lani-ho'one'enu'u,
Ia Niho'aikaulu,	To Niho-'ai-kaulu,
Ia Leihulunuiakamau,	To Lei-hulu-nui-a-Kamau,
Ia Ka'oa'oakaha'iaonuia'umi,	To Ka-'oa'oaka-ha'i-ao-nui-a-'Umi,
Ia Ahukiniokalani,	To Ahukini-o-ka-lani,
Ia Keahiolalo,	To Ke-ahi-olalo,
Ia Kamakaokeahi,	To Ka-maka-o-ke-ahi,
Ia Kapohinaokalani.	To Ka-pohina-o-ka-lani.
I na 'aumakua wahine a pau loa,	To all the female 'aumakua.
Ia 'oukou pale ka po, pale ka make, pale ka pilikia.	It is yours [the mana] to brush aside darkness, brush aside death, brush aside trouble.
Owau nei o Kiha ka pua keia i ke ao,	This is I, Kiha, your descendant in this world of the living.
Homai i mana.	Give me mana.
'Eli'eli kapu, 'eli'eli noa, ia lahonua;	The kapu has been profound, the freeing profound, in this earthly life;
'Amama, 'amama, ua noa.	It is finished; freed.[47]

E HOONA ANA KE 'AUMAKUA: PLACATING AN 'AUMAKUA

Every person has special obligations to his 'aumakua and every member of its species, be it animal, fish, bird, or insect. If by some accident one might harm a member of the species, immediate prayers must be said.

17

The following is a prayer said under such circumstances. It is a prayer for those occasions when a fisherman with a *kala* as an *'aumakua* might catch such a fish. The prayer is said after returning the fish to the sea. Kane-huna-moku, one of twelve paradisical islands, is the place Kane and Kanaloa went to live when they left Hawaii.

E Kane-ko-kala	O Kane-ko-kala
E Kane-ko-kala	O Kane-ko-kala
E ho'i, e ho'i	Return, return
I Kane-huna-moku.	To Kane-huna-moku.[48]

NOTES:

4. Taylor, Ahuena, December 1931, p. 78.
5. Kamakau 1964, p. 28-29. It should be noted that while entries citing Kamakau may show either 1961, 1964, or 1976 as the date of publication, this is the date that the English translation was published. The material was originally published in Hawaiian language newspapers during the 1860s and 1870s.
6. As Ku-nui-akea, "a national god," he was said to be the head of all the Ku gods. It was to worship him in this role that the *luakini heiau* was developed. This type of *heiau* could be built only by ruling chiefs and was the only type of *heiau* in which human sacrifice could be offered. When an especially pleasing human offering was laid on the altar, Ku would come in a cloud pillar, accompanied by thunder and lightning, as his thrusting tongue picked up the sacrifice and carried it away.

   Ku was often symbolized by a wooden image wrapped in layers of tapa. On the head of the image was a very fine feather which drooped and streamed down. When the god gave a favorable answer to a petition the feather stood straight up and twisted about as if full of lightning. The feather might even fly from its place and rest on the head of a person. When carried into battle, the figure known as Ku-ka-'ili-moku was said to utter a cry which could be heard above the sounds of fighting. (Malo, 1951, p. 114).

   The *ki'i* or god figures were not gods. The figures were reminders of the gods and their power. They might be receptacles for a stone or piece of wood that was imbued with the essence or aspect of a god.
7. Malo 1951, p. 177.
8. The *'aumakua* were individual or family guardians. (See pp. 14-18.)
9. The northern limit is the summer solstice, the longest day of the year. The southern limit is the winter solstice, the shortest day of the year.
10. In other parts of Polynesia the traditions of Kanaloa are stronger and there he is, perhaps, the most famous of the gods.
11. Emerson n.d.; Kelsey translation.
12. Malo 1951, pp. 110-111.
13. Lono was the child of Kane and Hina, according to Amalu.
14. A little piece of *'awa* was tied to the outside of the gourd. Mornings and evenings the family elder took the gourd and laid it at the door. He then faced outward and prayed, first for the chiefs and then the commoners and then his own family. After that he chewed the *'awa* and ate the food.
15. "*Kai uli* refers to the deep places of the ocean. *Kai kea* refers to the shallow places of the sea, the places of the waves. You see things at the bottom of the *kai kea*. You do not see the bottom of the dark sea." (Kuluwai-maka n.d.)
16. Wise, June 6, 1911; Kelsey translation.
17. Beckwith, 1970, pp. 53-54. This is part of a series of prayers collected by Theodore Kelsey from Robert Luahiwa and translated by Laura Green. The complete series may be found in Hawaiian Mythology.
18. This line refers to the handling of fish nets. *Kai-na* is to lift or ease the net, rather than pull. (Fornander 1919, p. 501)
19. This line calls upon Hina to give birth to or to supply fish.
20. The introduction of the mudhen identifies Hina as the mother of the demi-god Maui, who by cunning obtained the secret of fire from this bird.
21. Fornander 1919, pp. 501-503.
22. Human children who drool at the mouth are said to have been born from the brain of Haumea.
23. The mountain represents the chiefs and the earth the people.
24. "*Pa'i ku* represents an equilibrist. Haumea brings peace to the race, to seven islands. She is foremost." (Beckley)
25. Kia'aina n.d.; Kelsey translation.

26. Malo 1951, p. 90.
27. The so-called bitterness of the *'awa* was a desirable characteristic.
28. Pele, a late arrival in the Hawaiian Islands, was frequently referred to as a *malihini* or foreigner.
29. Kuluwaimaka n.d.; Kelsey translation.
30. Kia'aina n.d.; Kelsey translation.
31. For an extensive listing of the gods, see Pukui and Elbert 1975, pp. 381-400.
32. Fornander 1917, p. 606.
33. Traditional offerings for this wooing of a spirit were two *malo,* a *tapa,* an *'awa* cup, a choice piece of *'awa* as well as red fish that had been salted, and a small calabash of *poi.*
34. Titcomb 1948, p. 150.
35. Kamakau 1964, pp. 30-32.
36. Amalu 1979.
37. Kuluwaimaka n.d.; Kelsey translation. Kuluwaimaka received this chant from Ke-ahi-nui-o-ki-lau-ea.
38. The "solid above" refers to the heavens, the "solid below" refers to the earth.
39. Iokepa n.d.; Kelsey translation.
40. "Kele'ahona is a shark god who is the dread of those on land. You can sense his heat in the water." (Beckley)
41. "Ku-hai-moana is the father or patriarch of sharks. He made his home at Ka'ula where he became a petrified coral ledge. Wherever he goes it is his." (Beckley)
42. *"Kapa'i* pertains to Kua and company, the one for whom is this prayer." (Kuluwaimaka) "Sharks were separated into groups by circumstances or force of nature. Different branches of the shark family are in different seas." (Beckley)
43. "Kua came from Kahiki to Hawaii where he was accepted and came into control of the courses of peoples lives." (Beckley)
44. *I kupu ke ko'a 'ula,* etc., refers to Pearl Harbor and the red and white coral that was found there, which is said to provide food and shelter for the *kala* fish. The *kala* on the red side of Pearl Harbor is good and edible while that from the white coral reef on the Barber's Point side is rank. From Pearl Harbor outward you cannot eat the *kala.* The red coral is symbolically healthy, full of blood, teaming with fish. The white coral suggests old sharks, old blood." (Beckley)
45. "While this chant closes *He inoa,* as would a *mele inoa,* Kuluwaimaka repeatedly called it a *pule mano.*" (Kelsey)
46. Kuluwaimaka n.d.; Kelsey translation.
47. Kamakau 1964, pp. 30-32. These prayers originally appeared in the Hawaiian language paper *Ke Au 'Oko'a,* October 20, 1870.
48. Pukui n.d.

III NĀ PULE MOHAI
Offering Prayers

It has been said that food must be offered to any who come to the door, even an enemy. This also applies to the gods and the spirits whether they be friendly or evil. This is not just a matter of graciousness. If an evil god or spirit is offered hospitality, it may become friendly. If not, the friendly gods who have been generously received will drive the evil ones away.[49]

When preparing foods for the gods it is well to remember that the gods prefer the dark varieties of most plants and animals as well as red species of fish.[50]

NA MOHAI ʻAWA: ʻAWA OFFERINGS

Of all the offerings man has to give the gods, that of ʻawa is the most pleasing.[51] It is as essential for their nourishment and growth as fish and *poi* are essential for the nourishment and growth of man.

The following is a typical prayer said when offering ʻawa.

O Ku, O Kane, O Kanaloa, naʻliʻi,	O Ku, O Kane, O Kanaloa, the chiefs,
Na ʻaumakua i ka po,	To the *ʻaumakua* of the night,
Na ʻaumakua i ka ao,	To the *ʻaumakua* of the day,
Eia ka ʻawa.	Here is *ʻawa*.
E ola ia Kamehameha,[52]	Grant health to Kamehameha,[52]
E ola no hoi ia makou pulapula,	Grant health to us, thine offspring,
A kanikoʻo, a pala-lauhala,	Till the [time of the] sounding cane, the sprawling on the lauhala [mat],
A kolopupu, a haumakaʻiole,	The hitching along, bent with age, with eyes heavy and wrinkled as a rat's,
O ka ola ia e ke akua	That is the life from [dealt out by] the gods,
A hiki i ka puaneane.	Till breath gradually fades away.[53]

After saying the prayer, the drinker dips a finger into the *ʻawa* and snapping it upward says, *"Ke aka ka ʻoukou, ka ʻiʻo ka makou."* "The shadow (or essense) is yours, the substance ours." Then the *ʻawa* is served to all who are present.

The prayer said before a chief drinks *ʻawa* socially may be said either by the chief himself or by a *kahuna*. The following is an *ʻawa* drinking prayer for a chief.

E nuʻa iluna,	O thickly piled above,
E nuʻa ilalo,	O thickly piled below,
I mapunapuna,	Surging emotion,
I pae a maiʻa,	In the enclosure of a mountain banana patch,
I kuhi wale,	Who simply points out,
I hoopeʻa wale,	The one who crosses another,
I kuʻina o ka aahu,	As the joining of the garment.
Ka ihu o ka puaa;	The nose of the pig;
I ka aʻe pa,	Who surmounts obstructions,
I ka wawahi pa,	Who breaks up obstructions,
No kela kau ka hewa.	The wrong is of that (not this) season.
Mamuli oe o makou.	We people are because of you.
O Ku-i-ke-kala,	O Ku-in-the-forgiveness,
O Ku-pulupulu,	O Ku-kindling-in-the-forest,
O Ku-alana-wao,	O Ku-of-the-upland-offering,
O Ku-moku-halii,	O Ku-island-spreader,
O Laea, ka wahine,	O Laea the woman,
Nana e kua ka waa,	By him would be hewed the tree for a canoe,
A hina ilalo,	Until it falls down,
A no ke ʻeulu.	And cut off the top.
Ia ku-ele ka La,	Who causes the sun to stand darkly
Ia ku-ele ka Mahina,	Who causes the moon to stand darkly,
Ia Ku-poo-loa,	To Long-headed-Ku,
Ia Ku-maka-aka,	To Ku-with-laughing-eyes,
Ko loko, ko waho.	Of within, of without.
Eia ka ai la, e ke akua.	Here is the food, o deity.
O ko ola no koʻu a loihi,	May I have long life
A kolo-pupu, a hau-maka-iole,	Until I crawl with difficulty and with the blurred eyes of a rat,
A pala-lauhala, a kani-koʻo,	Until (I am) weak of old age and sound the cane,
A ka i ke koko.	Until (I am) thrust into a carrying net.
Amama, ua noa.	Amama, it is free of tabu.

If the drinker is a woman, the last four lines will be changed to the following:

A kani koʻo, a kolo pupu   Until the cane sounds, until bent with age
A hau maka ʻiole;   Until I have blurred eyes of a rat;
A ʻeia ke ola ia ʻoe, e ke akua.   And that is the life to you, o god.
Amama, ua noa.   Amama, it is free of tabu.[54]

Figures of the family gods are kept in the men's eating house. There in the evenings the men in the family gather and make offerings to those gods. The following prayer is said by the head of the household when offering ʻawa.

Na akua o ka po,   Ye gods of the night,
Na akua o ke ao,   Ye gods of the day,
E hoomau i ke ola   Perpetuate your scion
O ka oukou pulapula,   Until crouching old age,
A Kolopupu,   Till his features become peaked and pinched with age,
A Haumaka iole,   Resembling those of a rat,
Kanikookoo,   Till the rattle of his hobbling stick shall be heard,
Palalauhala,   And his skin shall become yellow as the ripened
                                              pandanus,
A ka i koko.   Till he is helpless with years, as to be hung up in a net.
(Na ka pulapula e pane mai)   (The son of the house responds)
E-O.   Here am I.
(A olelo aʻe la ka makua)   (The parent then closes with)
Amama ua noa.   So be it.
A lele wale aku la.   It is free.[55]

The following prayer is said when offering food to the family god. It was chanted in the style Kuluwaimaka called *leo oli kaholo*.

Eia ka ʻai e ke ʻkua e,   Here is the food, o deity
E Kahuli, e Kahela,   O Transformer, o Extender,
E ka wahine e moe ana iluna ke alo,   O woman lying face upward.
O Moe-a-hanuna, o Wili-kaa-mea, o Ka-lepo-ahulu,   A Moe-a-hanuna, o Wili-kaa-mea, o Ka-lepo-ahulu,
O Pahu-kini, o Pahu-lau, o Kulana a Pahu, O Pahu-kini, o Pahu-lau, o Kulana a Pahu,
O ka paepae ia Laka,   O the supporter of Laka,
O ka paepae nui alai moku e, e ala;   O great supporter that hides from view the island,
                                              awake;

E ala e ka ua, e ka la,   Arouse the rain, arouse the sun,
E ka makani, e ka pohu, e ke kaikoo,   The wind, the calm, the rough sea.
E ka ʻohu kolo mai uka e ka ʻohu kolo mai kai,
O kai kane, o kai wahine   O sea of the male, o sea of the female
O kai luu, o kai ea,   O sea of submersion, o sea of arising,
Kai piliaiku e, ua puni   Cramped sea, sea all around
Ua puni na moku i ke kai.   The islands are surrounded by sea.
O huʻehuʻe kai e Kaʻale-ʻi, e Kaʻale-moe, Twisting sea, great waves, waves of calm sea.
E ka ʻale hakoʻikoʻi e i Ka-hiki;   O the agitated waves in Ka-hiki
O kalana au a Ka-hiki ia ʻoe la-e, e Lono. O releaser of the current from Ka-hiki it is thee, o
                                              Lono.

E Lono i ka po, e Lono i ke ao,   O Lono in the night of antiquity, in the day of
                                              antiquity,

E Lono i ka ʻoʻiliʻili makakai nei la e, e Lono. O Lono in the occasional seawash here
O Pipipi, o Unauna, o ʻAlealea, o Naka, o Hee,   Small mollusks, hermit crabs, a shell fish, land shell,
                                              octopus

22

O Kualakai, o Kulipee-nui-'ai akua,	A sea slug, great *kulipee* that consumes deity.
O kike 'ala o Piikea,	Breaker open of the dense volcanic rock of Pii-kea
O ka uahi pookea i ka mauna.	The white-headed smoke on the mountain.
O Ku-pulupulu, o Ku-'alana-wao, O Ku-moku-halii,	O Ku-pulupulu, o Ku-'alana-wao, o Ku-moku-halii,
O Kupa-'ai-ku, o Kupa-'ai-kee,	O Ku-pa-'ai-ku, o Kupa-'ai-kee,
O na kua mai ka waokele.	The deities from the rain belt.
O Laka, o Lea,	O Laka, o Lea
O na wahine i ke kuahiwi, i ke kualono,	The woman in the mountain, near the top
I ka he'i, i ka manowai,	At the he'i, at the sluice gate
I ka wai ola loa a Kane e,	At the water of long life of Kane
O Kane-i-ka-po, o Kane i ke ao,	Kane in the night, Kane in the day
O Kane i ka ua loku, o Kane i ka ua kea,	Kane in the pouring rain, Kane in the misty rain
O Kane-kii, o Kane-lele, o Kane-pa,	Getting Kane, Flying Kane, Striking Kane,
O Kane i ka pualena,	Kane in the yellow light of dawn,
O Kane kilo pono, o Kane kilo hewa,	Kane who spies rightly, Kane who spies wrongly,
O Kane i ka halawai la e, halawai,	Kane in the meeting together, meet together
E halawai paha a'uane'i ua po'e hoole akua nei	Perhaps will meet together presently those people who deny deity.
Me kini akua o ka po la. . .	With multitudenous deities of the night
Akahi ka po, alua ka po,	One the night, two the night
Akolu ka po, 'aha ka po, 'alima ka po,	Three the night, four the night, five the night period.
Pale ka po, puka i ke ao.	Set aside the night, issue forth the day.
O Welona a ka la ka wahine nona ua pule;	Setting-of-the-sun is the woman of whom is this prayer.
Ka walina la;	She makes softness
Walina mai ana ho'i i ko pule e.	Making softness in your prayer.[56]

NOTES

49. If an enemy sees that one is careless in his duties to the gods he may go to a sorcerer and say, "That man does not have food for the gods in his house, he is a careless fellow. Send the gods to strike him dead." (Taylor n.d.)
50. All varieties of bananas excepting those of the *popo'ula* and *iho-lena* families were acceptable as offerings to the gods. Under the *kapu*, these two varieties, which included a number of subvarieties, were the only bananas women could eat.
51. The varieties of *'awa* most favored as gifts to the gods are the *mo'i, hiwa* and for the female gods the *papa*. The *'awa* itself is served from a coconut shell cut lengthwise. Only a dark-shelled coconut can be used when making offerings to the gods. The cup is never placed directly on the floor.
52. The name of the then currently ruling chief was used here. Today the name of the highest official of the nation, state, city, or of an organization may be used.
53. Titcomb 1948, p. 142.
54. Emerson, N. B., n.d. Kelsey translation.
55. Emerson, Oliver P. 1903
56. Kuluwaimaka n.d. Kelsey translation.

IV PO'INO, MAKE, MALU
Misfortune, Death, Protection

At some point, relationships between humans may become so stressed that the gods are asked to intervene. They may be asked to return a lover, to decide the outcome of a battle, and, in extreme cases, to cause misfortune or even the death of an enemy.

When seeking revenge, the petitioner should be very sure of the justice of his anger. If his revenge is not just, his victim can successfully return the intended misfortune or death. He should also be prepared to observe very strictly prescribed rituals and pay careful attention to the smallest details. If there is the slightest interruption in the ritual, such as any form of loud or distracting noise, the prayer will not only be unsuccessful but it may turn back on the sender.

HO'OPO'INO: TO CAUSE MISFORTUNE

The following is a prayer to cause misfortune:

Kaulia a Uli imua i ke kahuna.	Set by Uli in front of the *kahuna.*
Kaulia i Ke aloha lani, alia kupua oluna nei.	Stationed in the shining heaven, awaiting the demigod above.
'O wai kupua oluna nei?	Who are the demigods above here?
O 'Ilio uli o ka-lani,[57] o 'Ilio 'ehu, o 'Ilio mea.	O 'Ilio-uli-o-ka-lani,[57] O Ilio-'ehu, O 'Ilio-mea.
O Ku-ke-ao-iki, o Ku-ke-ao-nui	Maker of the small cloud, maker of the big cloud.
O Ku-ke-ao-loa, o Ku-ke-ao-poko	Maker of the long cloud, maker of the short cloud.
O Ku-ke-ao 'awihawiha-'ula-o-ka-lani	Maker of the faintly red cloud of the heavens.
Kanaka o ka mauna, na hoa o ka ulula'au	Men of the mountains, the companions of the forest.
Ha ke alo lani, kua 'ia 'e Laka ka 'omaka pule.	The face of the heavens breathes out the spirit.
Ua ka ua, kahe ka wai la e na ho'alii	Rains the rain, flows the water by the aids of the chiefs.
Nani wale ka pali makamaka o Wawa	Simply beautiful is the chief, companions of tumultuous roar.
O Kupina'i, O Ku wawa, O Ku-ha'ili'ili moe	Ku of the echo, Ku of the roar, Ku who curses sleep,
O Ha'iha'i-lau-ahea, o na wahine i ke ao ma'ukele.	O Ha'iha'i-lau-akea, the woman in the cloud always acts.
O ke kahuna i ka puoko o ke ahi	The *kahuna* in the raging of the fire,
O 'imi'imi, o nalowale, o loaa la e.	Seek lest it be lost, lest it be obtained.
Loa'a la ho'i ka hala, uku i ka 'oiwi.	Gotten is the wrong, compensated is the native son.
Na ke aloha i kono aku la hele mai la a	By love is he invited to come here
Elieli kapu, elieli noa.	Profound the *tabu,* profound its removal.[58]

E HO'I MAI A PALE I KA 'INO: TO RETURN AND PROTECT FROM EVIL

When the forces of misfortune seem to be gathering, one should examine his thoughts and actions to see what the cause might be. If nothing has been done to justify such troubles, it may only be necessary to so inform the trouble-bearing spirits and assure oneself that nothing has been done to merit the bad luck. Then the malevolent spirit can be ordered back to its keeper. It is often sufficient to say something such as, *"Ho'i no kau me 'oe."* "What you have given me, go, return to you (the sender)." Or one might say, *"Ho'i no'ai i kou kahu."* "Go back and destroy your keeper."

If, on examining his actions, the person suffering misfortune finds that he has offended a god, his *'aumakua,* a member of his family, or a friend, he must set things right before seeking relief. In the case of offending a god or *'aumakua,* the offender may require the help of a *kahuna.* In the case of offending a human, the offender must go to the person and seek his or her forgiveness.

Tradition demands that forgiveness be given. If a curse has been given, it must be lifted. Not to do so is to invite the gods to act in the same manner in the future when forgiveness might be sought from them.

If a person who gives a curse dies without removing it, the curse can still be removed by going to the corpse before it is buried and saying, *"I mea ho'ola no ka ma'i o mea."* "Now you are gone, take all curses with you." If for some reason this *pule kala* or cutting prayer can not be said before the body is buried, the curse can still be removed by sincere prayer. It can also be removed by the family senior of the deceased who may agree to take the curse with him when he dies. Although a curse may remain in effect after the death of the giver, it can not be inherited by the family of the cursed person.[59]

The following is a prayer that may be said when seeking forgiveness. It is said before making an offering of *'awa.* After the prayer, the *'awa* is shared with the family *'aumakua* and the person who gave the curse. After drinking the *'awa,* food is offered and shared by all present, including the *'aumakua.*

E Ku i ke kala,	Oh Ku, the forgiving,
E Lono i kau weke kala,	O Lono who grants pardon,
Weke puha ia,	Giving full pardon,
Kalakaua i Ahuena.	Undo the knot of our sins at Ahuena.
Kapu ka aha o ke makala au e Kane.	Tabu is the ceremony presided over by you, Kane.
Kala weke puha ia.	Pardon is wide and free.[60]

If the sufferer of misfortune has been possessed by a spirit sent from an enemy and he is not sufficiently strong to battle it by himself, he may enlist the help of a family member, his entire family, and/or the help of a *kahuna*.

The person chosen to help may kill and dress a white rooster, cooking it in an *imu*. He will then carefully feed the sufferer a part of the bird, telling the possessive spirit that the food is for it to eat. The spirit will then ask, perhaps so quietly that it can not be heard, *"Heaha ka uku ia oe no kou lokomaika'i?"* "What shall I do to repay you for your kindness?"

The one who prepared the chicken will answer, *"Hele oe i kou kahu, ka mea nana oe i houna mai, ilaila kou hale, kau'ai, kau mea inu, kau moena; e luku i kau Kahu, a kau uku ia ia makou."* That is, "Go to your keeper, the one who has sent you here, there find your home, your food, your drink, your mats, destroy your keeper and that will be your gift to me."[61]

The following two prayers are called *pule ho'ola*. They are said to save one from trouble or to heal or cure the problems caused by an evil spirit.

Ia Kane-hoa-lani, pau ko ka lani,	To Kane Companion of the Heavens, all things of the heavens,
Ia Kane-huli-honua, pau ko ka honua,	To Kane Overturner of the Earth, all things of the earth,
Ia Kane-huli-moana, pau ko ka moana,	To Kane Overturner of the Ocean, all things of the ocean,
Ia Ku la-uka, pau ko uka,	To Ku there of the Uplands, all things of the uplands,
Ia Ku la kai, pau ko kai,	To Ku there of the Sea, all things of the sea,
Na kane, na wahine, na keiki,	The men, the women, the children
I hanau i ka manawa a ku'u waha e kahea nei.	Born at the time that my mouth calls.
Ia Kihe-lau'i', ke-akua hele ma ke ala loa,	To Stripper of Ti Leaf, the deity that travels on the long road,
'A'ohe 'ai, 'a'ohe i'a, 'a'ohe hale e kipa ai.	No food, no fish, no house to be received at.
'Eia ka 'ai, 'eia ka i'a, 'eia ka hale, 'eia kahi e moe ai.	Here is the food, here is the fish, here is the house, here is the place to recline.
Hele mai a kipa i ka hale a.	Come and be a guest in the house.
Eia au la, ko kaohi pule,	Here am I the chanter of prayer,
Ho mai ka 'ike; ho mai ka mana maluna o ko kaohi pule,	Extend hither knowledge, extend hither spirit power unto thy chanter of prayer.
Elieli kapu, elieli noa.	Profound be the tabu, profound be its lifting.
Ua noa a.	It is free of tabu.[62]

Lu'ulu'u Hana-lei i ka ua nui	Hana-lei is downcast with heavy rains
Kaumaha i ka noe o Alaka'i.	Heavy with the mist of Alaka'i.
Ke hele au a Manu'a-kepa	I go to Manu'a-kepa
'Oi-ku i ka loa o Ko'i 'alana.	Pained by the distance of Ko'i-alana.
Ke alaka'i 'ia ka malihini	The stranger is led
Hina au e palaha	I fall over, and flat
Make au i ke akua hoounauna.	I die through the god of hoounauna.

Kii mai 'oe ia'u Hookala-ko'i,	You get me Hookala-ko'i,
Ala mai au a ku a hele,	I arose and stood up at the time to go,
Hele au me ku'u lanakila.	I went with my victory.
'Aole au make i koe	I have no death remaining
No ka mea ua kahea au ia Hookala-ko'i	Because I called Hookala-ko'i
A ku au a hele, a lanakila i ka la o kuu make.	And I stood up, and went, and was victorious on the day of my death.
Ke hele nei au me kuu lanakila.	I go with my victory.
A'ole au make i koe	I have no death remaining
Ke ho'i nei au a 'aha'aina ia'u.	I return and am feasted.
Ka 'awa, pua'a, ka 'uala	'Awa, pig, sweet potatoe
Ka mai'a, ke ko.	Bananas, sugarcane.
Pule au ia Hookalako'i	I pray to Hookala-ko'i
O kuu akua ia i ola ai.	My god through whom I live.
Elieli ku elieli moe.	Profound the standing, profound the lying down.
Kapu o, noa.	Kapu o. It is finished.[63]

This prayer calls on all the multitude of gods for protection and asks them to consider the great and little things done by man.

O kini o ke akua;	O ye forty thousand godlings;
E lehu o ke akua;	Ye four hundred thousand godlings;
Ka mano o ke akua;	The four thousand little gods;
Ka puku'i o ke akua,	The assembly of the gods,
O ka lalani o ke akua,	The ranks of the gods,
O ka mau o ke akua,	The endurance of the gods,
O ka oi o ke akua;	The superiority of the gods;
Eia ka hana o ke akua:	This is the task for you gods:
Kulia mai a nana i ka'i na wawae a ke akua;	Present yourselves and behold the strides of these hostile gods;
I ke kiei ana i ka mana'o ino,	Guard against their evil plans,
I ka nana ana i ka uhane ino o ka poe e.	Keep watch of these evil spirits of the night.
E ala mai a nana pono	Arise and consider diligently
I ka hana nui, hana iki, a kanaka po e.	The great things and the little things done by the men of the dark.
Elieli kapu, elieli noa.	Finished the tabu. Finished. It is free.
Amama, ua noa.	The tabu is lifted, removed.[64]

NA PULE 'ANA'ANA: DEATH PRAYERS

In the case of extreme offence, one may ask the gods to completely destroy an enemy. As with other similar acts of revenge, the seeker should be extremely certain of the justice of his anger and observe all the smallest details in his prayers and the accompanying rituals. Inaccuracy or injustice of any kind may cause the action to rebound back onto the sender, causing his death.

The following is a prayer used to cause the death of an enemy. Some say that a worm is eaten at the time of praying so that the spiritual power of the prayer might crawl to the one being prayed to death.[65]

Ea mai ka mano o ke Akua	The spirit power of the deity approaches
Kokooha o ke Akua	The companionship of the deity
Puku'i o ke Akua	The assembly of the god
Lalani Akua	The genealogical line of the god
Ke Akua ki'ei	The god that peeps
Ke Akua halo (inoa)	The god that turns the eyes on (name)

27

Halo i ka ia	Looks at the fish
Halo i ka ʻai	Looks at the food
Halo i ke kino	Looks at the body
Halo i ka hale.	Looks at the house.
ʻEia ka ʻalana, ka mohai	Here is the free-will offering, the sacrifice
O kaumaha ʻai ia ʻoukou	The food offering to your gods
Alaila a pau na Akua	Then to all the deities
I ka ʻakoʻakoʻa mai ana,	Upon the gathering together,
Akua i haʻi ʻia ka hana i makemake	God to whom is told the work desired
He ʻanaʻana paha	Perhaps a praying to death
O ke kanaka he iʻa wawae loloa.	Man to a long-legged fish.[66]

NA PALE I KA ʻANAʻANA: **PRAYERS AGAINST ʻANAʻANA**

When a person feels the impact of the troublemaking prayers of another he can attempt to return the evil. If he acts promptly he may succeed without seeking the help of a *kahuna*.

The following is a prayer of defense against *anaʻana* or praying to death. It is said to make a barrier "impossible to break." It can also be used against *hoʻopiʻopiʻo,* a form of sorcery, in which the practioner touches a part of his own body, thereby causing injury to his victim's body. The prayer may be said by either the intended victim or by a *kahuna.* If said by a *kahuna,* the victim makes offerings of *ʻawa* as well as black pig or red fish. It is necessary for the victim to say the prayer while away from home and then to sleep, eat, and change his clothing before returning home.

In this prayer the victim's body is compared to a house which, part by part, he seeks to protect.

Nana i ka pou kua,	Look at the back row of house-wall posts,
I ka pou alo,	At the front row of house-wall posts,
I ke kauhuhu,	At the ridge pole,
I ke kuaʻiole,	At the upper ridge pole,
I ke kunakuna,	At the side post of the door frame,
Ka lapauila,	Also at the other side post of the door frame,
I ka paepae,	At the platform on which the rafters rest,
Ka pou hana.	The post set in the middle of each end of the house.
Ka uila i ka lani.	The lightning in the heavens,
Hekili i ka lani,	Thunder in the heavens,
Ka hoʻi kua,	The return from the back,
Ka hoopaʻa,	The making fast,
Laʻi kau ʻaʻi,[67]	Ti leaves on the neck,[67]
Ka hoʻi kua la i ka ua i Ka-hiki,	The returning back to the rain in Ka-hiki,
Ia Kapa-ʻahu, Ka-hiki a Lono,	To Kapa-ʻahu, Ka-hiki of Lono,
Ku makaha i ka lani.	Stands as a sluice gate in the heavens.
ʻEwalu i Kauaʻi	Eight in Kauaʻi
Puʻu o manu ʻewalu i Hawaii	Puu-o-manu, eight in Hawaii
Malaila ʻe hoʻea mai ai na huaʻolelo,	There will arrive the words,
Ka-hiki a Lono la kau ai.	Ka-hiki of Lono in place.[68]

No matter how immediate the danger may be, innocence and quick action are all that are required to protect the intended victim. The following prayer saved an ancient warrior, Namakaokapaoo, when he was about to be killed by Puʻalii. As Puʻalii raised his axe to strike Namakaokapaoo, the axe slipped and killed the would-be killer.

Aloha wale ka maka o aʻu wahi paoo,	O how I long for the eyes of my little fishes (paoo's).
E hapupuu, e hapapaa mai nei,	For which I am undecided, wavering,
E ai paha, e waiho paha,	Whether to eat, or whether to leave.

E waiho paha Nakukuiaimakaokalani,
O Kukuiaimakaokalani kela,
O ku'u wahi aikane keia,
O Namakaokaia ke'lii nui o Hawaii.
E hee la, e hee ka hohewale,
O kanaka no me ka ihe,
O ka ihe no me ka pahu,
Make no ia Namakaokapaoo.

To leave for Kukuiaimakaokalani.
That is Kukuiaimakaokalani,
This is my little friend
Namakaokaia, the great chief of Hawaii.
Vanquished, yes, vanquished is the coward,
The man with the spear,
The spear and the drum,
Shall be vanquished by Namakaokapaoo.[69]

KUNI: PRAYER WITH FIRE

Kuni is a form of sending death or misfortune to a person who has unjustly used 'ana'ana to cause death or illness. There are two types of kuni: kuni ola and kuni 'ana'ana, and both use fire in their ritual. Kuni ola is used when a person is very ill and shows symptoms characteristic of being prayed to death. Kuni 'ana'ana is used after a person has been prayed to death.[70] The rituals in both cases are similar and take place for three successive days, the first of which is Kaloa-ku-kahi, which falls on the twenty-fourth of the moon-month. On the twenty-sixth of the moon-month, Kaloa-pau, the ashes of the burnt offerings are scattered at sea. Within five to ten days the person who caused the original illness or death will themselves die.[71]

When a person shows signs of having been prayed to death, a family member or friend takes an offering of 'awa and, depending on his importance, one or more pigs, dogs, and/or chickens to a kahuna kuni who specializes in 'ana'ana. When the gift is offered to Uli, a prayer such as the following is said.

Eia na puaa (moa, ilio, etc.) i na hoalewa.

Here is the pig (chicken, dog, etc.), o Uli in the heavens.

He puaa ke'ia, e no hia aku ana, e make ka mea nana i ana'ana kau mea aloha.

This pig is to cause the death of him who prayed to death my loved one.

O kau i'a e Uli, a me Maka-ku-koae, a me Ka-alae-a-Hina e hoelewa ai.

It is yours (to do) o Uli, and Maka-ku-koae and Ka-alae-a-Hina in the heavens.[72]

The pig or other animal that was brought as an offering is then released. If it roots or scratches in the earth the kahuna knows that the person who caused the death will die. If the animal goes to the left side of the kahuna, it is said that the death was caused by relatives of the wife. If it goes to the right of the kahuna, it is thought the problem is due to the "younger brother's people."

If the animal passes behind the kahuna, it is said that someone not of the family caused the death praying. If the animal raises its head in the air, a chiefly person is responsible, and if it stands by the man who brought it, then the death was caused by one of his "table companions."

Then the kahuna sends for 'auhuhu, 'akia, bitter gourd, and kukui to use for the ceremony. When all is ready, an ala stone wrapped in pink tapa is laid by the head of the dead person and a prayer such as the following is said.

Ka Ho'olua ka oa mai,
Ka Moae ke pa mai, pa mai, pa mai, pa mai,
Ke alo lolohi, lolohi, lolohi, lolohi,
No-no-pa, no-no-pa, no-no-pa,
Aia-la, aia-la, aia-la a pau i ka
'Oki'oki i ka 'ohe kapu a ke akua o Kane,

A-la, a hala a pa i ke kua au ai la.

O strong Hoolua wind, blow,
O Moae (trade) wind, blow,
Blow! Blow! Blow!
Blow slowly, slowly, slowly,
Gustily, gustily, gustily,
There! There! There! Till all is cut by the sacred bamboo knife of the god, Kane,

Awake! May the prayer and the food be acceptable to the god.

After the prayer, the *kahuna* walks around the body with a gourd in one hand and a bunch of *kukui* nuts in the other, praying over the body.

Penei ka pule ana, i ae penei ka hui,

Hui hano o ka hui ke'ia a ka 'aumakua e hoomana aku
 ana e make ka mea i 'ana'ana iaia i hoihoi ai e oe,
Oihaa lelea ka nui nei.
Penei ka hui, hui hano.
O ka hu'i keia a Uli, o ka-'alae a Hina, a Ku-koa'e,

E molia aku ana e make ka mea nana i 'ana'ana, i hoihoi
 ai e 'oe, oi haalelea ka hui nei.
Penei ka hui, hui hano.

Thus is the praying, thus the joining of the joining
 prayer
Thus is the uniting with the *'aumakua,* to give death
 to the one praying for your death,
And to return you to life.
Thus is the uniting prayer, uniting authority.
Thus is the uniting of Uli, of Ka-'alae a Hina, and
 Ku-koa'e,
Sacrificing to die the one who was praying to death.

Such is the uniting authority.

Then the *kahuna* strikes the gourd and the *kukui* nuts on the tapa-wrapped stone, causing them to break and scatter. The direction in which the pieces fly indicates where the person that caused the death praying may be found.

A wide fire pit is dug and lined with *'akia* and *'auhuhu.* Four *kapu* sticks are set up around the pit and a large fire built with *olomea* wood.

The animals brought for offering are then prepared for cooking. Some "bait" is stuffed into the body of each offering. In this case, the bait will be some part of the body of the dead person; liver or the other entrails are favored. Then each offering is placed in the fire while family and friends pray.

Eia mai o Mea, ke 'imi aku la i ka mea nana i 'ana'ana.

Here comes (name) seeking the one who did death
 praying.

Prayers continue, and before three days are over the *kahuna* will see the spector of the person who caused the death praying. On the third night he scatters the ashes of the offering at sea.[73]

NOTES

57. 'Ilio-uli-o-ka-lani is another *'aumakua* of *'ana'ana.*
58. Kuluwaimaka n.d.; Kelsey translation.
59. Pukui, et. al. 1972, pp. 32-33.
60. Malo 1951, p. 113.
61. Green & Beckwith 1926, pp. 206-207.
62. Emerson, N. B. n.d.; Kelsey translation.
63. Emerson, N.B. n.d.; Kelsey translation.
64. Emerson, J.S. 1917, pp. 35-36.
65. Nalimu n.d.
66. Emerson, N.B. n.d.; Kelsey translation.
67. Ti leaves torn in long strips are used to ward off evil. In this case, two leaves are tied together by their stems and worn around the neck.
68. Anonymous (1); Kelsey translation.
69. Fornander 1918, pp. 276-277.
70. Emerson, N.B. n.d. According to Iokepa (n.d.), one of the signs of having been prayed to death is that part or all the body turns black.
71. Anonymous (1).
72. Titcomb 1948, p. 148.
73. Holograph of the Hawaiian text of *Hawaiian Antiquities*; Kelsey translation.
     Malo 1951, pp. 100-104, Anonymous (1).

V LAPA'AU, OLA, MAKE
Medicine, Life, Death

As with other problems, sickness and damage to the body are caused by either external forces sent by an enemy or by internal forces brought into being by the improper actions of the sick individual or by members of his family. An examination by a family elder or by a *kahuna* will reveal which type of force is causing the problem. If the problem is external, the malevolent spirit is sent back to its keeper and then the body is treated. A minor problem of external origin may require only a prayer as simple as, *"Hele 'oe i kou kahu. E lawe aku i ka 'eha me 'oe."* "Return to your keeper. Take the pain with you."

If the problem is within the individual or his family, *ho'oponopono,* a form of spiritual cleansing, is performed with all members of the family present.[74] After matters have been "set right" and the guilty individual has made restitution for his improper act, the body is treated. This treatment may be by one or more of several methods such as *kahea,* calling spirits; *kuehu kapa,* removing the destructive spirit with a tapa; *lomilomi,* a system of massage; or with herbs called *la'au.*

KALANA: FORGIVENESS

The following prayer seeks forgiveness for actions that might have caused an illness.

31

E ke Akua, e aloha mai 'oe i ka mea i mai ia.

O deity, give love to the one who is sick.

E kala wale mai 'oe i kona hewa ana, a me kona haumia, a me kona ai-ku,

Forgive his sins, his impurities, his improprieties,

A me kona ai-a, a me kona waha-waha, a me kona ho'ohiki 'ino ana ia'oe.

His ungodliness, and his contempt, and his false vows.

E na mai kou lili ma keia mau mohai.

Let your anger be appeased with these sacrifices.

E maliu mai'oe.

Give heed.

A ho'ola mai iaia ma ke kino,

Give life in his body

A hele ku, a hele kolo, a hele nee, a kolo pupu

That he may walk standing, go creeping, go moving little by little, till bent with age

A hau-maka-'iole, a pala-lau-hala, a ola loa a ka pua-ane-ane.

Till with the blurred eyes of a rat and as a yellow pandanus leaf and live very long.

Kau ola ia, e ke Akua,

It is your life, o deity,

Pela kau waiha aku, a me kau waipa aku ia 'oe, e ke Akua.

Such is my breathing upon the water to give spiritual power and my prayer.

Pela kau ho'omana ia 'oe.

Such is my worship to thee.[75]

KUNI OLA

If, while diagnosing the illness, the *kahuna* finds the symptoms are those typical of a person being prayed to death, a specialist in *kuni ola* is consulted before continuing treatment. As with *kuni 'ana'ana,* an offering is made to the *kahuna* who observes its movement to determine in a general way the person who is causing the death praying. Then, as in the other form of *kuni,* a fire pit is built and a fire of *olomea* wood started with leaves of *'akia, 'auhuhu* or bitter gourd added. Then "bait" in the form of nail cuttings, clothing, hair, or spittle is mixed with the offerings which are put into the fire by members of the family or friends. The ceremony proceeds as for *kuni 'ana'ana* with prayers such as the following being said while the *kahuna* waits to see the person causing the death praying.

A kanu e Kane i ka 'ohe ka hikina

Plant, o Kane, the bamboo in the east

A kanu i ka 'ohe, a kapu e ka 'ohe,

And plant the bamboo and make it grow

A lau e ka 'ohe, a pona e ka 'ohe.

And cause the bamboo to leaf, and to have segments.

Lala e ka 'ohe, ka 'ohe laulii i heia.

Cause the bamboo to branch, the small-leaved bamboo

Heia i ke ake loa, i ke ake poko, i ke ake mama,

Offered to the great desire, the short desire, the quick desire

I kulana o hanai-pu, e Lono.

In the position of the feeder of the god, o Lono.

'Amama. Ua noa.

'Amama. The tabu is lifted.

  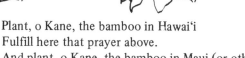

A kanu e Kane i ka 'ohe i Hawai'i

Plant, o Kane, the bamboo in Hawai'i

E hoopiha maane'i i kela pule maluna

Fulfill here that prayer above.

A kanu e Kane i ka 'ohe i Maui

And plant, o Kane, the bamboo in Maui (or other island).

A kanu e Kane i ka 'ohe i Kana-loa

And plant, o Kane, the bamboo in Kana-loa (Kahoolawe)

Pela no maane'i

And so here.

A kanu e Kane i ka 'ohe i La-nai

And plant, o Kane, the bamboo in La-nai

Pela no maane'i

And so here.

E kanu, e Kane i ka ʻohe i Molo-kaʻi,
A kanu, e Kane i ka ʻohe i Oʻahu,
A kanu, e Kane i ka ʻohe i Kauaʻi,
A kanu, e Kane i ka ʻoke i Nii-hau,
A kanu, e Kane i ka ʻohe i Lehua,
A kanu, e Kane i ka ʻohe i Kaʻula,
A kanu, e Kane i ka ʻohe i Nihoa,

Ka wai la ihea, e Kane,
Ka wai la i Kahiki, e Kane
Noa ka wai i ka ʻololi
Noa ka wai i ka ʻolola
Lumaʻia kulia holohiʻa luna
O lau mahuʻe luna
O lau mahuʻe lalo
O lau mahana, mahana huli honua
Hoouka ka i hoe, a ee o Kane
A holo e Kane, a kele e Kane
Kelekele e Kane, he kaua, he kaua
I helua e Lei-maa-loa hopu.
Hou hewa i ke aka i ke aka o Kane
Koloi kolo aʻe kolo anuenue
O ukuhi e ka hue i ka wai

Pakaha i ka lau naenae
I ka lau ʻala o ka nahele.

(The *kahuna* questions and the people answer)

Ka wai la ikea, e Kane?
Ka wai la i Hawaiʻi, e Kane.
Ka wai la ihea, e Kane?
Ka wai la i Maui, e Kane.
Ka wai la ihea, e Kane?
Ka wai la i Kana-loa, e Kane.
Ka wai la ihea, e Kane?
Ka wai la i La-naʻi, e Kane.
Ka wai la ihea, e Kane?
Ka wai la i Molo-kaʻi, e Kane.
Ka wai la ihea, e Kane?
Ka wai la i Oʻahu, e Kane.
Ka wai la ihea, e Kane?
Ka wai la i Kauaʻi, e Kane.
Ka wai la ihea, e Kane?
Ka wai la i Nii-hau, e Kane.
Ka wai la ihea, e Kane?
Ka wai la i Lehua, e Kane.
Ka wai la ihea, e Kane?
Ka wai la i Kaʻula, e Kane.
Ka wai la ihea, e Kane?
Ka wai la i Nihoa, e Kane.

Plant, o Kane, the bamboo in Molo-kaʻi,
And plant, o Kane, the bamboo in Oʻahu,
And plant, o Kane, the bamboo in Kauaʻi,
And plant, o Kane, the bamboo in Nii-hau,
And plant, o Kane, the bamboo in Lehua,
And plant, o Kane, the bamboo in Kaʻula,
And plant, o Kane, the bamboo in Nihoa.

The water where, o Kane?
The water at Ka-hiki, o Kane.
Free of tabu is the water at the narrow,
Free of tabu is the broad.
Drowning, standing, darting up
Take out above
Take out below.
Many are warm, warm throughout the earth.
Put in your paddle and get aboard, o Kane
And go, o Kane, and sail, o Kane.
Sail and sail, o Kane, there is a war, a battle.
It was counted by Lei-maa-loa-hopu
Grasp wrongly the reflection, the reflection of Kane
Crawl the best. Crawl onward. The rainbow crawls.
Lest poured out beforehand be the water of the
    gourd
Robbed of the many for whom my heart pants
The fragrant leaves of the forest.

(The *kahuna* questions and the people answer)

The water where, o Kane?
The water in Hawaiʻi, o Kane.
The water where, o Kane?
The water in Maui, o Kane.
The water where, o Kane?
The water in Kana-loa (Ka-haoolawe), o Kane.
The water where, o Kane?
The water in La-naʻi, o Kane.
The water where, o Kane?
The water in Molo-kaʻi, o Kane.
The water where, o Kane?
The water in Oʻahu, o Kane.
The water where, o Kane?
The water in Kauaʻi, o Kane.
The water where, o Kane?
The water in Nii-hau, o Kane.
The water where, o Kane?
The water in Lehua, o Kane.
The water where, o Kane?
The water in Kaʻula, o Kane.
The water where, o Kane?
The water in Nihoa, o Kane.

On the last of the three days of prayer the ashes of the offerings are scattered at sea and the person who has caused the death praying will die. In the meantime, the sick person can be treated with hopes of success.[76]

KAHEA I HE AKUA: CALL TO A GOD

This prayer is a *kahea* or call to the god Ku-mauna and seeks his attention to an illness. Similar prayers may be addressed to either the family *'aumakua* or to a god whose *kino lau* (alternate form)[77] is the plant that will be used in treating the illness. It may also be said to any god that might have an interest in the treatment.

E Ku-mauna, huli mai nana.
'Eia kau pulapula i hele mai nei i ou la no ka po'e
    pilikia.
Kane, wahine, a huli mai ka honua 'e 'ike.
'Eia au imua o 'oukou, na kua o ka lani, ka honua

Ka-mauna, ka moana pau loa, na kini a pau

Kahiki-ku, Ka-hiki-moe, ka paapaa lani, e Ku, e Hina
'Eia au kau pulapula. I ki'i mai nei i ola no ka po'e
    pilikia.
'Eli'eli kapu, 'eli'eli noa, ka hikina, ke komohana, ke
    kuahiwi, a me ke kai,
'Amama. Ua noa.

O Ku-mauna, turn this way and look
Here is your offspring who has come to you, the
    people in trouble.
Man, woman, and let the earth turn this way to see.
Here am I before You, the gods of the heavens, the
    earth
The mountain, all the ocean, all the multitudes (of
    men).
Kahiki-ku, Kahiki-moe, secure heaven of Ku, of Hina.
Here am I, your offspring. I have (you) to give life to
    the people in trouble.
Profound the tabu, profound its lifting, the east, the
    west, the mountain land, the sea.
'Amama. It is free of tabu.[78]

'OHI 'ANA E LA'AU: PICKING HERBS

The *kahuna,* who treats the sick person's body, will usually gather his herbs in the early hours of the morning to avoid the corruption of distracting noises or actions. When he finds the desired plant he prays to Ku and Hina, and then to the god of the plant he is collecting.

This prayer is for someone whose illness is in their eyes. It is to Kane-i-ka-popolo and is said by the *kahuna* when he has found a large, healthy *popolo* plant standing alone. He begins,

I hele mai nei au e noi ia 'oe, e Kane i-ka-popolo

I la'au e ola ai ku'u maka (a i 'ole, o mea)
I ulu iluna,
I ku iluna,
I lala iluna,
I liko iluna,
I 'opu iluna,
I mohala iluna,
I pua iluna,
I hua a 'o'o iluna,
I pala iluna.

I have come here to request you, o Kane in-the-
    popolo
Medicine that (name) eyes may be healed.
That grew above,
That stood above,
That branched above,
That budded and leafed above,
That opened its flowers above,
That full-bloomed above,
That flowered above,
That bore fruit and matured above,
That ripened above.

After saying the prayer the *kahuna* picks a leaf on the east (or right side) of the plant and then one on the west (or left side) and then one in the middle of the plant.[79] He continues picking in this pattern until he has picked the needed number of leaves, leaving some for another time. He then prays,

O ke ola o ka laʻau au, a Kane, no kuʻu maka. ʻAmama.

Grant the healing power of your medicine, o Kane, for my eyes. It is finished. I have been healed.

After this, the *kahuna* returns home and pounds five leaves[80] until they are mashed soft. Then he mixes them with the Water-of-Kane[81] and squeezes them through white tapa (cloth). The juice is put in the eyes every morning for five days.[82]

KAHEA I OLA: CALL TO HEAL

Sometimes either spirits or the injured part of the body are called to produce healing. Such prayers are called *kahea.* This *kahea* or call is for healing a broken bone.

E Ku! E Hina!

O Ku! O Hina!

Na akua hoʻokumu, hoʻokawowo, hoʻoulu, hoʻohua

The gods that bring into being, that cause to thrive, that cause to grow,

I na lahui kanaka a me na mea ulu o uka, a me ke kai.

Bring to fruition the races of mankind, and the things that grow on land and in the sea.

Ke kahea nei au i ke kanaka

I call to the man of the upland,

O uka o ke ola iloko na laʻau apau o uka.

Of the life in all the medicinal herbs of the upland.

Pela hoʻi ke kanaka o kai; na mea ulu a pau

So to the man of the sea, met by you two.

O ke kai a ʻolua i laʻau no ka (haki o kuʻu iwi).

As medicine for the (break of name of bone)

O ʻoukou maloko owau mawaho pela hoʻi o Ka-ʻonohi-o-ka-la

All of you within and I without, and also Ka-ʻonohi-o-ka-la.

E ʻike hoʻi i na ʻai hemahema a palahe o kuʻu kino

Know of course, the food taken wrongfully, the putrid food of my body.

Pela hoʻi kiʻi hoʻi mai ke kai miki a me ke kai kaha.

So bring, return hither the receding sea, the inrushing sea.

E lawe aku ke kuʻi, ke koni, ka ʻeha

Take away the aches, the throbbing pangs, the pains

A o ke ola a ʻolua me kuʻu kino.

And let the life of you two be within my body.

(Ha, ha, ha (ʻakolu mau ha).)

(The *kahuna* expels his breath three times[83] and then says),

ʻAmama, ua noa.

The prayer is said, it is free of tabu.[84]

The following is another *kahea* for a broken bone.

Ia ʻoe keʻia papa i ʻeha ai ka wawae o (inoa)

To thee is this board (or other object) that injured the foot of (name)

ʻE hoʻi mai ka ʻiʻo o ka ʻio i ke koko, i ke koko, i ka ʻaʻa, i ka ʻaʻa.

Return the flesh to the flesh, the blood to the blood, the vein to itself.

ʻE lawe ʻoe i ka ʻeha a pau

Take away all pain.

Konikoni ka maʻeʻele, ke kuʻi, na ʻeha a pau loa o ke ola.

Benumb the numbness, the hit, remove every pain. Grant recovery.

Nau no e ke Akua ʻe hoʻala mai iaia

It is for thee, O Deity, to restore him.

ʻAmama. Ua noa.

ʻAmama. It is free of tabu.[85]

KUEHU KAPA: DRIVING SICKNESS OFF WITH A TAPA

Keuhu kapa is a technique used to treat sickness caused by someone through "an act of striking to destroy," that is, a sickness sent by an enemy. In this treatment, a tapa is wrapped around various parts of the body and as the tapa is pulled away, the illness is pulled off and flipped away. During the treatment the patient's *ʻaumakua* sits on his body and talks with the *kahuna* while giving directions for the treatment.

The *kahuna* begins the treatment by having the sick person lay face up while he stands on the patient's left side. He then wraps a white tapa around and under the patient's head, binding the tapa crosswise with the left end on the top of the right end. While doing this, the *kahuna* says, *"Hanalei ke ka'ina."* or "Hanalei is the procedure." He throws the left end and then the right end of the tapa over the patient's body. After that he takes hold of the tapa on the left side and draws it along the body and flips off the sickness while saying,

Noho ana Kapo[86] i ka ulu wehiwehi	Kapo[86] is dwelling in the beautiful growth
Ku ana i Ma'ohe-laia	Standing at Ma'ohe-laia
Ohai ku i Mauna-loa	*'Ohai* trees standing on Mauna-loa
Aloha mai Kaulana-'ula	Kaulana-'ula celebrated gives aloha.
'Eia ka ula la, he mohai,	Here is what is red, a sacrifice,
He mohai, he makana na'u ia 'oe.	A sacrifice, a gift by me to you.
Maika'i.	Good.

The *kahuna* then places the tapa around and under the neck, crossing the left end over the right. Then, while standing on the left, he takes hold of the tapa and draws it along the body and flips off the sickness, saying *"O hapu'u ke ka'ina."* or "Hapu'u is the procedure." After that he prays,

Koko pilipili 'ula i ka la	Red sticky blood in the sun,
'I 'ula i ka Mokiha 'Ula a Kane.	Made red by the red *mo'o* of Kane.
I kane 'oe, i wahine au	You are the husband, I the wife.
Kane-aloha nau ke kaha ka 'aina-ko	A loving husband for you in the plain, the sugar cane land
Ke-anoano o Malae-koa i ka la.	The awesomeness of Malae-koa.

When this procedure has been completed, the *kahuna* again wraps the tapa around the patient's neck, this time saying, *"Pani ku ke ka'ina."* "Slamming shut is the procedure." He then pulls the tapa to the left and flips it fully open and prays,

'Ohai o Papio-huli	*'Ohai* trees of Papio-huli
Na hale o Lima-loa[87] i ke kahakai	The house of Lima-loa[87] at the sea shore
Ke ku wale la no i Wai-o-Lono[88]	That just stands there at Wai-o-Lono[88]
'A'ohe kanaka, aia i Mana	There are no people. They are at Mana
'Ohohia e Ka-i'a ike, ua pau	Delighted by Ka-i'a wind. It has ceased.
Ua miki ke ko'ona wai li'u-la.	It has dipped up the remainder of the water of the mirage.

The *kahuna* follows this by wrapping the tapa around the patient on the stomach at the navel, saying, *"Ka Piko o Wa-kea ke ka'ina."* "The navel of Wa-kea is the procedure." As he opens up the tapa he pulls it to the left and prays,

Ua wela Ka-'Ulu-o-Na'e i ka la,	The Breadfruit-of-Na'e are hot in the sun
Ua puhia mai la e Kala'e-loa	They are blown by the Kala'e-loa wind
Ulu loa Ho'olehua i ka makani.	Ho'olehua has grown most greatly in the wind.

The tapa is again wrapped around the patient, this time where the loin cloth is bound on. While the *kahuna* holds both ends of the tapa in his hands he prays, *"Hume-ku ke ka'ina."* "Hume-ku is the procedure." He then pulls the tapa to the left, flipping it open, praying,

Heaha ka uku o nei makani	What is the price of this wind
I kao ai 'oe i ke kai a waiho wale	That has forced you to the sea and left you
Pupu'u wale ua i'a la i ke anu	That fish is doubled up with cold,

| Alo ku'i, ku'iku'i, make. | The front of the body beaten, again and again, dead. |
| Ku'iku'i ola. Ua ola a'e la. | Beaten and beaten alive. He lives. |

The tapa is then wrapped around the thighs and the *kahuna* says, *"Ka-Opili ke ka'ina."* "The-Cramped is the procedure." As he opens up the tapa and pulls it along the left side, he prays,

A makani nu iluna o Ka-lama-'ula a ka'alele	At the wind that roars above Ka-lama-'ula and forsakes it
Iho a'e la i kai o Pa-la'au	Descends by the sea of Pa-la'au
Ko'o-lau wa'a o Molo-ka'i	Making trouble for the canoes of Molo-ka'i
O Molo-ka'i ka'u 'aina aloha.	Molo-ka'i is my beloved land.

Again the tapa is wrapped around the body, this time over the knees, while the *kahuna* says, *"O Kuli-lole ke ka'ina."* "The knee is the procedure." He then pulls the tapa away from the knees and prays,

| Uliuli kai pali o Kahiki-nui | Dark by the sea is the cliff of Kahiki-nui |
| Kokolo mai ka 'ohu e he 'ino. | The fog creeps up. There will be storm. |

Next the *kahuna* places the tapa over the calves of the leg and says, *"Piliaiku ke ka'ina."* "Cramped is the procedure." The tapa is then pulled off the left side while he prays,

| 'Ike i ka nehe a ke kai e | Observed is the rustle of the sea |
| O Papa-loa i Kahiki-nui. | Of Papa-loa at Kahiki-nui. |

Then the tapa is wrapped over the ankles, and the *kahuna* says, *"Ka-hu'a-lepo ke ka'ina."* "The-stirring-up-of-the-dust is the procedure." He then flips the tapa off the left side and prays,

Pupu'u wale ka uahi	Simply cramped up is the place
He ao wale ka'u moe	Just in daylight is my sleep
Moe au i Kani-ku e	I sleep at Kani-ku
I waenakonu o ka 'ino.	In the mist of evil.[89]

The tapa is then wrapped across and under the body, coming up on the right side, as the *kahuna* says, *"Ka-pe'a ke ka'ina."* "The crossing is the procedure." As he pulls the tapa from under the body on the right side, he prays,

Ku i ke 'a ka hale o Kau-po	Stand on stone the houses of Kau-po
'I ho'ohalike i ka hale pa pohaku	Like stone wall houses.
Pa'a 'ole ai ka hale a ka lauwili	Unstable is the house of the fickle person,
He lauwili.	A fickle person.

The tapa is then twisted about the right shoulder with the words, *"Ka-waha-o-ka-puhi ke ka'ina."* "The-mouth-of-the-eel is the procedure." Then standing on the left side of his patient, the *kahuna* pulls the tapa off and flips it while praying,

| He lauwili ka makani | Fickle is the wind |
| O ka puna loa ku aku Na-iwi e i ala e. | Blowing upward all the way as far as Na-iwi that you may arise. |

The tapa is then twisted up and placed on the left shoulder as the *kahuna* says, *"Kowali ke ka'ina."* "Morning Glory is the procedure." He then takes hold of the middle of the tapa and pulls straight up and flips it, praying,

Ko 'ai i 'ai 'ia	Your food that is eaten
Ko kapa 'e 'a'ahu 'ia	Your tapa that is worn
Ko hale 'i noho 'ia	Your house that is dwelt in
'Eia mai ka uku o ka hale la, o na iwi	Here is the payment of the house, the bones.

Finally the tapa is tightly covered over the sick person flatly, lengthwise from head to feet. When it is made fast, the *kahuna* says, *"Kauhi-pu ke ka'ina."* "Cover-all is the procedure." Then standing on the left side, the tapa is drawn off and flipped while praying,

A Kukui-lau-'aina au i Hilo	I am at Kukui-lau-aina in Hilo
Nana aku ia Wai-a-kea	Looking at Wai-a-kea outspread.
Ho'akea ka 'aha a ka ua i ka lani	It is shown widespread by the rains that have lifted.
Ke momoku la no i ka piko o ka hanauna	Cut stroke on stroke is the umbilical cord of one closely related.
Mea no a he loko'ino, a he loko wai akua.	That is the way with you, you are bad inside.
I kuhi paha i ku'u 'opio, he 'opio iluna ke alo.	You presumed that I was young, a young one lying face upward,
Iluna no ke alo, a hele no a.	I was indeed face upward, and I went.

This type of treatment is done in the morning and evenings for five times. When completed, a ceremonial closing is prepared with a mature white chicken, *pi'i-ali'i* taro, its *lu'au* greens, and some *'awa*. The *'awa* is for the *kahuna*. If the patient is a widow or widower, they are the only one to eat the food.[90]

HO'IHO'I ANA I KA 'UHANE: RECALLING THE SPIRIT

At times, when a man or woman dies, some member of the family, a lover, or some other interested person, will attempt to return the spirit to the body. They may do it either by themselves or with the aid of a spirit-capturing *kahuna*. To attract the spirit, sweet-smelling plants, such as *mokihana, maile, 'iliahi,* or *'olena,* are wrapped around the body. Other items attractive to the deceased are collected and brought to the room of the deceased.

When the spirit is contacted it is led, often reluctantly, back to the body. There it is forced to return into the body through the great (big) toe or some say the arch of the foot. The soul of a man is forced through the right foot and that of a woman through the left foot. Others say it leaves through the corner of the eye. After the soul is forced into the foot, the body is then massaged, working from the feet upward. Some say at this time the great toe (or arch) should be held to prevent the soul from escaping again. When the patient has recovered he takes a purifying bath in the ocean, followed by a feast with his family and friends.[91]

The following is a typical prayer to restore life. It was used by Kanaki to restore the life of Ka'ina-li'i.

Lani pipili i ka maka o ke akua,	Heaven-high one who adheres to the eyes of the god,
Lani 'oaka i ka maka o ke ahi,	Heaven-high one that flashes in the source of fire,
Hui papa-nu'u i ka maka o ka uila.	The group of highest royalty unites in the source of the lightning.
Lani kilo o ka maka o Wahi-lani	Heaven-high one of the spying eyes of Wahi-lani
Lani ki'ei a halo i ke kihi o ka malama,	Heaven-high one that peeps and peers at the beginning of the month,
Lani nui kui a mamao,	Heaven-high one of a line that extends afar
O lani Uli wahine, o Nu'u-mea-lani	Heaven-high woman of the Uli line of Nu'u-mea-lani.
O ka-meha-na-lani, o kameha'i-kana	The lone one of the heaven-high ones of multitudinous descendants,

O ku i ke akua i ka mahele nuu o Nuʻu-mea-lani- nui-manomano.	Who stands with the deity in the division of the highest place of royalty, Nuʻu-mea-lani,
E hoʻihoʻi ai ka ʻuhane kino aka wailua o ke kaikamahine	Return hither the spirit of the shadowy body of the deceased maiden.
Wahine uʻi la ʻe moe nei i ka moe niau ninoniolo niʻo hele kapu.	Beautiful, stately woman that lies here in the sleep of no return at the summit of the going of the tabu.
O Niolopua i ke ala koʻi ʻula a Kane	Handsome one in the rainbow-hued mist-cloud of Kane.
E ala aʻe ʻoe a.	O arise thee.[92]

Among the many gods appealed to in the times of illness is Hiʻiaka-i-ka-poli-o-Pele, a younger sister of Pele. The following is a prayer that was said by her while she worked to restore life to Lohiʻau.

Kulia, e Uli, ka pule kanaenae ola;	Speed, o Uli,[93] this prayer for health;
Kulia i ke Alohi-lani.	Speed it to the bright heavens.
Ui ʻa kupua o luna nei:	Is the *kupua* above there:
Owai kupua o luna nei?	Where flows the water of the royal ones?
O Ilio-uli o ka lani;	O Slate-blue-clouds of heaven;
O Ilio-mea, o Ilio-ʻehu;	O White-cloud, o Red-tinted-cloud;
O Ku-ke-ao-iki;	O Ku-of-the-mackerel-spotted-cloud;
O Ku-ke-ao-loa;	O Ku-of-the-long-cloud;
O Ku-ke-ao-poko;	O Ku-of-the-small-cloud;
O Ku-ke-ao-awihiwihi-ula o ka lani;	O Ku-of-the-pink-ragged-cloud of heaven;
O Kanaka o ka mauna,	O the men of the mountain,
Na Hoa hele o ka ulu-laau;	Those who travel the forest;
Ka Keo-lani, i ku ai, e Laka;	Women gods who heal;
O Makaʻa-pule	O Makaʻa-pule
Kahe ka wai o na Hoalii;	Flows the water of Hoʻalii;
Nei wale ka pili moku;	Last is the one attached to the island;
Wawa, kupinaʻi, kuwawa o Ku-haili-moe	Ku-haili-moe whose voice rumbles afar[94]
O Haʻihaʻi-lau-ahea;	O Haʻihaʻi-lau-ahea;
O na Wahine i kapa ku, i kapa eleele—	O women wearing black standing at the edge of the assembly—
Na ke aloha, kono e hele	Great love is their coming;
Hele mai la au, o Hiiaka,	I Hiʻiaka have come,
I ke aloha a ka hanau:	At the love of the one born:
Hanau ke ola;	Birth place of life;
A ola, a ola, e-e!	Life! Life![95]

Some births are not easy and the child is still-born. On those sad occasions every effort is made to bring life to the small body. When Keʻopu-o-lani was expecting the child that would later rule as Kamehameha III, she was at Ke-au-hou, Kona, Hawaii. One day, after swimming in the bay, she was seized with violent cramps as she walked back to her house on the grounds of Ka-lei-o-papa *heiau* and she gave birth in the open. The child appeared dead with afterbirth that was very flabby.

Ka-pihe, the high priest, was called. He instructed Keʻopu-o-lani's attendants to stand in a circle with their forefingers locked with each other. A fire was built in the center of the ring and after the embers were brushed aside the afterbirth was turned over and over above the hot rocks.

At one point, Ka-pihe looked up and saw the image of a child in the dark clouds and he knew that the baby would live. He gave the boy the name Kau-ike-ke-ao-uli, which means, "Stationed-in-the-firmament." Some say Ka-pihe used a kite in this ceremony.

The following is said to be one of the prayers used by Ka-pihe as he worked over the body.

Huila ka lani i ke akua	Flashes the heavens to the god,
Lapalapa ka honua i ke keiki	The earth blazes by the child.
E ke keiki e hoʻoua i ka punohu lani,	O child, cause the small black clouds of the heavens to give rain.
Aia i ka lani ka hoku e	The star is in the heavens
O kuʻu ʻuhane e kahe mau,	O my spirit continually flows,
I laʻa i kou kanawai.	That your ti leaves be sacred.[96]

MAKE: **DEATH**

When death is final and the first wails of loss are over, the body is prepared for burial. Only the family and close friends are allowed in the house where death occurred. As the body is being prepared, the foods that the deceased had been fond of are gathered and taken with the body to its burial place.

When members of the burial party arrive at the interment site they call out to the ancestors of the departed, *"(Inoa) ʻeia mai kou mano."* "(Name) here comes your descendant." They then place the body with the head towards the east and the feet to the west. The corpse is told, *"E (inoa), ʻeia no ʻoe ke hele nei! Hele no ʻoe, e hele loa!"* "(Name), here you are departing! Go, and be gone forever!"

If a wife, husband, lover, or other close person does not want to send the spirit completely away, they will say, *"E hele ʻoe, a i manaʻo e hoʻi mai, e hoʻi mai no! ʻEia ka ʻai, ka iʻa, ke kapa!"* "Go, but if you have a mind to return, come back! Here is vegetable food, fish, clothing!" A spirit thus invited to return may come back as a guest and provide protection, revenge, and other services to the loved one.

Just before the family leaves the burial site, sandalwood may be burned and a farewell prayer, such as the following, may be said.

Aloha na hale o maua i makamaka ʻole!	Grief for our home without our friend!
Ka alanuihele mauka o Huliwale.	The road that leads to the mountain Huliwale.
E huli au ana au i makana ia ʻoe, a-a-a!	I am seeking a gift for you, alas.
Aloha wale, e (inoa), kaua, a-a-a.	Boundless love, O (name), between us, alas.[97]

In the past, burial was generally done at night, and early the following morning all who took part went to the ocean, bathed, and then returned to the house in which the death occurred. There they were purified by a *kahuna*[98] who, after reciting a prayer such as the following, sprinkled all the people with sea water mixed with *limu-kala* and *ʻolena*.[99]

Lele Uli e! Lele wai e!	Hasten, O Uli; hasten, O water!
He Uli, he Uli, he wai, he wai!	Here is Uli, Uli; here is water, water!
Lele au i ka ahua e Kane mehani.	I fly to thy shrine, O Kane, the approachable one.
O Nehelani, nehe ia pikana ka lani.	A rustling in heaven—it rustles with the sprinkling.
A lama. He mu oia.	Light appears. The deity is silent.

Then the people responded:	Then the people responded:
He mu.	The deity is silent.

The kahuna resumed:	The *kahuna* resumed:
He-mu ka aiku,	Silent and attentive are the rude and unceremonious
He-mu ka aia,	Silent are the wicked and unbelievers
He-mu ka ahula,	Silent are the *hula* dancers,
He-mu ka paani,	Silent are those given to sports and games,

40

He-mu koko lana,　　　　　　　　　　Silent are the hot-blooded ones.
I koko puaa!　　　　　　　　　　　　Give us now the blood of swine!
I koko ilio!　　　　　　　　　　　　Give us now the blood of dogs!
I koko kanaka make!　　　　　　　　The blood of the human sacrifice!
He mu oia!　　　　　　　　　　　　The deity is silent!

The people responded:　　　　　　　The people responded:
　He mu.　　　　　　　　　　　　　The deity is silent.

The kahuna said:　　　　　　　　　The *kahuna* said:
　Elieli.　　　　　　　　　　　　　Profoundly.

The people responded:　　　　　　　The people responded:
　Kapu.　　　　　　　　　　　　　Tabu.

The kahuna said:　　　　　　　　　The *kahuna* said:
　Elieli.　　　　　　　　　　　　　Entirely, profoundly.

The people:　　　　　　　　　　　The people:
　Noa.　　　　　　　　　　　　　Free.

The kahuna:　　　　　　　　　　　The *kahuna:*
　Ia e!　　　　　　　　　　　　　O Ia!

The people:　　　　　　　　　　　The people:
　Noa honua.　　　　　　　　　　Freedom instant and complete.[100]

It should be noted that at various times, and in various families, different ways were used to care for the dead. Some were interred in caves, and some were buried, mostly in sand dunes. Other bodies were consigned, intact, either to the ocean or to the volcano. In some families, after the body was cleaned and the wailing over, the head was covered with tapa and then the body was buried. Others were embalmed with *pulu* fiber and salt before interment. Still other bodies, especially those of the chiefly class, were placed in an *imu* until the flesh could be stripped from the bones. Then the flesh and small bones were burned and the ashes sprinkled in the ocean or volcano. The skull and large bones were placed in a casket woven of fiber and then hidden.

NOTES:

74. For a discussion of the practice of *ho'oponopono*, see Pukui 1972, pp. 60-71.
75. Malo 1951, pp. 95-96; Kelsey translation.
76. Kupaiulu 1867; Kelsey translation. It might be noted that *kuni* rituals took place during the day and *'ana'ana* during the night.
77. All classes of *akua* could take on several forms or bodies. These might be animal, fish, bird, plant, or mineral. The bodies were called *kino lau*.
78. Kia'aina n.d.; Kelsey translation.
79. The right side and east are associated with the male while the left side and the west are associated with the female.
80. Although four is the number commonly used in counting, five is the unit used in Hawaiian medicine. Leaves are picked in units of five. The compounded prescription is administered in units of five: five times, five days, etc.
81. The Water-of-Kane is water that drips out of rocks.
82. William Kekoa n.d.; Kelsey translation.
83. The use of three in this prayer collected in the late 1920s reflects the intrusion of Christian beliefs as five would have been the ancient unit.

84. Mrs. Namakahelu Makaena.

85. Henderson n.d.; Kelsey translation.

86. Kapo is one of Pele's sisters. She is both a *hula* and a sorcery goddess.

87. Lima-loa is the god of mirages.

88. "Wai-o-Lono, or Water-of-Lono, is a spring on the plains." (Na-luahine Kaopua n.d.)

89. According to Kelsey, the chant used in this portion of the treatment is a parody of a chant by Hi'iaka when she was on her way to Kaua'i to bring Lohi'au to Pele. Hi'iaka was also a patron of medicine.

90. Kalama n.d.; Kelsey translation.

91. For a Hawaiian story of out-of-the-body death experiences, see Night Marchers (Hoyt 1976, pp. 43-46). Said to be a true story, it first appeared in the Hawaiian Annual in 1883.

92. Ke Auhou, March 8, 1911; Kelsey translation.

93. Uli, the chief goddess of sorcery, is also a healer.

94. Ku-kaili-moe is a healing god who is also worshiped by canoe makers.

95. Emerson, N.B. 1915, pp. 146-147.

96. The story of Kamehameha III's birth may be found in Liliuokalani, n.d. Kekahuna translation; Kama'u, n.d. Kelsey translation, and Kamakau 1951, pp. 263-264. It is said that Kamehameha I had hoped that one of his children by Ke'opu-lani might be born at Ku-kani-loko, the famous birth place on Oahu that assured the rank of those born there. However, none of his children were born there. For another story of giving life to a still-born child, see Gutmanis 1977, pp. 109–110. The story is based on the birth of Arthur K. Cathcart in 1903. In the last line of this chant used to revive the child, *kanawai* is "fig. ti leaves as used in religious ceremony as a plant respected by all spirits." Pukui 1965, p. 119.

97. Green & Beckwith 1926, pp. 180-181.

98. A *kahuna 'ana'ana* cannot perform this rite.

99. Certain plants are sources of *mana* and/or spiritual power. These included *'olena*, ti, bamboo, and *'ape*. Other plants are used because of their names and the power in words. In this case, *kala* means to forgive.

100. Malo 1951, p. 98.

VI ALOHA
Love

The joys of love are such an important part of life that the gods are often called upon to either set a love affair right, to attract a new love, intensify sexual pleasure, or end an unwanted affair.

HANA ALOHA: **LOVE WORK**

When a person needs help attracting or repelling a lover they may go directly to their ancestor gods or seek the help of an experienced member of his living family, a friend, or a *kahuna*. Sugar cane is often a part of the offerings at this time. Because of the power of words, the cane used is chosen according to the meaning of its name. The most commonly used canes for *hana aloha*, or love work, are *manu lele* (flying bird), *papaʻa* (burned or overdone), *laukona* (despised, unfriendly), *lahi* (thin, frail, delicate), and *pili mai* (clinging, held close). At times, other plants might be used to influence a love affair.[101]

The first two of the following prayers are to capture a new love. To make love fly to the hopeful suitor it should be accompanied by an offering of *manu lele* sugar cane. The third prayer is to recapture a straying or weak love and is to be accompanied by an offering of *papaʻa* cane to heat the love or *pili mai* cane to bring the love closer. The offering to accompany the fourth prayer, which is to sever an unwanted love affair, is *lau kona* cane.

Makani-keoe	Makani-keoe
Hono a lele	(The) joining flies
Lele ke aloha	The love flies
Pili ia (inoa)	This pertains to (name)
'Ilaila 'e pili ai	There it will be in contact
'A moe 'ole kona po.	And sleepless are his/her nights.[102]

Lele 'oe a loa'a o (inoa)	You fly until you get (name)
Ma kona wahi e noho ai	At his/her place at which he/she lives
Ho'okomo 'oe i ke aloha iloko ona	You put love into him/her
Ka hali'a, ke kuko, ka makalahia	The fond recollection, the strong desire
Moe 'ole ai kona po	That his/her nights may be without sleep
Ho'iho'i mai a pili a pa'a me ia'u	Return and join firmly with me
E pili a pa'a, mau a mau	Come together, fixedly, continually
A mau loa	And ever after
A kau i ka pua aneane	Till the last offspring is born.[103]

Uli iluna, Uli ilalo	Uli above, Uli below
Uli 'ai, Uli noho	Uli that eats, Uli that dwells
E ku 'oukou i ka wahine/kane	Get the woman/man, all four of you
Ho'iho'i mai 'e pili me a'u kana kane/wahine aloha.	Bring her back to join me, her loving man/woman.[104]

E ho'okonakona, e wehe, e kala	Hold in contempt, undo, release
Kiola hoohele'i i ka mana'o	Throw away, scatter the thought
Ho'opalaka, ho'opoina,	Indifferent, entirely forgotten
Ho'opoina loa i ku'u aloha ho'owahawaha aloha	Entirely forgotten my love, utterly despised
Ho'opauloa, me ka hi'a.[105]	Bring entirely to an end the rubbing back and forth[105]
'Amama, ua noa, lele wale aku la.	Amama, it is free of tabu. Simply flown away.[106]

HE MAHALO: **A THANK YOU**

A joyful love, whether an action of the moment or a life-long relationship, deserves appreciation. The following is an expression of thanksgiving to both the lover and the gods.

Ho'okahi no a'u 'oi Hawai'i moku o Ke-awe	One is my foremost Hawai'i island of Ke-awe
Kilohana ke 'ike iho i ka nani o Mauna Kea	The greatest if you behold the splendor of Mauna Kea
A ke kela o Mauna Loa	And Mauna Loa is excellent.
Hou pili o Hu-alalai	Close companion of Hu-alalai.
Kahiko Kilau-ea i ke ahi a ka wahine	Kilau-ea is ancient with the fire woman
He wahine mai no wau.	I am a woman after her
He ukali no ka makemake	A following of the desire
Makemake au i ka nani	I desire the beauty.
Maika'i o ke 'ala, ke 'ala o ia pua.	Time is the fragrance, the fragrance of that flower
Koni au a ho omau.	I kiss and continue on.[107]

44

HO'AO: MARRIAGE

In the ancient times when *hana aloha* had worked its spell there was no licensing or ritualizing the resulting relationship. Marriage as it is known today did not exist.[108] There were no life-long civil or religious contracts, although many couples formed enduring relationships. The ceremony known as *ho'ao* was normally a ritual of the chiefly class. Its principal purpose was not to bind a lasting relationship but to produce offspring whose rank was certain, whose reservoir of *mana* was assured, and in whom physical and mental perfection could be expected. While waiting for word of the woman having become pregnant, high-ranking *kahuna* of several classes, members of the chiefly families involved, and others with an interest in the line offered prayers, rituals, and chants suggestive of the qualities sought in the hoped-for offspring.

The following prayers are among the many that would be recited in the days, weeks, and occasionally months of waiting for confirmation of the woman's pregnancy. In these prayers, the purpose of the ritual is stated through suggestion and allusion. Today both prayers are used as marriage prayers.

'E'ele mimo ka lani
'Uwe'uwehe ke ao ho'okiki'i
Kiki'i ke ao 'opua lani e
'Ola'olapa ka uwila
Ho'oku'i, nei, nakolokolo ka hekili
Ke wawa kupina'i nei i Ku-haili-moe
O Haiha'ilauahea
O na wahine i ka puoko o ke ahi
O 'imi'imi, o nalowale a loa'a
Loa'a ho'i ka hoa e.
Pupu'u ako o ke anu o ka Ho'oilo
Ke 'iloli nei ka lani
Loa'a ka hale kipa maha o Hako'ilani

Na ke aloha i kono e hui 'olua e.
I ka hakamoa keia, ke halakau nei ka lani
O haka, o haka, i ka lani
O nei, o nakolo, o 'u'ina,
O nakolo i luna, o nehe i lalo
He nehe na ka 'ili'ili kaka'a o 'Ikuwa
A wawa 'ia no he hale kanaka
Nawai e wawa ke hale alaneo,
Pili olua e—
Moku ka pawa o ke ao
Ke moakaka nei ka hikina
Ua hiki ho'i,
Ua kapu i ka po
A ho'oma'ama'ama i ke ao
Ho'ao e! ua noa!
Lele wale aku la ka pule a ke kahuna,
Ua ao holi—amama ua noa.
Lele uli! lele wai!
Lele wale ka pule.

The sky is covered with darkness,
The tilting clouds begin to part,
The leaning bud-shaped clouds in the sky.
The lightning flashes here and there,
The thunder reverberates, rumbles and roars,
Sending echoes repeatedly to Ku-haili-moe,
To Ha'iha-'i-lau-ahea,
To the women in the rising flames.
There was a seeking of the lost, now it is found—
A mate is found,
One to share the chills of winter.
The sky is changing,
For Hakoi-lani, the house of welcome where rest is
     found.
Love has made a plea that you two become united.
Here is a perch, a heavenly resting place,
A perch, a perch in heaven.
There is a trembling, a rumbling, a crackling
A rattling above, a rattling below,
A rustling of the rolling pebbles of 'Ikuwa.
There are sounds of voices in an inhabited house,
But what voices are heard in any empty one?
You two are now one,
The darkness has begun to depart,
The east is beginning to brighten
For day is here at last!
The night has been made *kapu*
Until the light of day arrives.
You are wedded! Free (to each other),
The prayer of the priest has taken flight.
Day is here! *Amama*, the *kapu* is freed!
It has flown to the darkness! flown to the waters!
The prayer has gone its way.[109]

O Wanahili ka po loa la Manuʻa,	Wanahili bides the whole night with Manuʻa,
O ka pu kau kama i Hawaii akea;	By trumpet hailed through broad Hawaii,.
O ka pu leina kea a Kiha—	By the white vaulting conch of Kiha—
O Kiha nui a Pii-lani—	Great Kiha, offspring of Pii-lani,
O Kauhi kalana-honu-a-Kama;	Father of eight-branched Kama-lala-walu.
O ka maka lolena ke hoohaulani i-o!	The far-roaming eye now sparkles with joy,
O kela kanaka hoali mauna.	Whose energy erstwhile shook mountains,
O Ka Lani kuʻi hono i ka moku.	The king who firm-bound the isles in one state,
I waihona kapuahi kanaka eha,	His glory, symboled by four human altars,
Ai i Kauai, i Oahu, i Maui,	Reaches Kauai, Oahu, Maui,
I Hawaii kahiko o Keawe enaena,	Hawaii the eld of Keawe,
Ke a-a mai la me ke o-koko,	Whose tabu, burning with blood-red blaze,
Ke lapa-lapa la i ka makani,	Shoots flame-tongues that leap with the wind,
Makani kua, he Naulu.	The breeze from the mountain, the Naulu.
Kua ka Waihoa i ka Mikioi,	Waihoa humps its back, while cold Mikioi
Pua-a ia lalo o Hala-liʻi,	Blows fierce and swift across Hala-liʻi.
Me he alii, alii, la no ka hele i Kekaha,	It vaunts like a king at Kekaha,
Ka hookiekie i ka liʻu-la,	Flaunting itself in the sun's heat,
Ka hele i ke alia-lia la, alia!	And lifts itself up in mirage,
Alia-lia laʻa-laau Kekaha.	Ghost-forms of woods and trees in Kekaha—
Ke kaha o Kaia-ihi, Wai-o-lono.	Sweeping o'er waste Kala-ihi, Water-of-Lono;
Ke olo la ke pihe a ka La, e!	While the sun shoots forth its fierce rays—
Ke nu la paha i Honua-ula.	Its heat, perchance, reaches to Honua-ula.[110]

HOʻIHOʻI HOU I KE KULANA MUA: RESTORING SEXUAL POTENCY

Sometimes the joys of sexual fulfillment are denied men and they lose their power to function sexually. At such times the gods may be called on to help. The following is a series of prayers used to restore sexual potency.

Ia Waiwai-ʻole[111]	To Worthless[111]
Pale ka po,	Ward off the period of night,
Puka i ke ao.	Bring forth the period of day.
ʻOwau nei, o Ka-noho-aloha.[112]	It is I here, The-Dweller-With-Love.[112]
Ho mai he ʻike,	Extend forth knowledge,
Ho mai he mana,	Extend forth power,
Ho mai he ola	Extend forth well-being
I nui ka ikaika.	That great be strength.

This prayer is followed by a prayer to the women of the volcano pit.

ʻE Pele, ʻe Hiʻi-aka, ʻe Hau-mea,	O Pele, O Hiʻi-aka, O Hau-mea,
ʻE na wahine o ka wai,	O women of the water,
O na wahine alo ka hikina a ka la,	The women that face the rising of the sun,
ʻAu na wahine makaʻikaʻi ia ʻoe, ʻe Laka.	The women who visit you travel by sea, O Laka
ʻE Laka i ka maʻi kane, i ka maʻi wahine,	O Laka at the genitals of the man, at the genitals of the woman,
ʻE Hina puku ʻai, ʻe Hina-puka iʻa,	O Hina who makes a final offering of food, O Hina who makes a final offering of fish.
ʻE Hina puku maʻi, i kela maʻi, keia maʻi.	O Hina who decreases that genital, this genital,
ʻE Hina puku ola,	O Hina make a final offering of life,
Pale ka po; puka i ka ao.	Set aside the period of night, bring forth the period of day.

'Owau nei a Ka-noho, ola ma'i.   Here am I, The-Dweller, cure (the) genital.
He 'ike, he mana, he ola, i nui ka ikaika.   Grant knowledge, power, life, that great be strength.

When that prayer is completed the following prayer is said.

'E 'ike i ka la loa, i ka mama,	See the distance, the speed,
'I ku nana hiku au, e Kane,	I stand beholding you, turn to me o Kane,
Ke'ia pu'u nei[113] e ku nei.	This great hill[113] that stands here,
Ke'eke'ehia,[114] holahola 'ia,	Let it be stamped[114] upon, outspread,
Ke'ia ma'i nui 'e ku nei.	This great sickness that stands here,
Ke'eke'ehia, holahola 'ia,	Let it be stamped upon, flattened,
Mana ia 'oe, mana ia'u;	Power to you, power to me;
Ia 'oe 'e Ka-la, e Ka-la-hau-mania,	To you a Ka-la, O Ka-la of shuddery sensation
A ka la pa i ke ku'e'e 'auwai la,	By the sun that strikes the stream of opposition,
'Amama; ua noa, i nui ka ikaika.	It is free of tabu; great is the strength.

When the above prayer is completed the following prayer is said.

Ke kaha imua, ke kaha ihope,	Devastate in front, devastate behind,
Ke kaha 'iwaena nei o'u nei la,	The devastation between me here
'Opihi 'ula iki Pele a palo 'auwai la.	A little red limpet is Pele, and reveals a water stream.
'Amama, ua noa, i nui ka ikaika.	It is free of tabu, that great be the strength.

When this prayer is ended, then the patient is given medicine to drink. It might be *'ala'ala-wai-nui*. If so, he will also be given *'a'ala-'ula limu* and *'ala'ala he'e*, possibly at the closing of the treatment or as part of the final meal.

If the patient belches ten times he will soon return to health. If he does not belch, then he repeats the treatment. If he does not belch after the second treatment, "the work for the patient is done."

After the medicine has been given the patient, the following prayer is said.

He ola imua,	A life forward,
He ola ihope,	A life behind,
He ola iwaena,	A life between,
He ola, he ola loa;	A life, a long life;
Ho'opuka 'ia ke ola.	Let the life be brought forth.
He hemo imua;	A discharge forward;
He hemo ihope;	A discharge behind;
He hemo loa, 'auwai la.	A long discharge, like a stream.
'Amama. Ua noa. I nani ka ikaika.	*Amama*. It is free of tabu. Beautiful is the strength.

The following is the last prayer and completes the treatment.

Aia i Ka-hua, i Ka-wai-hae,[115]	At Ka-hua, at Ka-wai-hae,[115]
'I Wai-mea, i Pohaku-loa.	At Wai-mea, at Pohaku-loa.
Pau Kani-ku i ka 'a'ina,	Kani-ku is completely devoured by the explosive sound,
'A'ina no i Kua-hewa,	Explosive sound indeed at Kua-hewa,
'A'ina iuka, 'a'ina i kai	Explosive sound upland, explosive sound seaward,
'A'ina i kekepa o wahine,	Explosive sound at the snapping of the woman,
A lele na ho'ali'i	And those acting as chiefs are sent flying,
Maka'u ka la'au, mauka Pahoehoe, 'ai 'oe	Fearful is the medicine upland of Pahoehoe, eat it,
'Ai 'oe i Kiholo,	You eat at Kiholo,
I ke ala a'e pau na wai ho'olike,	Upon arousing the waters of comparison are at an end

47

A Ka'u-pulehu, i Manini-'owali	At Ka'u-pulehu, at Manini-'owali
A Ku-ki'i-a-ka-ua noho mau i 'Alana-po,	At Ku-ki'i-a-ka-ua continually dwell at 'Alana-po,
A Ka-ho'opulu, na 'ulu i Ka-la-hiki,	At Ka-ho'opulu, the breadfruits at Ka-la-hiki,
I kuli na e Ka Wahine,	In the deafening noise by the Woman,
No ke kua i Pili-wale.	For the deity at Pili-wale.
Mai Pili-wale mai owaho o ka piko,	From Pili-wale outside of the umbilicus,
Ua hemo, ua hemo loa,	It is withdrawn, entirely withdrawn,
A kala pa i ke ku'e la, 'auwai la,	To forgiveness that strikes at opposition, like a stream.
'Amama. Ua noa. Nui ka ikaika.	'Amama. The tabu is lifted. Great is the strength.[125]

NOTES

101. *Manu lele* is a sugar cane with yellowish-green stripes. *Papa'a* cane has a mottled, dark-red skin and brownish fiber. *Laukona* is a yellow and green striped sugar cane. *Lahi* is the yellow mutation of *laukona*. It is also called *'uala-lehu*. This was the offering when seeking a short-term affair. *Pili mai* is a yellow-green mutant of *'aki-lolo* cane. It is sometimes called *'uala*. Besides sugar cane, a number of other plants, such as *ka-manomano* grass (*Cenchrus L. agrimonioides*), *'ape ke'oke'o (Alocasia macrorrhiza)*, and the fruit of the *hinahina (Heliotropium anomalum)* are also used in *hana aloha*. Fish such as *ulua* and *ahole* are also sometimes used. To intensify sexual pleasure, the pollen from the male *hala* blossom, called *hinano,* or from the all-white hibiscus may be applied before love making.

102. Tom Cook n.d.; Kelsey translation. *Makani-ke-oe* (Wind-that-does) in the first line of this *pule* is a god of *hana aloha*.

103. Kia'aina n.d.; Kelsey translation.

104. Kia'aina n.d.; Kelsey translation.

105. *Hi'a* is the rubbing back and forth to make fire and is symbolic of passion.

106. Kia'aina n.d.; Kelsey translation.

107. Ke-ahi-nui-o-Kilau-ea n.d.; Kelsey translation.

108. In some matings, such as the first *pi'o* mating, an effort was made to assure that the mother-to-be was a virgin, thus assuring the certainty of the blood line. This was probably the only time virginity was valued among the people of old Hawaii. The extent to which women were sexually active may be gathered from the Hawaiian saying, *"Maopopo ka makuahine; maopopo ole ka makuakane."* "There is certainty as to the mother, uncertainty as to the father."

The term *po'o lua,* "two-headed," a play on words, was used of a child when it was uncertain as to which of two men was the father. A *po'o lua* child, if acknowledged by both fathers, acquired prestige from the lines of both fathers as well as that of the mother.

109. Handy 1958, pp. 111-112.

110. Emerson, N.B. 1965, pp. 100-101.

111. Worthless in this case refers to the non-functioning organ.

112. According to Cathcart, this line should be translated as "I, here, the seat of love."

113. The word *pu'u,* meaning hill, may also mean desire or obstruction.

114. Stamped upon refers to ending the problem.

115. Ka-wai-hae refers to wild rough water, according to Cathcart, and by projection refers to strong sexual action.

116. Emerson, N.B. n.d.; Kelsey translation.

VII KĀMĀLI'I
Children

A child belongs not only to his parents, but also to his gods, his ancestors, and his community. While the entire community has the responsibility of aiding in the care and development of all children, the bearing of a child in Hawai'i has traditionally been a matter of personal choice. From ancient times the *kahuna* could prescribe practical methods of contraception and abortion. "Any *wahine* (woman) who had too many babies in too little time was fair target for every *waha ko'u* (clucking mouth) in the neighborhood."[117]

KO'U: CONCEPTION

For many, especially those of the chiefly class, the conception of a child was accompanied by rituals, offerings, and prayers. The following is a prayer that is used to effect a pregnancy either in a woman who has had trouble getting pregnant or a woman who is making a first attempt at conceiving. The prayer is said before eating eight fruit of the *kanawao*[118] with two eggs, all of which are broiled.

49

E Ku a me Hina, na 'aumakua ho'olaupa'i kanaka,	O Ku, o Hina, the family gods that cause human increase,
Ho'oulu kanaka, ho'olehulehu kanaka,	Cause humans to grow, cause them to be multitudinous,
E ha'awi mai 'olua i keiki na (name of parents and sex of child desired)	You two, give a child for (name of parents and sex of child desired)
(Work of parent-to-be) i ola ka malihini kipa i ko kaua hale nei la	(Work of parent-to-be) grant life to the stranger who enjoys the hospitality of the house of us two
E Ku; e Ho'ohapai 'ia iloko o (name of mother) i keiki na kaua,	O Ku, cause impregnation in (name of mother) as a child for us two.
O Ku a me Hina.	O Ku and Hina.
'Eli'eli kapu, 'eli'eli noa i a'e honua,	Profound is the tabu, profound the freedom from tabu.
Kapu i ka lani, noa i ka honua	Tabu the heavens. Let the earth be free of tabu.
Ku kane ka wahine.	May the woman have a man.
'Amama. Ua noa.	'Amama. It is free of tabu.

For five days the woman eats the *kanawao* and eggs while repeating the prayer. After this she becomes pregnant.

A woman with a history of miscarriages is directed to regularly eat the dry fruit of the *kanawao,* starting from the time of conception and continuing until after giving birth. Both the mother and child are to eat the *'anae* or *aholehole*[119] fish until the child is "big."[120]

HAPAINA: PREGNANCY

For all the family, the joyful but serious process of assuring an unborn child a strong, healthy body and mind begins with the first signs of pregnancy. This includes prayers, offerings, and chants describing the lineage of the family and the hoped-for attributes of the child. These prayers may be composed by a *kahuna,* the expectant parents, or other family members or friends.

Both parents are expected to maintain positive attitudes and avoid any actions that might be destructive to the forming child.[121]

The prayers for the unborn child are often full of suggestions. This may be seen in the following *mele pule* which was composed for the famous ancient Chief Kua-li'i while he was still in his mother's womb. It may be used as a guide when composing a *mele pule* for an unborn child.

E Ku, e Kawelo-ai-kanaka,	O Ku of the strain that controls common man,
Kala i ka lili wehe ai ka hala,	Forgive the jealousy,
Ka inaina o na moku,	The enmity of the islands,
Ka leo huli i kahua o Ku,	The voice that overturns the foundation of Ku
Ka leo kaha i ka 'opu,[122]	The voice that cuts open the belly of life,[122]
Ka inoa o na Ku i pakele;	The name of the Ku(s) that was saved;
Na ka leo 'ino e ui make;	By the stormy voice to question death;
He kilo ke kahi iluna;	There is, too, one above that watches closely;
O ka alo ka Ku i ka ihe,	The dodging of the spears by Ku,
Ke kuhai Ku-malae,	Who stands feigning friendship,
Ka pule he kaha kahuna imua;	The prayer that draws a *kahuna* forward.
Puni ai ke au ia Ku.	The period caused to be surrounded by Ku.
'Eia Ku la, he kumu ali'i,	Here is Ku, a hereditary chief,
A 'oe i 'a'ea kona kapu.	His tabu is not overstepped.
Na kana Ku i a'e mai,	His god Ku oversteps it,
Na ka la i kau maluna o Nono-muku.	By the sun above Nono-muku.
O ko ho'i Ku-malae,	Yours to be sure Ku-malae,

50

Ka Ku hiapo la 'e ke akua,
I hume Ku i ka malo,
'A'ahu i ke kapa ho'okahi?
Hi'i Ku ma ka uha,
I hanai Ku ma ka 'ai?
I hana i ha'awe i kua-mo'o.
O Kaua'i kona lua-hiwa,
O Lili-ha'a i kona 'a-'i alea,
O Ka-lani-nui lei-moku,
Ka mea nana i ho'o-hanohano;
I luku mai ilaila,
I kupapa i ka 'opu,
I ke kauhua 'ana o Mahu-lua.
Kauhua Ku, make kanaka;
Poha ka 'ina'ina, make kanaka;
Hanau mai Ku, make kanaka;
'Ai Ku i ka 'ai, make kanaka;
I kupu ai ka niho, make kanaka.
I ka lukuna mai 'a 'ahu ke oka.
Noho a pohaku Ku i ke ao.
Hahana aku la paha Kaua'i;
He lu'a mai Maui me Hawai'i.
Ua mo'a ka i'a iloko o ka wai.
Ke puka mai Ku me he ua nui la no ka ho'oilo,
Ke aha ke puka mai me he la no ka Makali'i.

Anoano Ku, ke puka mai,
Me he mea la o Lono-i-ka-makahiki la.
I pa'apa'a ai kuahiwi ke ahu nei ke oka i kai;

Ua loa'a i na 'aina o Honomunu me Waikiki,
A nui mai ka ho'o-wahawaha, 'ohumu.
E ho'i mai, ho'i mai ka lani, ho'i ke aka-mea.
Ua ikiiki makou i ka hana nui,
I maka'u makou i ka uliuli o Ku, e. . . .

Belonging to Ku is the first born child by the deity,
Who girded Ku with the loin cloth,
Garbed him with a single garment?
God Ku embraces the thighs,
Who fed Ku with food?
He made a bundle on the back on the backbone.
Kaua'i is his precious and entirely black pit,
Jealous of a dwarf with his towering neck,
O Ka-lani-nui, lei of the island,
The one who honored;
Who slaughtered there,
To Ku who holds fast the stomach,
In the fruiting season of Mahu-lua.
Ku bears fruit; men die;
Wrath bursts forth, men are sacrificed;
Ku is born, men are sacrificed;
Ku eats, men are sacrificed;
When the teeth grow, men are sacrificed.
In slaughtering the pieces heap up.
Ku stays as stone in the daytime.
Kaua'i becomes hot perhaps;
Maui is a second island with Hawai'i.
The fish in the water is cooked.
Ku comes forth like a great rain of the winter season,
Your pains come forth like a sun of the Maka-li'i
    season.
Ku is in sacredness,
As if he were a Lono-i-ka-makahiki.
Parched the mountains and the refuse heaps up by
    the sea;
He has the lands of Hono-manu and Wai-kiki,
Great is the contempt, the finding fault.
O return, return heaven high one.
We are acutely discomforted with great work;
We were in fear because of the early stage in the
    development of the fetus of Ku.

HE 'OKI

Kaua moku e e. . . . .
Moku e ka hanauna.
'A'ole i hui ka makani i Kaua'i.
O Kaua'i hea Maka-li'i.
Ka haha ia nei au ke aloha,
Ke a'e nei au maluna.
Alia wale ami ai 'a;
A kau maluna o kahi ali'i.
He puhala, he puhala ali'i.
He ku no.

A CUTTING OFF

His island,
Island of the ancestor(s).
The wind did not unite at Kaua'i.
Kaua'i companion of Maka-li'i.
Now groped for by me is love,
I get on top.
I simply wait to have hip movement;
And get on top of a royal one.
A pandanus tree, a chiefly pandanus tree.
A standing indeed.[123]

HANAU: BIRTH

In the ancient times, as soon as a child was born the figure representing the father's god was brought to the place of delivery. If the child was a commoner or a girl, its navel string would be cut at the place of birth. If of the chiefly class, a boy would be carried to a *heiau* for the cutting of his navel string. After the new father had made an offering, which might have included a pure black pig, dark-shelled coconuts, and some tapa, the *kahuna*, holding a length of bamboo, prayed *"O ka 'ohe ke'ia o ka piko o ka 'aiwaiwa lani."* "This is the bamboo for the navel string of the heaven-born chief." Then, using his teeth, the *kahuna* split the bamboo in two to get a sharp cutting edge while praying, *"O ka hahae ke'ia o ka ohe o ka piko o ka 'aiwaiwa lani. O ka moku ke'ia o ka piko o ka aiwaiwa lani."* "This is the splitting of the bamboo for the navel string of the heaven-born one."

When the cord was severed, the *kahuna* prayed as follows.

Kupenu 'ula;	Cleanse the red blood from the stump;
Kupenu lei;	Cleanse it from the cord;
Kumu lei.	Bind up the cord.
A ka halapa i ke akua i laau wai la.	It is for the god to safeguard this child, to make him flourish like a well-watered plant.[124]

WAIU NO KE KEIKI: MILK FOR THE CHILD

If a new mother does not have sufficient milk to nurse her child she will seek the help of the gods. At dawn she will gather a bowl of spring water which she takes to a sweet potato patch. There, while praying to Ku, she will pick a vine with her right hand. While praying to Hina she will pick another vine with her left hand. Dipping the sweet potato vine in the spring water, she will strike her right breast with the vine picked with her right hand and her left breast with the vine picked with her left hand. Some women perform this ceremony in the doorway of their home. In both cases, the women face the rising sun and say a prayer such as the following.

Ia ola 'e Ku a me Hina.	That life o Ku and Hina.
Ho mai ka waiu a nui a lawe a helehele'i.	Extend (give) the milk till there is much and sufficient and scattered about.
'Oia ka 'olua e ha'awi mai ai ka 'olua pulapula.	That is for you to give to your offspring to multiply.[125]

When the time for weaning seems to have come, the mother and a grandparent, *kahuna,* or other interested person perform a ceremony called *ukuhi.* Seated on a mat, holding the child, the mother faces the person performing the ceremony, who asks the child, *"(Inoa) makemake anei 'oe 'e hele o waiu mai 'oe aku?"* "(Name) do you wish the desire for milk to go away from you?" The mother, acting as a spokesman for her child, replies, *"Ae."* "Yes." The *kahuna* then asks the child, *" 'A'ole loa e makemake 'ia ma ke'ia mua aku?"* "Nevermore to desire it?" The mother, again speaking for the child, says, *" 'A'ole loa."* "Never."

Since in ancient times a child was generally nursed much longer than today and consequently was older when weaned, he has a part in the ceremony which is in the form of a test.

Depending upon the family, the test may take any of several forms. While the child is still sitting on the mat, two polished stones may be placed in front of the child. If he ignores them or picks one up and throws it inside the house or, if outside, on the mat, the child is not considered ready for weaning. If the stone is thrown away from the mat the ceremony continues. In some families the test is made with two *lele* bananas. If the child grabs one and attempts to eat it he is considered ready to wean. In other families a bowl of spring water may be placed in front of the child, and if he places his hands in the water he is ready for weaning. Still other families may place a pure white rooster in front of the child and if he grabs it he is ready for weaning. Other versions of this testing is used, depending upon family traditions. Some use introduced foods or modern objects.

Following the test, a prayer such as the following is said in behalf of the child.

E, Ku, e! e lawe aku i	O Ku, listen! take away
Ka ono, ana o ka waiu,	The sweetness of the milk,
Ka makemake o ka waiu,	The desire for the milk,
Ka hoopuni i ka waiu.	The teasing for the milk.
'Amama, ua noa.	So be it, it is free.[126]

Then the mother prays to the goddess Nu'a-kea to stop the flow of her milk. (One such prayer may be found on page 11 of this book.) Following this, there is a celebration feast.

MA'I 'EA: 'EA SICKNESS

One of the most common sicknesses of children is *'ea,* a form of thrush, which is often the signal for the onset of other diseases. The following treatment and prayer were gathered by Elia Helekunihi in the 1870s. The herbs to be used are sought out during the day but gathered at night to avoid the distractions that would be a sign that the treatment would not be successful. Only a *kahuna* is to gather and prepare the herbs for this particular treatment

The herb is the bark of a *kukui* tree which is first gathered from the east side of the tree, which is the side of Ku. Three pieces are cut off and Ku prayed to:

E Ku e,	O Ku
Ke lawe nei au i ka 'ili, o ke'ia laau	I take the bark of this tree
I mea hoola no ka ma'i o (mea)	For the purpose of curing the sickness of (name)
Wehe aku 'oe i na pilikia a me na po'ino a pau,	Undo all the troubles and afflictions,
A me na ma'i a pau maluna o kona kino,	And all the sickness upon his/her body
A lilo ke'ia laau i laau hoola nona (or no'u)	And may this medicine become the healing medicine for him/her.
E Ku e.	O Ku.

Then, three pieces are cut from the side of Hina, which is the western side. She is prayed to in the same manner as Ku. The *kahuna* then returns home and puts all the pieces together, pounding them thoroughly. After straining the liquid, he gives it to the child who is turned face down for a few minutes. This treatment is repeated for five days, always in the morning.[127]

HO'OLA'A E LONO: DEDICATION TO LONO

In the ancient times, when men and women ate apart, a boy-child stayed with the women until he had been weaned, taught the niceties of eating, how to handle his body wastes, and the observation of applicable tabus. All of these were usually learned by the time he was four or five years old. At that time he was ceremonially taken from the women' eating house and established in the eating house of the men. There he was dedicated to the god Lono.

The ceremony of dedication was planned for the night of Lono, the twenty-eighth night of the lunar month. Before it began, an altar was prepared. Each item that went on the altar was chosen because of the power in its name and the influence it would have on the boy's future life. There were the dark-green leaves of the *'ama'u* fern, symbolic of a long life, and the large fronds of the *hapu'u, hapu'u makua,* or the *hapu'upu'u pulu* ferns, which suggest a mighty physique. The *hapu'u 'i'i,* typifying little children, was included as a pledge that as this child had followed his forebears, so other little children would follow him when he was full grown. There were also a number of plants that were chosen to assure the boy of his choice of attractive women. These included the *hala pepe*,[128] the *'ie'ie*, and the *'awapuhi*.[129] "Twining over all, that the entanglement of the new life be sweet, ran lengths of fragrant, glossy-leafed *maile*."

As the altar was being decorated, food was prepared. The pig that was used as an offering was baked in an *imu* in the presence of the worshiping assembly and, being sacred, only those who took part in the ceremony ate of it. When the pig was removed from the *imu*, the head was cut off and set aside as an offering to Lono. Then the following dedicatory prayer was said.

E Ku, E Kane, E Lono,	O Ku, O Kane, O Lono,
'Eia ke keiki, o (inoa)	Here is the child (name),
He kane.	A boy.
E malama iaia a nui,	Take care of him till big,
A 'imi i kana hana,	Till he seeks his work,
E malama i kona ola a kani ko'o,	Preserve his life till he taps with a cane,
A pala lauhala,	Till he doesn't leave his *lauhala* mat,
A haumaka 'iole,	Till his eyes are dim, and small as a rat's,
A ka i koko,	Till he's borne in a calabash net,
A pili i ka moena.	Till he cleaves to his mat.
O kau ia, e ke kua, 'e ha'awi ai!	It is thine to grant, o deity!
'Amama, ua noa.	*'Amama*, ended is the tabu.[130]

After the prayer, the ear of the pig was cut off and placed in a gourd that hung around the neck of a carved image of Lono. Then the boy's father prayed, " *'Eia mai kou pua'a, na niu, ka 'awa, e na akua Ku, Lono, Kane, Kanaloa, a me na 'aumakua.*" "Here is the pig, the coconuts, the *'awa*, O you gods Ku, Lono, Kane, Kanaloa, and you ancestral guardians."[131]

When this offering was completed, the father prayed the following, called a *pule ipu*.

Ala mai, e Lono, i kou haina awa, haina awa nui nou, e Lono.	Arise, O Lono, eat of the sacrificial feast of *awa* set for you, an abundant feast for you, O Lono!
He ulu mai, e Kea, he pepeiao puaa, he pepeiao ilio, he pepeiao aina nui—nou, e Lono!	Provide, O Kea, swine and dogs in abundance! and of land a large territory—for you, O Lono!
Halapa i ke mauli! Kukala ia hale-hau! mau, malewa i ka po; molia ia hai ka po.	Make propitious the cloud-omens! Make proclamation for the building of a prayer-shrine! Peaceful, transparent is the night, night sacred to the gods.
O kuu ka-ipu; o kuu hua i ka-ipu; hua i kakala ka-ipu kakala; he kalana ipu!	My vine-branch this; and this the fruit on my vine-branch. Thick set with fruit are the shooting branches, a plantation of gourds.
O kua i na moo a Hii! I au ia ko ia.	Be fruitful in the heaped up rows! fruit bitter as fish-gall.
Ahia la anoano a ke ahi-kanu, a kanu la, i pua i Hawaii?	How many seeds from this gourd, pray, have been planted in this land cleared-by-fire? have been planted and flowered out in Hawaii?
A kanu la o ka ipu nei; a ulu; a lau; a pua; a hua la o ka ipu nei.	Planted is this seed. It grows; it leafs; it flowers; lo! it fruits—this gourd-vine.
Hoonoho la o ka ipu nei. Kekela o ka ipu nei.	The gourd is placed in position; a shapely gourd it is.
O uhai o ka ipu nei. Kalai la a ka ipu nei.	Plucked is the gourd; it is cut open.
O oki, o kua i o ka piha o ka ipu.	The core within is cut up and emptied out.
O ka ipu ka honua nui nei; o poi o ka lani o Kuakini.	The gourd is this great world; its cover the heavens of Kuakini.
A hou i ka hakaokao, kakai i ke anuenue.	Thrust it into the netting! Attach it to the rainbow for a handle!
O uhao i ka lili, o uhao i ka hala; o uhao i ka la mano-lele i ona!	Imprison within it the jealousies, the sins, the monsters of iniquity!

54

O ka ipu o ka lua mu-a-Iku, o ka ipu a makani koha, a kau ka hoku aiai.	Within this gourd from the cavern of Mu-a-Iku, calabash of explosive wind-squalls—till the serene star shines down.
Owahi! o kani mai, a hea o ka uka manu!	Make haste! lest the calabash sound, and the mountain bird utter its call!
Ka lalau a haa ka manu; ka lalau kulia i Wawau.	Take hold of it and it crouches; take hold of it and it displays itself at Vavau.
He malino a po, e Lono, i ka haunaele;	It has been calm and free from disturbances into the night, o Lono,
Na lili la i ka haunaele, na hala la i ka haunaele o mau kahuna o ke makala ulua.	Free from the turbulent enmities and bickerings of the *kahuna*, hunters after men.
Ulua mai, o Lono, ulua kolea ino o Maa-ku-newa awa lilelile!	Arrest them, O Lono! arrest the malicious sea-birds of Maa-ku-newa, with their flashing wings!
O makia, Lono, a hano, a hano wale no!	Confirm this and make it sacred, wholly sacred, O Lono!
Kila i nei; muli o hala, muli ke kani o Waioha!	Bind it securely here! The faults will be put in the background; the babbling waters of Waioha will take a second place.[132]

When the prayer was finished, the father sucked the dry *'awa* root as symbolic of the gods drinking. Then he mixed a bowl of strong *'awa*, drinking it while he ate of the foods that had been offered up. After that he declared the occasion *noa* or free. Then the general feasting began. However, the boy did not eat of the pork at this time as the eating of pork required a special consecration which would occur later.[133]

KAHE ULE: SUBINCISION

To enhance the pleasure of intercourse, a boy's foreskin was slit before he entered adolescence. The prayers and tabus associated with the operation, which is often confused with circumcision, were simple and "might be compared with the consecrating of a new tool."

The boy was prepared for the operation by having his foreskin daily blown into to loosen the skin. When the child could urinate in an arch, the operation was performed.[134]

When the operation began, four men held the boy. One on each side seized the preputial skin, pulling the prepuce taut. Then the *kahuna,* with a split piece of bamboo in his hand, prayed,

E Ki'i ka 'ohe i Ho-mai-ka-'ohe.	Bring the bamboo from Ho-mai-ka-'ohe.
Eia ka 'ohe lauli'i a Kane.	Here is the small-leafed bamboo of Kane.
'Okia i ka maka o ka ma'i	Cut now the foreskin
Ua moku.	It is divided.

After the prayer the *kahuna* gave the bamboo to the man who was to perform the operation. When the foreskin was cut, the blood was removed by sucking. A dressing of a fresh morning glory flower was placed over the cut and the boy was dressed in a white *malo*. After this an offering was made that was similar to that which had been performed when the boy had been taken to the men's eating house. This was followed by a feast in the men's eating house.[135]

NOTES

117. Pukui n.d.
118. *Kanawao* or *Broussaisia* is a small, endemic tree.
119. *Ahole* or *aholehole* fish, called the sea-pig, could be used as a ceremonial substitute for pig.
120. Spencer 1895; Kelsey translation.

121. On the practical side the mother's diet is also important. From ancient times she has been instructed to consume large amounts of greens, such as sweet potato and *popolo* leaves, throughout her pregnancy, changing from *poi* to sweet potatoes at about six months.

122. Before the time of Hau-mea women were said to be cut open for every delivery.

123. Emerson, N.B. n.d.; Kelsey translation.

124. Malo 1951, p. 136.

125. Gutmanis 1977, p. 112.

126. Green & Beckwith 1924, p. 244.

127. Spencer 1895; Kelsey translation. The use of three is probably a modern change from the ancient use of five.

128. *Pepe* means to crush down; *ho'opepe*, to cause the termination of virginity.

129. The *'awapuhi* was sometimes used to rupture the maidenhead (hymen) if a girl was still a virgin.

130. Kelsey collection and translation.

131. Malo 1951, pp. 87-88.

132. Malo 1951, pp. 88-89.

133. Handy & Pukui 1958, p. 97.

134. This operation might be done either at home or at a *heiau*. Thrum, in his extensive survey of *heiau*, cited two on Kaua'i that were used for subincision. Thrum 1907, pp. 36-44, 60-69.

135. Emerson n.d.; Kelsey translation.

VIII KE KĀUHALE
The Home

The house, which provides shelter and acts as a gathering place for the family, is important as the center in which the family develops its *mana* or spiritual forces. Consequently, the gods play an important part in the choice of the house sites, its construction, and the daily life within the home.

HO'OMAIKA'I I KA HALE: BLESSING THE HOUSE

Once the house is completed, the ceremonial cutting of the *piko* (umbilical cord) takes place. The *piko* in ancient times was a small tuft of thatch. Today it may be a board left protruding to be cut in the same ceremonial way. Some say that the ceremony takes place before the house is furnished; others say that it takes place after the house is completely furnished.[136] In either case, the first blessing is done with only members of the family present so that their *mana* will take possession of every part of the house. If an outsider is present, he will also leave some of his *mana,* giving him future claim on the house.

As part of the blessing, the family makes an offering of fresh-water fish, such as mullet, or red ocean fish, chicken, eggs, taro greens, *'awa,* and salt. This food will supply the needs of the gods of the elements: fresh water, sea, earth, fire, and air. The prayers that accompany these offerings may be quite informal; any religious man may say them. He need only talk with the gods as a family member.

MOKU 'ANA I KA PIKO: CUTTING THE UMBILICAL CORD

After the family blessing is over a feast is prepared. According to some traditions, the *imu* in which the food is cooked must be on either the side or front of the house. While the food is cooking, a red *kumu* or *weke* fish and a white *'ama'ama* or *aholehole* fish are placed under the threshold. Then the *piko* is cut. The following are four ancient prayers that might have been said at the time.

Today, if the family is moving into a previously occupied house, they will first sprinkle all the rooms and the outside of the house with salt or *'olena* water using ti leaves. Then changing the first line of the prayer to *"Ua ku ka hale, ua pa'a ka hale,"* "The house stands, the house is solid," they will say a prayer such as one of the first three of the following prayers. In the fourth prayer the second line will be changed.

Moku ka piko o ka hale	Cut the *piko* of the house
I 'eleua i 'ele ao,	At the time of the dark to the time of the light,
I kai 'eleua,[137]	At the time of the partial blackness,[137]
I kai mimiki,	At the time of the receding sea,
I kai ho'ea,	At the time of the arrival (of the sea)
Iluna,	Above,
Ilalo,	Below,
I manawa iki 'o'o e,	At the time that has come to an end,
A noa ka hale.	(It is time) to free the house of tabu.
E ola e.	Live.
E ola ka hu,[138]	Give life to the *hu*.[138]
E ola ku maka'ainana,	Give life to the *maka'ainana*,
E Ku, e Hina,	O Ku, O Hina,
Eia ka 'ai, na mea a pau.	Here is the food, everything.
E komo iloko o ka hale	Come into the house
O hale Mauli ola.	Into the house of Mauli-ola.
E ola!	Give life!
'Eli'eli kapu,	Profound *kapu*,
'Eli'eli noa.	Profound be the removal of the *kapu*.
Ua noa e.	It is free of *kapu*.[139]

A moku ka piko i ele-ua, i ele-ao,	Severed is the *piko* of the house, the thatch that sheds the rain, that wards off the evil influences of the heavens,
I ka wai i Kaakula-manu la!	The water-spout of Haakula-manu, oh!
E moku!	Cut now!
A moku ka piko o kou hale la, E Mauli-ola!	Cut the *piko* of your house, O Mauli-ola!
I ola i ka nono-hale,	That the house-dweller may prosper,
I ola i ke kanaka kipa mai,	That the guest who enters it may have health,
I ola i ka haku-aina,	That the lord of the land may have health,
I ola i na lii.	That the chiefs may have long life.
Oia ke ola o kau hale, e Mauli-ola;	Grant these blessings to your house, O Mauli-ola.
Ola a kolo-pupu, a haumaka-iole,	To live till one crawls hunched up, till one becomes blear-eyed,
A pala-lau-hala, a ka i koko.	Till one lies on the mat, till one has to be carried about in a net.
'Amama. Ua noa.	Amen. It is free.[140]

58

E 'oki i ka piko o ka hale
He hale ku i ka 'ele-ua, i ka 'ele ao
He hale noho ho'i no ke kanaka.
E Lono e, eia ka hale la,
Ua ku i Mauli-ola.
E ola i ka noho hale,
E ola i ke kanaka kipa mai
E ola i ka haku-'aina
E ola i na 'li'i
Oia ke ola o kauhale e Mauli-ola,
Ola a kolo-pupu, a haumaka 'iole
A pala lauhala, a ka i koko
A kau i ka puaneane.
Oia ke ola au e ke akua-Amama ua noa.
E Ku, e Kane, e Lono
Ku'ua mai i ke ola,
I na pomaika'i,
A ea ka lani, ka honua
Ea ia Kane-i-ka-wai-ola
E ola mai kahi pae a kahi pae,
E ola mai luna a lalo,
Mai kaupoku a ke kahua—
E ola—a ola loa no.

Cut the umbilical cord of the house
A house that resists the rains and stormy elements.
A house for man to dwell in.
O Lono, behold the house,
A house in the presence of the giver of life
Grant life to those who dwell therein,
Grant life to the visitors that come,
Grant life to the landlord.
Grant life to the chiefs,
Let that be the life from the life-giver,
Life until one creeps and is weak-eyed with age
Until one sprawls like a withered hala leaf,
Until one reaches the very extremity of life.
Let this be the life granted to us by the gods.
O Ku, O Kane, O Lono,
Let down the gift of life,
And all the blessings with it.
Till the heavens and earth be heaped,
Let them be raised up by Kane of the living waters.
May there be life from one boundary to the other
From above to below
From roof to foundation,
May there be life—everlasting life.[141]

E Kane, e Ku, e Lono
Ke 'o'oki nei au i ka piko o ka hale, e ke akua,
He hale i kamauliola,
He hale i kalana a ola,
Ola he kanaka ma'i a komo i keia hale ola.
He kanaka pilikia a komo i keia hale ola,
He kanaka make a komo i keia hale ola
E ola ia'u i ka pulapula i ke ao,

E ola i ka'u wahine,
E ola i ka'u mau keiki,
E ola i ko'u mau hoahanau,
E ola i ko'u mau makua,
E ola i ko'u 'ohana.
Ia lanahonua (ola honua).
'Amama, ua noa.

O Kane, O Ku, O Lono,
I am cutting the navel cord of the house, O gods,
A house to revive life,
A house to extend life.
Grant life to a sick man who enters this "house of life,"
A person in trouble who enters this *hale ola,*
A person near death who enters this *hale ola.*
Grant life (well-being) to me, your descendant in this
     world,
Grant life to my wife,
Grant life to my children,
Grant life to my sibs,
Grant life to my parents,
Grant life to my entire family.
May there be well-being in this earthly life.
'Amama; the *kapu* of the prayer is freed.[142]

When the prayer is over and the *piko* cut, fresh greenery is placed around the house. These greens are gathered early in the morning in the forest. Great care is taken in their gathering, avoiding excessive damage to the plants from which they are taken and leaving the parent plant intact. During the gathering, informal prayers are said to the various gods of the forest, explaining the use for which the plants are being taken. Ferns, *maile, 'ilima, 'ie'ie* and ti are the most desirable greens for the interior of the house, while bananas and *'awa* are laid on the *paepae, lanai,* or today the porch. After the greens are in place, the *imu* is opened and the feasting begins. No part may be left. No part of the pig may be given the dogs. Bones are burned or buried and all uneaten food is wrapped and given to the guests to take home with them.[143]

HE PULE NO KELA A ME KEIA LA: A DAILY PRAYER

The prayers to the gods do not stop with the dedication of the home but should continue on a daily basis. The following is an appropriate daily house prayer.

E o'u mau kia'i mai ka po mai	O my guardians, from remote antiquity,
E nana ia mai ka hale o kakou	Watch over our home
Mai luna a lalo	From top to bottom;
Mai kahi kihi a kahi kihi	From one corner to the other;
Mai ka hikina a ke komohana	From east to west;
Mai ka uka a he kai	From (the side facing) the upland to the (side facing the) sea;
Mai loko a waho	From the inside to the outside.
Kia'i 'ia, malama 'ia	Watch over and protect it;
E pale aku i na ho'opilikia ana i ko kakou nohona	Ward off all that may trouble our life here.
'Amama. Ua noa.	*'Amama*—(the prayer) is freed.[144]

NOTES

136. Taylor n.d. and Handy & Pukui 1958, pp. 113-114.
137. The Hawaiian in this line, *kai-'eleua*, refers to bad-tempered, angry, and improper thoughts. *Kai-mimiki* in the following line refers to grumbling. *Kai ho'ea* in line five refers to the bad people outside, all of which will be removed when the blessing has been completed and the *kapu* removed.
138. *Hu* is a class of commoners.
139. Kalama n.d.; Kelsey translation.
140. Malo 1951, p. 125.
141. Handy & Pukui 1958, pp. 113-114.
142. Kamakau 1976, p. 106.
143. In ancient times men and women would not have eaten together nor would their food have been cooked in the same *imu*.
144. Handy & Pukui 1958, p. 141.

IX KĀNUʻANA A MAHIʻAIʻANA
Planting and Farming

The plants are each a gift of the gods. As such their planting and cultivating is appropriate work for everyone from the lowest to the highest.[145] The techniques and prayers are not the same on every island, but the gods always play a part in successful farming.

KA ʻOʻO: THE DIGGING STICK

In ancient times, the soil was prepared by first burning off the land and then digging with an ʻoʻo or hard wood digging stick. If the crops planted in soil prepared by a particular ʻoʻo were especially bountiful for several seasons, then that digging stick might be carefully put away and used ceremonially at the beginning of each future planting season. Such an ʻoʻo would be passed down in a family for generations.

The tree chosen to make into an ʻoʻo had to be strong and straight. Any weakness would be transmitted to the plants that might grow in the field prepared by such an ʻoʻo.

The first of the following prayers addressed to Ku was said after the tree to make the ʻoʻo had been selected. The second prayer was said when making the ʻoʻo.

E Kumokuhali'i	O Ku-who-spreads-greenery,
E Kupulupulu,	O Ku-of-the-thickets,
E Kualanawao,	O Ku-in-the-mountain-regions,
E Kupa'aike'e,	O (Ku) Kupa-who-eats-defects,
E Kuho'oholopali,	O Ku-who-makes-slippery-the-pali,
Ke kua nei au i ke kumu o ka la'au,	I am hewing the trunk of the tree,
I ka eulu, i ka 'ala;	And cropping off the top with (an adz of) *'ala;*
E 'ike mai ia'u i kalai 'o'o,	Look toward me as I carve an *'o'o,*
He kauila ka 'o'o mahi'ai au i ka 'aina kula,	An *'o'o* of *kauila* to be used on *kula* lands,
He 'uala ka 'ai,	To plant sweet potatoes for food,
He kalo malo'o ka 'ai,	Dry land taro for food,
He uhi ka 'ai,	Yams for food,
He mai'a ka 'ai,	Bananas for food,
He wauke ka 'ai,	*Wauke* for "food,"
He ko ka 'ai.	Sugar cane for food.
E 'ike mai ia'u, i ka mahi'ai nui,	Look toward me, the mighty planter,
Ho'i i ka pulapula i ke ao,	Turn to your offspring of this world,
'Amama, ua noa.	*'Amama,* the *kapu* of the prayer is freed.[146]

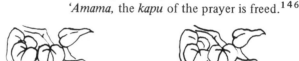

E Ku-alanawao,	O Ku-of-the-upland,
E Ku-mauna,	O Ku-of-the-mountain,
E Ku-oia-na-kia-i,	O Ku-the-watcher,
Ku ka mea nana i ha'awi i na lala 'oole'a a 'owili 'ia	Ku, giver of strong and twisted branches,
Aia ho'i ke kalai 'ana o ko kakou mau mea kalai	Behold the hewing of our implements
'Oi ka 'o'o no na mala, a me na kula wauke (or other plant(s))	Sharp cut the *'o'o* for the fields, for fields of wauke.[147]

In digging a new patch, a farmer called to the gods as he raised his digging stick to strike the first blow. This is one such call.

Ku-moku-hali'i, Ku-pulu-pulu,	Ku-moku-hali'i, Ku-pulu-pulu,
Ku-alana-wao, Ku-pa-'ai-ke'e,	Ku-alana-wao, Ku-pa-'ai-ke'e,
Kua i ke kumu, kua i kaelau,	Supporters of the foundation, supporters of the top (of the plant)
Kua i ka lala, e 'ike	Supporters of the branch, take notice!
E nana i ke kalai ana o ka 'o'o,	Observe the manner in which the spade digs,
He lapa ka 'o'o mahi au i ka 'aina kula,	This farming implement of mine is applied to the farm lands,
He uwala ka 'ai, he uhi ka 'ai,	The (sweet) potato crop, the yam crop,
He kalo malo'o ka 'ai,	The dry-land taro crop,
Me na 'ai ku pono i ka 'aina malo'o ke kanu.	And all crops suitable for dry cultivation.[148]

KANU 'ANA: **PLANTING**

Whatever the crop to be planted, the planter should carry the seed or cutting to the planting area in such a manner as to appear to be carrying an excessively heavy burden. This will suggest to the plants that they are to bear abundantly.[149]

The following prayer is used when planting on the thirteenth night of the moon called *Hua. Hua* means fruit and, through the power found in words, crops planted on this day will bear abundantly. This prayer may be used with any type of food-producing plant.

62

O mahina o ka po a Hua,	O moon of the night of Hua,
Lawe mai ka hua a me ka mea 'ai 'ula	Bring fruit and the food of growing things
No ke akua a me ke kanaka.	For the god and the human.
Eia ke kalo, ke ola o ka 'aina	Here is the taro, the life of the land
Ke ha'awi nei au i ka lepo honua.	I here give the soil of the earth.
Eia ka lau 'uala	Here is the leaf of sweet potato
E kanu au no 'oe a me a'u.	I will plant for you and me.
Eia ka maka o ke ko momona ke 'ai aku	Here is the sprout of the sugar cane that is delicious to eat
Ka ho'ailona o ka 'i'ini holo mua.	The sign of the desire to progress
Ke kanu nei au iloko o ka lepo, lepo makuahine.	I plant in the soil, mother soil.
O mahina o ka po o Hua	O moon of the night of Hua
'E ulu a hua no kia a me kia.	Grow till there is fruit for you and me.[150]

KALO: TARO

Planting a taro patch is a festive occasion. Family, friends and, in ancient times, even chiefs joined in the work. After the land is dug up and dirt walls formed, the area is left fallow for several weeks. Then a feast is prepared and eaten, after which the *huli kalo* or slips are planted. When the taro planting is completed, the walls of the patch are planted with bananas, sugar cane, and ti. Fish such as *'awa, pua, 'ama'ama, 'o'opu,* and *aholehole* are released into the water of the patch. When the new plants have three or four leaves, the planter picks a handful of these leaves and makes two or more bundles of them which he takes home and cooks. Before eating the taro greens he gives thanks to the gods.

After eating his fill of the greens and *poi,* the planter gives the leftovers to his pigs to show, through suggestion, that the crop will be large enough to provide for both the planter and his stock.

The following is a prayer said when planting the taro starts.

E Ku-ike-olo-walu-e,	O Ku-ike-olo-walu,
I olowalu ka huli i ka makalua a kaua.	May the taro top in our planting hole grow large.
I olowalu ke kalo i ola au i ka mahi'ai,	May they grow large that I the planter may live,
I ola ka noho hale,	That the dwellers in the house may live,
I ola ka 'ohua	That the dependants may live,
I ola ka 'ohana,	That the family may live,
I ola na malihini kipa mai,	That the visiting stranger may live,
A i ola ia'u ia (ka inoa o ka mahi'ai).	That I (the name of the planter) may live.
'Amama. Ua noa.	'Amama. It is free of tabu.[151]

After the taro is growing vigorously the patch is weeded, and as needed, the young plants pressed into the earth. This is a prayer that may be said when weeding the taro.

O ka 'omea hiwa uli pahapaha ka lani	With blue-black omen the heavens display themselves
He lani ia la, he la wela iluna, na ka makani	The heavens and a hot day above from the wind,
I wele ho'omaka, he mala na ka 'ino	As a commencement of weeding a garden of storm.
I kanu i na huli we'o mua e ka ua	That the first taro-tops commencing to grow from the rain
Lau ai ke kupu, kapa'ipa'i ka ha.	That many grow and the stalks be large.
Loliloli ka lani ke hiki i ka la'aulu	Of poor growth are the heavens when the time of good growth arrives.
O ka ulu o ka moe kai ha'ina 'ia	The growth of sleep is that declared,
Koi hailona 'ia, kai hea ia i ke kihi	A forceful sign is proclaimed at the outer edge
E mana iho ia 'oe a, ha'ina mai ke ole a	May you have power, declare denial
Oia ia ike a;	That's it, you know.[152]

63

After this, it is *kapu* for anyone to go into the field, even to cultivate it, until the taro is mature. However, the bananas, sugar cane, and ti planted on the walls of the patch are constantly cared for. When the taro growth slackens and some of the leaves begin to turn yellow the farmer collects some leaves and a taro shoot. After cooking them he prays as follows.

E ku'u akua i ke o'o ana o ke kalo,	O my god of the maturing of the taro,
E Kukeolowalu,	O Ku-of-joint-effort,
A kakahiaka e uhuki ka 'ai a kakou,	In the morning our taro will be pulled up,
E huihui ka 'ai, e auamo ka 'ai;	Clustered together, carried on poles;
E ho-'a ka umu o ka 'ai,	The *imu* for the taro will be lighted,
E kalua ka umu ka 'ai,	The taro baked in the *imu,*
E hua'i ka umu o ka 'ai,	The *imu* opened,
E 'ihi ka 'ili o ka 'ai;	The taro peeled;
E ku'i ka 'ai a kakou,	Our taro will be pounded,
E hahao ka 'ai i ka 'umeke;	Placed in a calabash;
E ho'owali ka 'ai a kakou	It will be mixed, this taro of ours
A Kukeolowalu la.	And of Ku-of-joint-effort.
E kaka ka wahie,	Firewood will be chopped,
E ho-'a ka imu,	The *imu* lighted,
E 'u'umi ka pua'a,	The pig strangled,
E unuunu ka hulu o ka pua'a,	The bristles of the pig singed off,
E kua'i ka pua'a,	The pig disemboweled,
E kalua ka imu o ka pua'a a kakou,	And our pig baked in the *imu,*
O Kukeolawalu.	O Ku-of-joint-effort.
Ua mo-'a ka pua'a, e 'oki'oki ka pua'a;	When the pig is cooked, it will be cut up;
E 'ai kane, e 'ai ka wahine, e 'ai kamali'i	Men, women, and children will eat
I ka pua'a, i ka poi, i ke kalo a kaua—	Of the pig, of the *poi,* of our taro—
A ka mahi'ai nui, e Kukeolowalu.	The mighty planter's and yours, O Ku-of-joint-effort.
A papa iki, a papa nui:	To (the gods of) the lesser ranks and the greater ranks:
'Eli'eli kapu, 'eli'eli noa,	Reverent has been the *kapu,* reverent the freeing,
I ola ka honua.	That life may be given to the earth.
'Amama, ua noa; lele wale aku la.	'Amama, the kapu is freed; the prayer has gone on its way.[153]

After his private prayer, the farmer prepares a feast for all those who have helped prepare and work the field.

MAI'A: BANANAS

Before planting bananas the holes are prepared by digging them about a foot and a half deep to hold the shoot so that it will not be blown down by high winds. Then a large meal is cooked and the planter eats until he cannot eat anymore. After this, the banana starts are carried to the holes. Some say this should be done while completely nude. All agree that one should carry the start as though it is extremely heavy, puffing and panting along the way.

While planting, a prayer such as one of the following is said.

Eia ka pohuli mai'a,	Here is the banana sprout,
Eia ka lua a kau pulapula i ho'omakaukau ai e kama.	Here is the hole that your descendant has prepared, o offspring.
E kama e, eeku iho a ho'oulu a'e i ka mai'a a kaua e kanu nei.	O offspring, dig and cause to grow the banana that we plant.
E hanai i nui, i halala ka 'ahui	Take care of it till large and the bunch oversized.
E haluapou ka pa'a o ka ahui	That it be sturdy and the bunch firm

64

E koʻikoʻi ka hiki o ka ʻahui
I lau, i mano, e lawa ai ka ʻahui.

That heavy be the bunch at its arrival
That there be many, and the bunch be thick and
    ample.[154]

E Kama e! E ʻeku iho a hoolu aʻe i
Ka maiʻa a kaua ʻe kanu nei.
E hanai nui, i halala ka ʻahui.
E haluapou ka paa o ka ʻahui,
E koʻikoʻi ka hiki o ka ʻahui,
I lau, i mano, e lawa ai ka ʻahui.

O Kama, root and scatter
The banana we two plant to grow.
Take great care of it that the bunch be large.
Make sturdy the stem of the bunch,
Make heavy the coming of the bunch,
That four hundred, four thousand have enough.[155]

ʻUALA: SWEET POTATOES

When the farmer decides to plant sweet potatoes, he gathers the slips and ties them into bundles.
He then leaves them until the day he is ready to plant. On that day, after calling on the gods, he
goes into the field and, making mounds in the already dug-up soil, plants the slips. When the plants
begin to send out runners the farmer winds them around the mounds. He then prays to Kama-
puaʻa[156] as follows.

He molia he mohai, he makana,
He ʻalana ia ʻoe, e ke Akua;
O na kino puaʻa ou, e Kane ia ka lani,
I ka lewa, i ka honua:
E ka puaʻa hiwa, olomea, kiʻoki,
Hahaikea, lawakea, kakalawela,
Pukoʻa, mahamahakea, huluʻiwi,
ʻOpulepule i kikokiko;
O ka puaʻa hiwapuni i manea keʻokeʻo Kahiki;

E Kanepuaʻa, e mau e, e huli.
E Kanepuaʻa, e ʻeʻeku, e kulapa e hoʻowali;
E mehelu i ka lepo i nenelu i ʻaeʻae;
E ʻeku i uka, e ʻeku i kai,
E ʻeku i naʻe, e ʻeku i lalo,
E ʻeku i waena o ko kakou hikapai ʻuala nei,
E Kanepuaʻa;
E ʻeku ʻoe mai kela kihi a keia kihi,
E ʻeku ʻoe mai kela ka ika a keia ka ika.
Mai kela iwi a keia iwi,
I hua i ka mole,
I hua i ke kano,
I hua i ke aʻakolo,
I hua i ke kakiwi,
I hua i ka wa,
I hua i ka lala,
I hua i ka lau,
Mai ʻeku ʻoe i ko haʻi waena,
O nou ʻia ʻoe i ka pohaku,
A hou ʻia ʻoe i ka ʻoʻo,
A ku ʻoe i ka ʻoʻo,

Set apart is a sacrifice, a gift,
An offering to you, O god;
(To) your pig forms, O Kane in the heavens,
In space, and on earth:
O black pig, brown-striped pig, barred pig,
Shoulder-spotted pig, all-white pig, black-and-brown pig,
Spotted pig, white-jowled pig, pig with reddish hams,
Pig speckled with dots;
O black pig with white hoofs, white, bright-eyed pig of
    Kahiki;
O Kanepuaʻa, stay, turn.
O Kanepuaʻa, root, dig, soften;
Dig the earth to soften and pulverize it;
Root toward the uplands, root toward the sea;
Root to windward, root to leeward,
Root in the midst of our potato patch here,
O Kanepuaʻa;
Root from that corner to this,
Root from that side to this,
From that border to this,
So that the taproots will fruit,
The stalks will fruit,
The creeping roots will fruit,
The layered vines will fruit,
The vine stems will fruit,
The branching vines will fruit,
The planting slips will fruit,
Do not root in the patches of others,
Lest you be pelted with stones,
Stabbed with an ʻoʻo,
Struck with an ʻoʻo,

65

A pa 'oe i ka pohaku a 'eha 'oe,	Hit by a stone and hurt,
A mainoino 'oe i ko ha'i waena.	And suffer harm in their patches.
E Kanepua'a e ho'i mai no 'oe a kakou waena,	O Kanepua'a, come to our patch,
Ilaila no 'oe e 'eku ai;	Dig here;
E malama i ko kaua waena,	Take care of our patch,
I kupu, i ulu, i hua,	So that it will sprout, grow, bear,
I ola na 'ohana, i ola na malihini kipa i ko kakou hale.	And bring "life" to the family, "life" to the strangers welcomed at our house.
He ho'oulu 'ai, he ho'olulu i'a na Kanepua'a.	(May there be) abundant "food," abundant "fish" from Kanepua'a.
'Amama, ua noa.	'Amama, the kapu of the prayer is freed.[157]

A shorter prayer to Kamapua'a as a patron of sweet potato planters follows. It might be said at any time during the plants' growth.

E Kama-pua'a,	O Kama-pua'a,
'Eia ka mala a kaua;	Here is our garden;
Ma'ane'i 'oe 'e 'eku-ai,	Here is where you should dig,
Mai kela ika 'a kela 'ika	From one edge of the patch to the other
A hiki 'i ke'ia kuaiwi.	Until you reach this boundary-wall of piled stones.
Mai hele–aku 'oe mawaho,	Do not go outside,
O pa 'oe–i ka pohaku!	Lest a rock should strike you.[158]

After the farmer prays to Kamapua'a, the patch becomes tabu and no one is to walk in it for a month or two. Throwing stones or putting sticks into the patch is also forbidden. When the sweet potatoes have set, the farmer brings fish and *poi* to the fields and eats. He may also bring a pig which is cooked there and shared with his friends.

WAUKE: PAPERBARK MULBERRY

Among the plants important to the people of old was the *wauke* or paperbark mulberry. Its bark was the principal source of material for making tapa, the cloth used for *malo, pa'u, kikepa,* and bedding.

In ancient times, when planting *wauke,* the farmer would place a fish into the hole before setting in the young start. In more modern times eggs have been placed in the planting hole.

The following is a prayer to Ku and Hina used when planting *wauke.*

O kokolo ke a'a i ka po loa,	That its roots will grow during the nights,
O puka ka maka i ke ao loa.	So that its eyes may be seen during the long days.
O 'oukou i ka po,	You during the night,
Owau nei la ke ao,	I during the day,
E ulu e, e ulu,	Shall cause it to grow, grow,
E ihi, e ihi,	To creep, to branch,
E kokolo ke a'a a paa i ka honua.	That its roots sink firmly to earth.
'Amama, ua noa–lele wale a.	It is over-gone is the message.[159]

NA IPU: GOURDS

Gourds require great care in planting and cultivating. They also require the constant attention of the gods. The most successful planters are potbellied men who eat a large meal before planting, suggesting to the gourds that they fill out like his stomach. This suggestion should be reinforced by carrying the seeds to the planting area, acting as though it requires great effort. At the already prepared planting spot, the farmer drops the seed with a sudden outward motion of his hands with his palm up. If the palms are down, the gourds will grow crooked and shriveled. While dropping the seeds, the farmer says a prayer-suggestion like the following.

He ipu nui!	A huge ipu!
O hiki ku mauna	Growing like a mountain
O hiki kua,	To be carried on the back,
Nui maoli keia ipu!	Really huge is this gourd![160]

Like other plants, the gourd is not to be disturbed during its growth period. Not even the planter's shadow is to fall on the plant once it blooms.[161]

NA PULE UA: RAIN PRAYERS

When a farmer inspects any of his crops and sees that they need rain, he prays to the gods. Two such prayers follow. The first is said to have been a rain prayer of Kamehameha I.

Iho mai ana ka ua i lalo nei,	The rain is descending below,
E kuu kino Akua i ka lani,	My deity body in the heavens,
E ka haka lei o Paoa,	O wreath shelf of Paoa,
E mahele ana e ka ua e ka la;	Dividing by the rain, by the sun;
E ka alewalewa,	O the floating,
E ka Punohu nui a kea,	O the great rising cloud far and wide,
I haule ai ka lani i ka honua,	That the heavens fall to the earth,
I hookaakaa ai ka lani e ua,	The rains split the heavens,
Hanau Kiouli Kiomea;	Born was Dark-blue-pool, Reddish-pool;
Hanau Kauakahi-iki-poo-waiku,	Born was The-single-rain at the head of standing water,
O Kahakaakelu-e,	O Kaha-kaa-kelu,
O Kepolohaina,	O Ke-polo-haina,
O Kuliaikekaua,	O Kulia-i-ke-kaua,
O Lonomakaihe,	O Lono-maka-ihe,
O Lono-ikiaweawealoha,	O Lono-iki-aweawe-aloha,
O Lonoopuakau,	O Lono-'opua-kau,
O Apanapoo e Pooilolea,	O Apanapoo, o Pooilolea,
E Kanikawi e Kanikawa,	O Sound-the-high-note, O Sound-the-low-note,
E Kumahumahukolo e Kolokaaka,	O Ku-mahumahu-kolo, o Kolo-ka-'aka,
E na Akua hooheu o Kama la-e,	The gods that sprout, o Kama,
Homai ana he ua.	Let rain be extended.[162]

O wahi mai, e Lono	Break through, O Lono
O wahi o luna	Break through above
O wahi o lalo	Break through below
O wahi ka uka	On the uplands
O wahi ke kai.	On the sea shores.[163]

NA PULE HO'OULU: GROWTH PRAYERS

While the crops are growing, many prayers are offered to the gods seeking their blessings. The following is one of many prayers for growth.

E Kane auloli ka honua!	O Kane, transform the earth!
Honu nee pu ka aina.	Let the earth move as one piece.
Ulu nakaka, kawahawaha ka honua.	The land is cracked and fissured.
Ulu ka ai hapuu, e Lono.	The edible fern yet grows, O Lono.
Ohi maloo, kupukupu.	Let *kupukupu* cover the dry land.
Ohi aa na uala o na pali.	Gather potatoes as stones on the side-hills.
Pali-ku kawahawaha ka ua,	The rain comes like the side of a *pali,*
Ka ua haule lani.	The rain falling from heaven.
He haule lani ka uala.	The potato also falls from heaven,
He aweu ke kalo,	The wild taro is the only taro now,
He lauloa pili kanawao.	The taro of the mountain patches.
O wao-akua ka ai, e Kane!	The only food is that of the wilds, O Kane!
E Kane! e Lono! na akua mahiai,	O Kane and Lono! Gods of the husbandmen,
Hoola i ka aina!	Give life to the land!
A poho ka ai,	Until the food goes to waste,
A ulu kupukupu,	Until it sprouts in the ground,
A ulu lau poo-ole;	Until the leaves cover the land;
A o ka nui ia o ka ai	And such be the plenty
Au, e Kane a me Lono.	Of you, O Kane and Lono.
'Amama. Ua noa.	The burden is lifted. We are free.[164]

NOTES

145. There are many traditions of great chiefs such as Kamehameha I and, in more recent times, Kamehameha III working in the taro patches.
146. Kamakau 1964, p. 26.
147. Anonymous (2)
148. Pouge & Kenn 1978, pp. 10, 12-13.
149. Planting is done according to the phases of the moon. The moon month starts with the first appearance of the new moon, called Hilo. It is considered a good time for planting, as is Ku-kahi, the third night of the moon. This is especially true for root crops. Ku-pau, the sixth night of the month, is also good for planting sweet potatoes. 'Ole-ku-pau, the tenth night, is good for planting bananas and breadfruit. Huna, the eleventh, is good for planting gourds, while Hua, the thirteenth, is good for all planting. Akua, the fourteenth moon-night, is also good for all planting, being especially good for sugar cane. Hoku, the full moon, that occurs on the fifteenth night, is considered by many as the best of all times for planting. The La'au days, the eighteenth, nineteenth, and twentieth, are all good for planting bananas. The Kaloa days, the twenty-fourth, twenty-fifth, and twenty-sixth, are good for planting bamboo, sugar cane, and *wauke*. Mauli, the twenty-ninth, is considered a good day for planting trees. Muku, the last day of the moon-month, is another day for planting bananas.
150. Ashdown n.d.; Kelsey translation.
151. Ho'olapa n.d.; Kelsey translation.
152. Kuluwaimaka n.d.; Kelsey translation.
153. Kamakau 1976, p. 36.
154. Kekahuna n.d.
155. Kelsey collection and translation.
156. Kama-pua'a is "the pig demigod whose rootings created valleys and springs . . . He had many affairs and is a symbol of lechery. He exchanged ribald taunts with Pele and then called on his plant forms—*olomea, hala* (pandanus), *'uha-loa, 'ama'ama'u* (ferns)—to block her advancing fires, which they did. He finally mated with Pele. . . ." (Pukui 1975, p. 386) Because of his rootings, he was also a patron of farmers.
157. Kamakau 1976, p. 28.
158. Koomoa n.d.; Kelsey translation.
159. Kalauaokalani n.d.; Beckley translation.
160. Ka Nupepa Kuokoa, March 24, 1922; Kelsey translation.
161. Maunakea n.d.
162. Hukilani 1864; Kelsey translation.
163. Ashdown n.d.
164. Malo 1951, pp. 158-159.

X LĀWAI‘A
Fishing

Of the many gods that give their help to fishermen, the most important is Ku‘ula, who is sometimes called Ku‘ula-kai. He taught his son, ‘Ai‘ai, how to set up fish altars and how to address the gods.[165]

After his father's death, ‘Ai‘ai traveled around the islands building fishing shrines which, today, are called *ku‘ula* in honor of his father. At these shrines, ‘Ai‘ai established the custom of offering two fish from each catch, one for his father, Ku, and one for his mother, Hina. He also established *ko‘a* or fishing stations where fish come to feed.

Besides Ku‘ula, other gods that watch over fishermen are Kane-makua, Kane-koa, Kane-kokala, Kane-‘apua, Ka-moho-alii, Hauma-kapu‘u, Hauwahine, and Malei.

KE PULE NEI NA ALI‘I:
THE CHIEFS PRAY

In ancient times, ruling chiefs might go to the gods to seek special consideration for their people. These considerations could include providing abundant fish. At those times, the chief would direct his people to build a *heiau loulu*. This was a temporary building with a flat roof and thatched with *loulu* palm fronds. The following is one of the prayers said at one of these services.

69

E Kane i ke au hulihia,	O Kane of the time of overturning,
Hulihia i ke ale ula.	Overturn the bright sea waves.
I ke ale lani,	The high-arching sea waves,
I ke pu-koa,	The coral reefs,
I ka aaka,	The bare reefs,
I ke ahua o Lonomuku.	The cave-floor of Lono-muku.
Moku ka pawa o ka po e Kane.	Severed is the milky way of the night, O Kane!
Eia ka alana la, e Kane,	Here is an offering, O Kane,
He puaa, he moa uakea.	A pig, a white fowl.
E ku ka ia mai Ka-hiki mai,	Drive hither the fish from Tahiti,
He opelu, ka ia hele pu me ka la,	The *opelu*, fish that travels with the sun,
He aku koki ia,	The *aku* pulled in by the line,
He uwiuwi, he ia lana kai,	The *uwiuwi* that swims near the surface,
He aweoweo ku i ke kaheka,	The *aweoweo* that haunts the pools,
E Kane, e ku ka ia,	O Kane send us fish,
E ai ka maka-pehu.	That the swollen-eyed may eat it.
E ola ka aina.	Life to the land.
'Amama. Ua noa.	Amen. It is free.

After this prayer, a feast was held. If anyone came near and looked into the structure, he had to come in and eat with the group. A light rain during the feast was considered a good omen. Before the eating began, the *kahuna* said the following prayer.

E Kane i ka wai ola,	O Kane of the water of life,
E ola ia makou kau mau pulapula.	Preserve us, thy offspring.
Eia ka mohai, he puaa,	Here is an offering, a hog,
He moa uakea, he niu,	A white fowl, coconuts,
He uala, he kalo mana,	Potatoes, a *mana taro*.
E mana ia oe Kane,	The power is thine, O Kane,
E houlu i ka ia	To collect for us the fish
I ola ka maka-pehu o ka aina.	And relieve the gauntness of the land.
E komo, e ai,	Come in and eat of the feast.
Eia ka ihu o ka puaa,	Here is the snout of the pig,
Ka huelo o ka puaa,	The tail of the pig,
Ke ake niau o ka puaa,	The spleen of the pig,
Ka puu o ka moa,	The neck of the fowl,
Ka wai o ka niu,	The juice of the coconut,
Ka limu koko,	The red sea moss,
Ke kalo mana uakea.	The white-leafed *mana taro*,
'Amama. Ua noa.	Amen. It is free.

The leftover food was made up into five parcels and placed at each of the four corner posts and in the center of the *heiau*. If, within the next ten days, a good haul of fish was not taken, there had been something wrong with the service and it had to be repeated.[166]

NA PULE O NA MAKA'AINANA: THE PRAYERS OF THE PEOPLE

While the chiefs might go to the gods with elaborate rituals and the aid of a *kahuna*, the ordinary fisherman, fishing for his family's daily needs, could approach the gods with simple prayers. The following are typical prayers said by an individual or a small group of fishermen.

E Kane, eia ka alana, ka mohai,	O Kane, here is the free-will offering, the prescribed offering,

He mai'a no Wai-'ololo e mana 'oe ia Ala-iki-punia
  i Ku'ula,
He pohaku mana i poni 'ia i ka niu, ka maile, ke
  kupaoa, la'au o na i'a.

E ka i'a nui, e ka i'a ku, e ka i'a ka'i, e ka i'a puni,

A ola ka makapehu, ke 'u-nu—
A ola ka 'aina, a pau ka wi i'a o ka 'aina.

'Amama.

A banana of Wai-'ololo, that you may give spirit power
  by Ala-iki-punia at Ku'ula,
A stone with spirit power anointed with the coconut,
  the *maile* vine, the *kupaoa,* plant that intoxicates
  fish.
O the big fish, o the fish in schools, o the journeying
  fish, o the surrounded fish,
And live the sufferers from lack of fish.
And live the land and ended be the famine of fish of
  the land.
'Amama.[167]

E Kane i Wai-'ololi i kani a ka pupu kai,
E 'a'au, naholo ka i'a a puni ka lau,

Hahai a holo ka i'a o kai uli a Ku'ula,

A ku, a 'ahu, a mokaki,
A ku ka paoa i ka pohaku Ala-iki-punia,

Ke Ku'ula a Kane-i-ka-poha-kea, e moe.
A noa. 'Amama, e noa. Ua noa.

O Kane at Wai-'ololi, who sounded the conch shell,
Make the fish go here and there, chase the fish
  around the dragnet.
Chase so that the fish run, the fish of the deep blue sea
  of Ku'ula.
Till in school, till in heaps, till scattered here and there,
And may the fragrance remain in the stone Ala-iki-
  punia,
The Ku'ula belonging to Kane-i-ka-poha-kea, lie quietly.
'Amama. Let it be free of tabu. It is free of tabu.[168]

Kani mai, e Lono, i ka leo, ka ualo au,
A ka pulapula e noho ana i ke ao nei.
'Owau, O Mano-ka-lani-po
Ia Ku, ia Hina.
Ka 'oukou ola ho'opa'a 'ia mai.
Na i'a o kela 'ano, ke'ia 'ano.
E ola ka 'oukou pulapula e noho nei i ke ao nei,
Kani ko'o, pala lauhala,
Haumaka 'iole, kau i ka pua aneane.
A kau, i ka pua aneane.

Sound, my calling out, O Lono-i-ka-leo,
By the descendant dwelling on the earth here.
I am Mano-ka-lani-po
To Ku, to Hina.
Let the life that belongs to you be made firm.
May the fish of that kind, this kind, be held fast.
Grant life to your progeny who dwell here on the earth
Till the cane sounds, till like *hala* leaves turned yellow,
Till they have the blurred eyes of a rat,
Till the offspring is exhausted.[169]

When a fish takes the fishhook, the fisherman might say a brief prayer such as the following to secure the fish.

E Ku; e ku'u Akua-i ke aho a kaua ea.
A i ai ka i'a i ka maunu a kaua;
Pa'a ae a pa'a i ka hoau—ke aho a kaua ea.
E Ku; e ku'u Akua i ka moana nei la e.
'Amama oe, e Ku.

O Ku, o my deity here in the ocean,
The fish ate our bait
Held fast by swimming is our fishline, isn't it.
O Ku, my god in the ocean here.
'Amama to you, O Ku.[170]

71

The following prayer is one that is said by a fisherman when seeking shellfish.

Monia, monia 'alealea | Be swallowed, be swallowed, shellfish
Pa'a i ka humu pihapiha lawe 'ia mai | Made fast by complete binding and brought here
O ka 'olua ola ia 'e Ku, a me Hina; | It is your life, o Ku and Hina;
O ko'u ola ho'i ia | It is my life, of course
O ka 'olua pulapula i ke'ia ao | Offspring of you two in this world.
'Amama, ua noa. | 'Amama. It is free of tabu.[171]

The following is a prayer of thanksgiving said by a fisherman after he catches a fish.

E kahikina, e ke komohana, | O the east, o the west,
E ka akau, e ka hema, | O the north, o the south
E luna, e lalo, e ka la. | O above, o below, o the sun,
E ike iau i ka lawai'a | Recognize me the fisherman
E nana i ka ohumu, i ka huahua, | Look at the grumbling, at the fruitfulness
He mua kaua, he hope ko kaua. | We are first; ours is last.
E ike oe ia'u e ka la ua, e ka la makani, e ka la malie, | Give recognition to me o the sun, the rain, the windy day, the quiet day

O ko'u la ho'i ia ko ke kanaka lawai'a, | My day of course is that of the fisherman.
I lako i ke aho me ka makau, | Provided with line and hook,
E ka la e-e ola i a'u | O sun give me life
I ka'u wahine, i ku'u keiki, i ko'u mau makua. | And to my wife, my children, my parents.
'Amama ua noa. | 'Amama. It is free of tabu.[172]

NA AHO: FISH LINES

Fishing, as all other aspects of life, is a cooperative effort between man and his ancestor-gods. While the gods provide the fish, man has the responsibility to prepare his equipment and to learn the techniques of fishing. In the ancient times, the preparation of fishlines and nets was an important part of man's responsibilities. These were generally made from *olona*, which is said to be the strongest vegetable fiber known. After the plants were cut and stripped, offerings were made before spinning the fibers began. Prayers such as the following were also said.

Kuhi kuu ka lani | I, a chief, willingly
Keaweawekaokai honua, | Cast my net of *olona*,
Kupu ola ua ulu ke ipuu. | The *olona* springs up, it grows,
Ke kahi 'ke olona. | It branches and is cut down.
Kahoekukama kohi lani, | The paddles of the chief beat the sea.
O kia ka piko o ke olona | Stripped off is the bark of the *olona*,
Ihi a ka ili no moki no lena, | Peeled is the bark of the yellow *moki*.
Ahi kuni ka aala, | The fire exhales a sweet odor.
Kunia, haina, paia, | The sacrifice is ready.
Holea, hoomoe ka papa, | The bark is peeled, the board is made ready,
Ke kahi ke olona, | The *olona* is carded,
Ke kau ko opua, | And laid on the board.
Ke kea ka maawe | White is the cord,
Kau hae ka ilo ka uha, | The cord is twisted on the thigh,
Ke kaakalawa ka upena: | Finished is the net:
O kuu aku i kai, | Cast it into the sea.
I kai a Papa; ua hina, | Into the sea of Papa; let him fall,
E hina, kohia i ka aa | Let him fall, that I may strangle the neck
Of Uhumakaikai. | Of Uhumakaikai.[173]

72

NOTES:

165. Ancient stories tell of Kuʻula living with his wife Hina-puku-iʻa on East Maui on the land named Alea-mai at a place called Lehoʻula on the side of the hill Ka-iwi-o-Pele. Kuʻula gave his son four objects with which he could control the fish. These were a decoy stick, called Pahiaku-kahui (or kahuoi); a cowry shell, called Lehoʻula; a fish hook, called Manai-a-ka-lani; and a stone, called Kuʻula, which had the power to draw fish to it.
166. Malo 1951, pp. 157-158.
167. Emerson, N.B., from J. P. Keawe n.d.; Kelsey translation.
168. Emerson, N.B., from J. P. Keawe n.d.; Kelsey translation.
169. Kelsey collection and translation.
170. Kelsey collection and translation.
171. Kelsey collection and translation.
172. Kelsey collection and translation.
173. Remy 1868, p. 44; MacCaughey 1918, p. 237; Kepler 1980, p. B 13.

XI NĀ WAʻA
The Canoes

The gods gave man the knowledge of canoe making and sailing so long ago that no one knows where or when it was. Man has, in turn, over the generations composed many prayers for the trees from which canoes are constructed and for the work of building canoes, as well as for launching and sailing canoes. The first of the prayers for a canoe may be said as much as a generation before it is to be built when a *kahuna kalai waʻa* (canoe building *kahuna*) visits the upper forest checking the growth of *koa* trees.[174] There he prays to the various gods of the forest and canoe building, reminding them of their ties to man and asking their care of the trees until they are to be made into canoes.

NĀ KOʻI: THE ADZES

In ancient times, when a canoe was to be built, the canoe-making *kahuna* went to the forest and chose a tree, perhaps a tree his family had watched for years. He then returned to the *heiau* and prepared the tools and offerings that would be used in cutting the tree. When all was ready as sunset ended the Hilo and began Hoaka (the second night of the moon-month), he called all the men who were to work on the canoe to the *heiau*. There the *kahuna* prepared and baked three chickens, one for the canoe-making god, one for the person the canoe was to be made for, and one for the *kahuna* himself. After a prayer, the adzes were put to sleep within the lintels of "the door of *mana*" of the house of the god images. After the fowls were eaten, all the men went to sleep in the *heiau*.

The following is a prayer said before the adzes were "put to sleep."

E Kane uakea,
Eia ka alana,
He moa ualehu,
He moa uakea,
He moa, ulahiwa,
He alana keia ia oe Kane,
No ke ko'i kalai wa'a,
Ko'i kua,
Ko'i kikoni,
Ko'i lou,
He ko'i e kai e kalai ai ka wa'a
E Kane, ke akua ola,
Ke akua mana,
Ke akua noho i ka 'iu'iu,
Ke akua i ke ao polohiwa.
E ike iau ia (inoa)
Ke kahuna kalai wa'a.
E ola ia, ke ali'i heiau,
E ola iau ia (inoa), ke kahuna,
E ola i na kahuna.
He 'ai kapu ka moa o ke ali'i.
E 'ai noa ka moa o ke akua me ke kahuna.

A lele, ua noa.
A noa i ke akua.
'Amama, lele wale.

O Kane the white one,
Here is the free-will offering,
An ashy-gray fowl,
A light-colored fowl,
A dark-red fowl,
These are offerings for you, O Kane,
For the cane carver's adze,
Hewing adze,
Little adze,
Reversible adze,
An adze to finish the canoe.
O Kane, the god of life,
The god of power,
The god who dwells in the distant realm,
The god surrounded with dark clouds.
See me (name)
The canoe-carving *kahuna.*
Give life to the chief of the *heiau,*
Give life to me (name), the priest
Give life to the priests.
A consecreted food is the chicken of the chief.
A food released from restrictions is the chicken of the god and the priest
And the prayer has flown, it is free of restrictions.
Free of tabu to the god.
'Amama, it is free of tabu, only flown away.[175]

I KA UKA: **TO THE MOUNTAINS**

The next morning the adzes were awakened by dipping them in the ocean as the *kahuna* called out *"E ala i hana no Kane."* "Awake to work for Kane." They were then dried and wrapped in *tapa.* After that, the workmen, the *kahuna kalai wa'a,* and any other men with an interest in the canoe set out for the forest carrying the adzes and other supplies.

On the way to the forest, prayers such as the following would have been said.

Ke amo la ke ko'i ke akua la i-uka;
Haki nu'a-nu'a mai ka nalu mai Kahiki,
Po-po'i aku la i ke alo o Kilauea.
Kanaka hea i ka lakou puaa kanu;
He wahine kui lei lehua i uka o Olaa,
Ku'u moku lehua i ke alo o He-eia.
O Kuku-ena wahine,
Komo i ka lau-ki,
A'e-a'e a noho.
Eia makou, kou lau kaula la.
Eli-eli, kau mai!

They bear the god's ax up the mountain;
Trampling the mire, like waves from Kahiki
That beat on the front of Kilauea.
The people with offerings lift up a prayer;
A woman strings wreaths in Olaa—
Lehua grove mine bord'ring He-eia.
And now Kukuena, mother god,
Covers her loins with a pa-u of ti leaf;
She mounts the altar; she sits,
Behold us, your conclave of priests.
Enter in, possess us![176]

KALAI 'ANA I KA LA'AU: **CUTTING THE TREE**

When the canoe-building party reached the tree they were going to cut, they made camp and prepared offerings to the gods. According to some this first offering was a black pig and red fish[177]

75

that had been carried alive to the spot. The pig was a small one so that the *kahuna* could eat it all by himself. It was not killed in the usual manner but by the power of prayer. Holding the pig firmly, the *kahuna* said a prayer such as the following. When he completed the prayer the pig would be dead.

Pupu weuweu e Laka e![178]	Gather together your greenery, o Laka,[178]
O au ko kahu, e ke akua.	I am your keeper, o deity.
Kaumaha e ia Laka,	First make a sacrifice to Laka
A o Laka ka pule ikaika.	And of Laka is the powerful prayer
Ikaika ke pule i ka pua'a.	Powerful if you pray to the pig
E lawe i ke ola o ka pua'a.	To take the life of the pig.
Ua make ka pua'a e Laka e	The pig is dead, o Laka.
Ua noa ke kahua.	The grounds are free of tabu.
Ua lulu ka maile.	The *maile* vine is scattered.
Noa ia Kaha-'ula papalua,	Free of tabu by a sensual dream, doubly free.
Ua noa.	It is free of tabu.[179]

The following morning, an *imu* was built as close to the root of the chosen tree as possible and a pig was baked. When cooked, the spleen was removed and offered as the *kahuna* prayed, *"He ho'o-mama ke'ia na'au na ke kahuna ia 'oe, e Moku-hali'i. 'Amama, ua noa."* "This spleen from the *kahuna* is a thing made light for thee, O Moku-hali'i. *'Amama.* It is free of tabu."[180]

After eating, the *kahuna* took a ceremonial adze and called the male canoe-making gods, *"O Ku-pulupulu, O Ku-'alana-wao, O Ku-moku-hali'i, O Ku-ka-'ie'ie, O Ku-palalake, O Ku-ka-'ohi'a-Laka."* Then he called on the female canoe-making gods, *"O Lea, O Ka-pua-o-alaka'i, e hoolohe ano i ke ko'i."* "O Lea, O Ka-pua-o-alakai, listen now to the adze."

After this brief address to the gods, the *kahuna* would say a prayer such as one of the two following prayers.

E Lea,	O Lea
E ku'u akua,	O my goddess,
'Eia wau ke 'oki nei i ku'u la'au koa.	Here am I who now cuts my *koa* tree.
Nana pono mai 'oe i ku'u ko'i	Look well at my adze,
Malaila 'oe 'e ho'opili mau ai.	There you are to continually remain.
'A'ole 'oe 'e ho'opa kua.	Do not let it strike crookedly.
'A'ole 'oe 'e ho'ohina i ku'u la'au	You are not to cause my tree to fall
Iluna o ka pu'ulu koa 'e ulu nei.	Up where the *koas* are growing.
Ho'ohina a'e 'oe ma kahi mala'ela'e.	Cause it to fall in a clear place.
'A'ole no ho'i 'oe 'e hou 'ia i kuu la'au.	Do not cut it all the way until it falls and splits.[181]

Koa la'au ke kua nei he koa la'au wa'a	*Koa* trees, I now hew a *koa* canoe
Ho'opololei mai 'oe i ka maka o ko'u ko'i	Make straight the edge of my adze
Ma kahi e pa mau ai	At the place where it always strikes.
E ho'oka'awale a'e 'oe i na hili a pau	Set aside all entanglements
E pili ana i ka la'au wa'a	Pertaining to the canoe tree
No ka mea ua waiho aku la au i ka'u alana ia 'oukou	Because I have left my free-will offering for you
He uku, he mohai, he makana ia 'oukou.	A payment, a sacrifice, a gift to you.
'Amama. Ua noa.	*'Amama.* It is free of tabu.[182]

The *kahuna* then struck the first blow as he prayed the following or a similar prayer.

Ho mai he wa'a, e ku a i'a!
He wa e ulu,
Ulu i ka 'ao'ao a nui!

Grant a canoe that shall be swift as a fish!
To sail in stormy seas,
When the storm tosses on all sides![183]

When the tree was nearly cut through, all the workmen paused to rest. Then the *kahuna* called for absolute quiet. Going to the side opposite to where the tree was to fall, he called to the gods asking them to let the tree fall without splitting. The following is such a prayer.

O Ku-pulupulu
O Ku-alanawao,
O Ku-pa'aike'e,
O Ku-mokuhali'i,
'Eia ka wa'a no ke ali'i,
He wa'a ku i ka moku,
Ku i ka moana kai akea
Ku ia (inoa)
Ku ia Ku-kaili-moku
Ku ia Olopue.
'Amama, ua noa.

Ku with many offerings,
Ku of the mountain wilderness,
Ku of the beveled adze,
Ku that bedecks the island,
Here is the canoe for the chief,
A canoe that belongs to the island
That belongs to the wide ocean
That belongs to (name)
To glorify Ku-ka'ili-moku,
To glorify Olopue.
'Amama. It is freed.[184]

When the tree was on the ground an offering was made immediately to the god of the tree. Some canoe-makers made this offering immediately after the branches were trimmed off. In either case, the offering included food, a red fish, and the *malo* of the *kahuna*.[185] All this was buried as near to the stump of the tree as possible.

The following is a prayer that might have been said before the trimming of the branches began.

O Lea ka wahine kua wa'a,
Akua kalaiwa'a,
A me Mokuhali'i, Kupaaike'e,
Na akua kane kalai wa'a,
Eia ka pua'a,
He pua'a uku, mohai, 'alana,
Ia oukou na Kalokuokamaile[186]
E ha'awi i ka 'ike a nui,
Ka 'ike mana, ka mana palena 'ole,
A nolaila, ke 'ai'e nei 'oukou i ka pua'a a
    Kalokuokamaile,[186]
'Amama, ua noa.

O Lea, woman who builds canoes,
Goddess of canoe making,
And Mokuhali'i and Kupaaike'e,
Male gods of canoe building.
Here is pork,
A pork gift, a sacrifice, an offering,
From Kalokuokamaile.[186]
Grant him much skill,
Skill and *mana*, unlimited *mana*,
So therefore you are obligated to Kalokuokamaile[186]
    for his pork.
'Amama, it is freed.[187]

Some *kahuna* included Pele in their prayers when building a canoe. They would say a prayer such as the following before trimming the tree.

Na Pele 'oni ke kumu o ke kuahiwi,
Kuahiwi ke koa e ku nei.
Kapakahi huli lalaha ka eulu.
E ulu ke akua iki, ke akua nui,
Ke akua loa, ke akua poko
Poke i ka lala, ka eulu, pa i ka lani.
Nou ho'i, e ka lani, ua wa'a la, ke loki 'ia nei.
Malu ka la'au, kapu ke aka,
He aka iki, he aka loa.

Pele shakes the base of the mountains
Mountains of the *koa* trees that stand here.
Crookedly turn flat the tree tops.
May the lesser deity, the major deity, cause growth,
The long god, the short god
Cut off the branches, the tops that reach to the heavens.
Yours, to be sure, o heaven high one, is that canoe.
Protected is the tree, tabu its shadow
A little shadow, a long shadow.

77

| Poke iho ka wa'a i hina la. | Trim the canoe that has fallen. |
| Noa. | It is free of tabu.[188] |

Before the trimming started some *kahuna* covered the stump of the tree with bird's-nest fern, others draped bunches of *'ie'ie* around the tree. After that, the *kahuna,* taking his adze, called to the gods, *"E kua ea, homai he wa'a."* 'O god(s) give us a canoe." He then trimmed off the top of the tree, after which the *kapu* for silence was lifted. After the tree was trimmed and the canoe roughed out, the following was a prayer that might have been said.

Ua pau na mea a pau loa	Everything is completed.
He pua'a ke'ia, he pani keia no ka laau	A pig is this, a closing ceremony for the tree
Wa'a i 'oki 'ia.	For the canoe that is cut down.
Nolaila ko makou lawelawe 'ana i keia wa'a.	This our service for the canoe.
Ha'awi mai 'oe ia makou i ka 'ike	Give knowledge to us,
Ke akamai, ka no'ono'o	Skill, thoughtfulness,
Ka ikaika, a me ka ho'oholo mua 'ana	Strength and advancement
I ka makou hana	In our work.
'Amama. Ua noa.	*'Amama.* It is free of tabu.[189]

KE KAUO 'ANA I KA WA'A: HAULING THE CANOE

After the canoe was roughed out it was normally left to cure or age at the spot where it had been cut.[190] When the time came to haul the canoe to the shore for its completion, the *kahuna kalai wa'a* and his crew again returned to the mountains carrying offerings and supplies. Prayers on the way up were similar to those said on the way to cut the trees. After offering food to the gods and eating with the men, the *kahuna* chewed a small portion of *'awa.* Then he spit in the hollow of his hand and rubbed it over the cut on the stern end of the canoe to which the hauling rope would be attached. While doing this he said, *"Ua noa ka 'aha, ua lele aku la."* "The assembly is free of tabu. It has flown away." He then said a prayer such as the following.

E Ku-pulupulu,	O Ku-pulupulu,
E Ku-alana-wao,	O Ku-alana-wao,
E Ku-moku-hali'i,	O Ku-moku-hali'i,
E malama 'oe i keia wa'a;	Care for this canoe;
E malama 'oe ia mua o ka wa'a;	Care for its bow;
E malama 'oe ia hope o ka wa'a;	Care for its stern;
A hiki ma kahakai;	Until it reaches the shore;
E malama 'oe a kau ma ka halau.	Care for it until it is placed in the *halau.*[191]

Hauling the canoe down the rough mountain trails was hard work and may have taken several days. Along the way, many prayers were offered to make the work of hauling easier. The following are two such prayers.

I Kahiki e ka po!	In Kahiki was the night,
I Kahiki e ke ao!	In Kahiki was the dawning:
He mau maka hia-a kou,	You have sleepless eyes,
No Kane iki poki'i.	Little grandchild of Kane.
Na Kula-uka, na Kula-kai,	By Kula-uka and Kula-kai
Na Kanikanihia e kani aku ana;	And Kanikanihia, was sounded the call.
He kai au, no muli, no wa'a,	I am a sea for the younger born, for canoes
No ke apapa nu'u, Ke-apapa-lani.	For the level of the place of highest royalty, Ke-apapa-lani.
E ala, e, e ala, e!	This way, that way.[192]

78

'E huki ana, ha!	Hauling, ha!
'E huki kau lani, ha!	Hauling to place in the heavens, ha!
'E huki papapa ka 'aina, ha!	Hauling on flat land, ha!
Ha'aha'a ka lani, ha!	The heavens are low, ha!
Ku-moku-hali'i, ha!	Ku-moku-hali'i, ha!
Kupa-'ai-ke'e, ha!	Kupa-'ai-ke'e, ha!
Ku-pulupulu-i-ka-nahele, ha!	Ku-pulupulu, ha!
Ku-'alana-wao, ha!	Ku-'alana-wao, ha!
Ku-o-Lono-wao, ha!	Ku-o-Lono-wao, ha!
O Laea-waha-'ula'ula o ka nahele	Laea-waha-'ula'ula, the wanderer
Ia ia ka holo o ka wa'a.	To her is the sailing of the canoe.
Ia Laea holo ka wa'a, holo!	To Laea is the sailing of the canoe, ha![193]

LOLO 'ANA I KA WA'A: LAUNCHING THE CANOE

As time passed and canoe-building materials and techniques changed, most of the foregoing prayers ceased to be applicable. Today, however the canoe may be built, the gods are still called on to consecrate it.

The ceremony of consecrating a canoe is called *lolo ana i ka wa'a,* or imparting brains to the canoe. According to some traditions, the canoe was held in the *halau* for four *anahulu,* that is forty days after its completion. During that time it was bathed with salt water periodically. Other traditions called for immediate launching.[194]

Today, as in the past, whichever tradition is followed, the consecration takes place on the beach near where the new canoe rests. There an *imu* is built and food prepared while the canoe is decorated with ti, fern, *maile,* and other forest greens. Then the *kahuna,* with a coconut shell filled with sea water, sprinkles the canoe, praying *"E kia'i, e alaka'i, e ho'ona'auao, e ho'olanakila, a pae ka wa'a i ke kula me ka lanakila."* "Guard, guide, instruct, give success, until the canoe lands on the plain of the seashore with victory."

The *kahuna* then drinks a mouthful of the sea water and pours the remainder into the sand at the bow of the canoe. After that the *imu* is opened and the *kahuna* takes the ceremonial pieces of the pig's snout, tail, and four feet, a piece of meat, a red fish, a banana, and a piece of *'awa* as an offering. The following is a prayer to accompany this offering.

E Mokuhali'i, Kupa'aike'e, Lea	O Mokuhali'i, Kupa'aike'e, Lea
Eia ka pua'a,	Here is the pig,
He uku, he makana, he 'alana,	A payment, a gift, an offering,
He mohai ia 'oukou.	A sacrifice to all of you.
Ua pa'a ka wa'a (inoa) ('ano)	The canoe (name) is completed,
A e ho'olana 'ia aku ana i ke kai	A (type of canoe) floating in the sea.
O kana i'a e huli ai i ka loa'a a me ka waiwai.	It is his fish to seek, to obtain wealth.
E nana pono loa 'oukou	Look very closely all of you.
E maka'ala i na puko'a, na pu'upohaku o kahi laupapa	Beware of the coral heads, the stone hills of the reef,
Na nalu, na 'ale o ka moana.	The waves, the billows of the ocean.
Ho'oholo no 'oukou i ka wa'a ma kahi hohonu o ke kai,	All of you direct the canoe to places of deep sea
I hele ai ka wa'a a nalukai	That the canoe goes over the waves of the sea.

79

A 'apulu, a ulu ka limu pakaiea, a kaniko'oko'o.	That the canoe may go till weather-worn, till worn out, and covered with *limu* and the cane sounds.
'Amama, ua noa.	'Amama. It is free of taboo.[195]

When the prayer is over, all join in the feasting,[196] eating until they can eat no more. After that, all the leftovers are gathered and placed in a coconut frond basket with a few rocks from the *imu.* Then the basket is placed on the canoe and all the men join in hauling it into the water. During a brief sail the basket is dropped in the water as an offering. The canoe then returns to shore where it is again hauled onto the sand and a prayer such as the following is said.

O kuwa o ka lani, o kuwa o ka honua,	Uplifter of the heavens, uplifter of the earth,
O kuwa o ka mauna, o kuwa o ka moana,	Uplifter of the mountains, uplifter of the ocean,
O kuwa o ka po, o kuwa o ke ao,	Who has appointed the night, appointed the day,
O Malualani ke kuwa, o Maluahopu ke kuwa,	Malualani is the *kuwa* and Maluahopu,
Aia no ia koi la ke kuwa.	That ax also is a *kuwa.*
Ka waa nei o ka luahine makua.	This is the ax of our venerable ancestral dame.
Ka luahine! Owai?	Venerable dame! What dame?
O ka luahine o Papa, wahine a Wakea.	Dame Papa, the wife of Wakea.
Nana i kuwa, nana i hainu,	She set apart and consecrated, she turned the tree about,
Nana i hele, nana i ae,	She impelled it, she guided it,
Nana i hoonoanoa.	She lifted the tabu from it.
Noa ke kuwa o ka waa o Wakea.	Gone is the tabu from the canoe of Wakea.
O ka waa nei o ka luahine makua.	The canoe this of our ancestral dame.
Ka luahine! Owai?	Ancestral dame! What dame?
Ka luahine o Lea, wahine o Moku-halii.	Dame Lea, wife of Moku-halii.
Nana i kuwa, nana i hainu,	She initiated, she pointed the canoe,
Nana i hele, nana i ae;	She started it, she guided it;
Nana i hoonoanoa.	She lifted the tabu from it.
Noa ke kuwa o ka wao o Mokuhalii.	Lifted was the tabu from the canoe of Mokuhalii.
Hinu helelei aku,	Fat dripping here,
Hinu helelei mai.	Fat dripping there.
He miki oe Kane;	Active art thou Kane;
He miki oe Kanaloa.	Active art thou Kanaloa.
O Kanaloa hea oe?	What Kanaloa art thou?
O Kanaloa inu awa.	Kanaloa the *awa* drinker.
Mai Kahiki ka awa,	*Awa* from Tahiti,
Mai Upolu ka awa,	*Awa* from Upolu,
Mai Wawau ka awa.	*Awa* from Wawau.
E hano awa hua,	Bottle up the frothy *awa,*
E hano awa puaka.	Bottle up the well-strained *awa.*
Halapa i ke akua i laau wai la!	Praise be to the God in the highest heaven *(laau)*!
Amama, ua noa.	The tabu is lifted, removed.
Lele wale aku la.	It flies away.[197]

When the *kahuna* finishes the prayer, he asks, *"Pehea ke'ia lawelawe 'ana, a kakou."* "How is this service of ours?" If no disturbance has been made during the prayer, the owner of the canoe will answer, *"Maika'i ka lolo 'ana."* "Our service is good!" The *kahuna* will then say, *E 'au ana 'oe iloko o ke'ia wa'a me ka palekana, no ka mea ua maika'i ka lawelawe 'ana a kakou."* "You will travel inside of this canoe with safety because it is good."

E HO'OHOLO ANA I KA WA'A: SAILING THE CANOE

Sailing the canoe, although under the protection of the gods, also required training. A part of that training was learning how to handle a canoe in rough water. The following is a graduation prayer said by a *kahuna*-teacher when a student was ready to demonstrate his ability to right a swamped canoe.

Ia oukou e na 'aumakua o ke kai.	To you, the *'aumakua* of the sea.
Ia 'Ale-nui,	To 'Ale-nui,
Ia 'Ale-iki,	To 'Ale-iki,
Ia 'Ale-loa,	To 'Ale-loa,
Ia 'Ale-poko,	To 'Ale-poko,
Ia 'Ale-aki,	To 'Ale-aki,
Ia 'Ale-kupipi,	To 'Ale-kupipi,
Ia 'Ale 'olowalu,	To 'Ale-'olowalu,
A me 'Ale-kualoloa o ka moana,	And 'Ale-kualoloa of the ocean,
'Ala-kuamakani hoi.	And 'Ala-kuamakani of course.
Ka mea nana e hoala mai i na kino ale o 'oukou a lilo i akua make no ka wa'a holo.	The one that stirred up you wave-bodies and made them deadly deities of sailing canoes.
Aia Hina-ke-ka hoi ka puuhonua o ka moana.	And here is Hina-ke-ka, the place of refuge of the ocean.
Eia ka pua'a, ka 'awa, a me ka luau.	Here is the pig, the *'awa*, and the *lu'au*.
He pua'a ailolo, he 'awa, ailolo, a he lu'au ailolo,	A pig for graduation, *'awa* for graduation, and *lu'au* for graduation,
Na ku'u haumana ho'olana wa'a na (inoa).	For my canoe-sailing student (inoa).
A he alana hoi ia 'oukou a pau.	And of course a free-will offering for all of you.
Ma'anei waiho iho ka huna, a me ka lokoloa,	Here let us leave the hidden things and the motes in the eyes
E ike i ka 'oukou pulapula, e lawe a'e 'oukou i ke kino aka o ka ailolo,	To set your offering and take the *kino aka* of graduation
A o ka 'i'o ka 'ailolo na (inoa) ku'u haumana a'o hoalana wa'a.	And the meat of the graduation from (name), my canoe-sailing student.
'Amama ua noa.	*'Amama.* The tabu is lifted.[198]

KA HOLO ANA: **THE VOYAGE**

Each voyage, however long or short, is begun with a prayer. The following prayer honors the ancient voyage of Kaha'i, who went to Kahiki to find his father, and the modern voyaging canoe Hoku-le'a.

O Ku o na mauna, o ka uka, o na nahele,	O Ku of the mountains, of the uplands, of the forests;
O Ku ke kupuna o ka waa,	O Ku, the ancestor of the canoe,
O Ku ka mea lokomaikai o na kalai waa,	O Ku, the benefactor of canoe builders
O Ku ka mea i haawi i ka makana.	O Ku who has given the gift,
O Ku o alaka'i i na ko'i,	O Ku who has guided the adzes,
O Ku nana i hoolaa ka molina, nana i hana me na mea 'ole keia waa pukonakona,	O Ku who has consecrated the molding, who has formed out of nothing this mighty vessel
O Ku ka mea nana i hoonoa i kona kapu,	O Ku who has lifted the *kapu* from it
E ae mai i ka mahalo o kakou.	Accept our gratitude
E alakai keia waa i ko kakou 'aina hanau o Kahiki.	Guide this vessel to our ancestral homeland Tahiti.
O Kane o ke ao holo 'oko'a	O Kane of the universe
E hoomakaukau i na hoku iloko o ka lani	Prepare the stars in the heavens
E hoomalamalama i ke ala i Kahiki.	That light the way to Tahiti.
E Lono o na ao, e ho'alaneo ka lani,	O Lono of the clouds
E ho'akaka na hoku alaka'i.	Clear the heavens
Moakaka na hoku alaka'i.	Make clear the guiding stars.
E Kana-loa o ke kai	O Kanaloa of the sea

E hooma'ema'e i ke kuahu	Purify the altar
E ho'opono i keia waa e hoolaaia	Accept this consecrated canoe
E hoomakaukau i ke ala i kauhale o ko kakou mau kapuna.	Pave the way to the home of our ancestors.
Amama. Ua noa. Lele wale aku la.	'Amama. The kapu is freed.[199]

The following is a prayer said when a loved one sails away. It was used by King Kalakaua when his wife Kapi'olani and his sister Lili'uokalani sailed from Hawaii to attend the celebration of Queen Victoria's Jubilee. It was sung to them at the time of their departure by the Healani Glee Club.

E ka moana nui	O thou great ocean,
Kai hohonu,	Thou deep seas,
'E lana malie kou mau ale.	Let thy waves flow gently.
'E ka makani nui ikaika,	O thou strong winds blowing,
'E pa kolonahe, malie 'oe.	Breathe softly and tenderly.
'E nihi e ka hele,	Go thou with serenity and peace,
Mai hoopa.	Let nothing arise to bar your way.[200]

This prayer is for the canoe of "the man who does much sailing." It is also a prayer said when a canoe is launched from a cliff such as along the Hamakua and Puna coasts of the island of Hawaii. It is said with an offering of pork.

Lea ka wahine kua kalai wa'a,	Lea, the woman who hews down the canoe tree, who carves the canoe,
Akua wahine noho kuahiwi.	Goddess who dwells in the mountain.
Ku-moku-hali'i	Ku-of-the-outspread-island
Ku-pulupulu	Ku-of-the-tinder
Ku-alana-wao	Ku-of-the-free-will-offering
Ku-pepeiao-loa	Long-eared Ku
Ku-hooholo-pali	Ku-that-runs-up-the-cliff
Kupa-'ai-ke'e	Swivel adze,
Ku-nea-luka	Ku-nea-luka.
Na akua ka ai wa'a apau;	All the deities that control canoes;
Ke kahea ia aku nei 'oukou apau loa.	All of you are called upon.
No ka uku, ala ka ia 'oukou.	For the reward of your leadership
Eia ku pua'a a Keanuenue e mohai aku ana ia 'oukou no kona wa'a,	Here is the pig of The Rainbow being sacrificed to you for his canoe.
No kona holo ana i ka moana	For his journeying upon the ocean
E na na pono 'oukou, e malama	For the benefit of you all to keep
E kiai me ka maka ala i na pu'u pohaku,	Watch with vigilance for heaps of stones and coral heads
Na ako'ako'a, na nalu po'i,	The gathered together, the breaking waves,
Na ale o ka moana,	The crashing waves, the waves of the ocean.
E lilo kahi e holo ai keia wa'a,	That were destined for the place that this canoe travels.
He pohu, a he malu.	A calm, a shelter.
E hoalo 'ana i na puu pohaku,	Escaping rock heaps.
Ume na moku ako'ako'a e holoi 'ia ana i ke ao	Draw away the coral islands that are being moved in the day
A me ka po.	And in the night.
E malama loa 'oukou i ke kino holo'oko'a o ka wa'a,	All of you take good care of the complete body of the canoe,
A lu'alu'a,	Till it is aged and weatherworn
A nalu kai,	To the sea waves
A ulu kohekohe	And it develops grooves
A me ko limu iluna o ka wa'a.	And seaweed on the canoe.

O ka 'oukou makana ia e like me kana mohai,   It is your gift like its sacrifice.
E nonoi ana ia 'oukou i ka 'oukou kiai.   Requesting you for your guardianship.
A malama i kona wa'a.   Take care of his canoe.
'Amama.   'Amama.[201]

KA 'AU 'ANA O KA WA'A: SAILING THE CANOE

If the wind dies down while sailing, the following prayer may be said to bring it up again.[202]

Pa mai, pa mai ka makani nui o Hilo,   Blow, blow great wind of Hilo,
Ka ipu nui lawe mai   Bring the large wind calabash
Ka ipu iki waiho aku.   Leave the small one.[203]

If the winds become too violent and endanger the canoe, this prayer will calm the ocean.

Pa mai, pa mai, ka makani nui o Hilo,[204]   Blow, blow, ye winds of Hilo,[204]
Waiho aku ka ipu nui,   Put away the big wind gourd,
Ho mai ka ipu li'ili'i.   Bring on the little wind gourd.[205]

NOTES

174. Canoe bodies were also built from drift logs. In the case of smaller canoes, lower elevation woods such as breadfruit might have been used.
175. Anonymous (2).
176. Emerson, N.B. 1965, pp. 190-191.
177. *Kumu* and *'aweoweo* were the favored fish for this offering.
178. Laka was one of the patrons of canoe builders. See footnotes 206 and 232 in the Hula Section.
179. Emerson, N.B. n.d.; Kelsey translation.
180. At the time a student *kahuna kalai wa'a* graduated he chose a god as his special patron. His choice was made from such gods as Moku-hali'i (also called Ku-moku-hali'i), Lea, Kupa'aike'e, Ku-pulupulu, Ku-alanawao, Ku-pepeiaoloa, Ku-ho'oholopali, or Kane-aluka. Whatever he prays for, the *kahuna* includes prayers to his chosen god. This prayer was by a *kahuna* who had chosen (Ku) Moku-hali'i.
181. Kalokuokamaile n.d.; Kelsey translation.
182. Mossman n.d.; Kelsey translation.
183. Malo 1951, p. 133.
184. Emerson, N.B. n.d.; Kelsey translation.
185. Kalokuokamaile spoke of wearing a red *malo* while one of Emerson's informants spoke of wearing a white *malo*. It seems that the color of the *malo* had family, religious, or other significance.
186. This prayer from Kalokuokamaile uses his name. However, each new canoe maker will substitute his own name.
187. Kalokuokamaile, December 7, 1922; Pukui translation n.d.
188. Emerson, N. B. n.d.; Kelsey translation.
189. Anonymous (2).
190. Canoe bodies were left to age in the mountains before they were brought to the shore for finishing. Captain Charles Clerke, commander of the "Discovery" under Captain Cook, wrote, when a man wanted a canoe he went "to the wood and looks about him till he has found a tree fit for his purpose . . . and goes to work upon his Canoe, which they in general completely finish before it's moved from the spot where its materials had birth. Our people who made excursions about the Country saw many of these Canoes in different states of forwardness, but what is somewhat singular, if one of their vessels want repairing she is immediately removed into the woods though at the distance of 5 or 6 miles." (Beaglehole 1967, p. 592.)
191. Emerson, N.B., from Peleioholani n.d.; Kelsey translation.
192. Emerson, N.B., from Luika Kaheakulani n.d.; Kelsey translation.
193. Kalokuokamaile, December 7, 1922, Pukui translation n.d.
194. John Haone 1980; Anonymous (2).
195. Anonymous (2); Kelsey translation.
196. In ancient times no women were allowed at this feast.
197. Malo 1951, pp. 129-130.

198. Kaelemakule 1929; Kelsey translation.

199. This prayer was composed in English by Stanley Kapepe (1976) and translated into Hawaiian by Theodore Kelsey.

200. Amalu, May 6, 1976. As a popular song the following eleven lines are added.

6. Mai pulale i ka 'ike a ka maka.	6. Do not hasten the sight of the eyes.
7. Ho'oakahi no makemake 'o ke aloha.	7. Just one desire, love.
8. A hea mai 'o ka lani, a e kipa.	8. And call a chiefly one, and be a guest.
9. 'Ike ia Keleponi he 'aina anu,	9. See California, a cold land,
10. Ke hau ho'okuakea i ka 'ili,	10. With dew that bleaches the skin,
11. Lamalama i ka 'ili o ke kama,	11. Make bright looking the skin of the offspring,
12. Ka wahine i ka 'iu o luna.	12. The woman in the loftiness above.
13. E hele me ka poina 'ole	13. Go without forgetting
14. E huli 'e ke alo i hope nei	14. Turn back here, o ocean waves
15. Eia ko lei kalaunu,	15. Here is the crown wreath,
16. 'O ka 'onohi o Hawai'i.	16. The eyeball of Hawai'i.

201. Kalokuokamaile n.d.; Kelsey translation.

202. This is the same chant used to call for wind to fly a kite.

203. Kelsey collection.

204. Hilo (or Whiro, as he was known elsewhere in Polynesia) was both a navigator and the patron of navigation as well as a famous voyager. Some say he held dominion over the winds which he kept confined in his wind gourd. Others say La'a-maomao controls the winds.

205. Emerson, J.S. 1926.

XII KĀ HULA
The Hula

The origins of the *hula* are ancient and lost in the mists of time. How the dance was brought to Hawaii is uncertain. Some say the *hula* was originally a form of worship performed only by men whose patron was a male god named Laka.[206] Others say that two gods, one male and one female, both named Laka, came to Hawaii bringing the *hula* with them. They say that in time Laka *kane* left the islands, leaving Laka *wahine* to preside over the *hula*.

Still others say that the knowledge of the *hula* was brought to Hawaii by Hopoe, a friend of Pele's youngest sister Hiʻiaka-i-ka-poli-o-Pele. They do not say where she learned the dance. They do say that, unknown to Pele and other members of her family, Hiʻiaka was taught the dance by Hopoe. When Pele heard of the *hula* she begged her sisters to perform the new dance for her. All excused themselves, saying they did not know the *hula*. When Hiʻiaka arrived she too was asked to dance and, to the surprise of all, she performed a beautiful *hula*.

There are even others who say that the *hula* was brought to Hawaii by Kapo-ʻula-kinaʻu, another sister of Pele. Traveling with an older brother, Ka-huila-o-ka-lani, and a younger sister, Kewelani,[207] she arrived at Niʻihau where the group was hosted by a local chief. As part of the entertainment, Kewelani danced what was the first *hula* in Hawaii.

There are also those who speculate that perhaps each of these ancestral beings may have brought to Hawaii a different style of *hula*. In any case, all are remembered in prayers associated with the dance.

KA WEUWEU NO KE KUAHU: GREENS FOR THE ALTAR

The *hula* may be danced spontaneously as an expression of the feelings of the moment or as a formal performance that requires prayerful preparation. The first prayers of a formal performance are said before going to gather the *'ie'ie, hala pepe,* ti, *maile, lehua, palai* ferns,[208] and other greens which will be placed on the altar.[209] This is one such prayer.

Haki pu o ka nahelehele,	Pluck together the greenery,
Haki hana maile o ka wao,	Pluck, preparing the *maile* of the upland,
Hooulu lei ou, o Laka, e!	Increase your wreaths, o Laka!
O Hiiaka ke kaula nana e hooulu na ma'i,	Hi'iaka is the seer that will gather together the sick ones,
A aeae a ulu a noho i kou kuahu,	And will rise, and cause the growth, and dwell in your altar.
Eia ka pule la, he pule ola,	Here is the prayer, a prayer for life,
He noi ola nou, e-e!	A request to you for life.
E ola ia makou, aohe hala!	Grant life to us, without fail.[210]

While the workers are in the forest gathering the greens they recite simple prayers. Some are to the gods of particular plants; some are general prayers such as the following.

Pupu weuweu au, e Laka e	I am gathering bunches of greens, o Laka
O kona weuweu ke ku nei	Her greenery that stands here
'A 'o Laka me Lau-ka-'ie'ie	For Laka and Lau-ka'ie'ie
Laua me ka 'awapuhi	Together with *'awapuhi*
Noa.	Free of tabu.[211]

When the dancers return with the carefully gathered mountain greenery it is placed around the altar.[212] While they work, the *kumu* (teacher or leader) says a prayer such as the following.

Noho ana Laka i ka ulu wehiwehi;	Laka dwells in the adornment of beautiful growth;
Ku ana iluna o Mo'o-helaia	That stands above Mo'o-helaia
Ka 'ohi'a ku iluna o Mauna Loa.	The *'ohia* trees that stand on the top of Mauna Loa.
Aloha mai Kaulana-a-'ula ia'u;	Kaulana-a-'ula gives love to me;
Eia ka 'ula la he 'ula leo,	Here is the *'ula,* a chant of affection,
He mohai e kanaenae na'u ia 'oe e Laka e;	An offering a chant of supplication from me to thee, o Laka;
E Laka e, ho'oulu 'ia.	O Laka, prayed to for inspiration.[213]

PULE HO'OULU: GROWTH PRAYER

After the greens have been placed around the altar,[214] the dancers retire to dress. As they prepare themselves, the *kumu* chants a prayer beginning with *E ulu, e ulu. Ulu* may mean growth in any form. In the case of the *hula,* the growth sought is that of talent and inspiration. The following is such a prayer.

E ulu, e ulu kini o ke akua;	Congregate, inspire, ye hosts of gods!
Ulu a'e o Kane me Kana-loa;	Come together, inspire O Kane, Kanaloa!
Ula ka 'ohi'a[215] lau ka wai, ka 'ie'ie;[216]	Live the *ohi'a,*[215] the *'ie'ie,* till many their sprinkling[216]
Ulu a'e ke kua a noho i kona kahu	Inspire the goddess to dwell within her keeper.
Eia ka wai la, ka 'awa, he wai ola.[217]	Here is the water- the *'awa*—the water of life.[217]
E ola ia'u i ke kumu	Give life to the teacher

E ola i ke poo puaa	Give life to the leader of the class
E ola i ka paepae	Give life to the leader's classmates
E ola i na haumana a pau	Give life to all the students.
Elieli kapu; elieli noa.	Profound the tabu; profound its lifting.[218]

NA PULE HOOKOMO LOLE: DRESSING PRAYERS

As the dancers actually dress, special prayers are said. This is a prayer chanted while putting on the pa'u.[219] The length of the prayer reflects the time it takes to put on the pa'u.

Ia kakua pa'u 'ahu na kikepa i ka pa'u,	Gird on the pa'u, put on the sarongs,
No'ano'a i ho'olu'ua, i ho'okakua 'ia a pa'a luna o ka imu.[220]	Beautifully dyed and girded tightly over the imu.[220]
Ku ka hu'a o ka pali o Ka-wai-kapu	Stands the rim of the cliff of Ka-wai-kapu[221]
He kuina pa'u pali no Ku-pahu	A pa'u strung together of the cliff of Ku-pahu
I holoa, pa'alia, pa'a 'e Hono-kane.	That extended and was made fast, made fast by Hono-kane.
Malama 'e Hilo i ka pa'u[222]	Hilo first took care of the pa'u.[222]
Holo iho la ke 'ala o ka manu[223] i na pali.	The fragrance of the bird[223] travels to the cliffs.
Pali ku kaha ko; ha ka 'a'i i ke keiki pa'u pali o Kau-kini	Cliff that stands sheer, a shelf for the necks of the children of the pa'u cliffs of Kau-kini.
I ho'onu'anu'a iluna o Ka-'au-ana	That are stacked above the moving bodies.
Akahi ke ana, ka luhi i ka pa'u,	This is the first time of having enough, the weariness of the pa'u,
O ka ho'oio i na kapa ko'ele wai o 'Apua,	At the showing off of the tapa dyed in (the) water of 'Apua,
I hopua i ka ua a noe Holo-po'opo'o	That is seized by the rain Holo-po'opo'o
Me he pa'u 'ele hiwa ala i na pali.	Like a pure black pa'u on the cliffs.
'Ohi'ohi ka pali, ku ka liko o ka lama,	The cliffs collect their dues, the new leaves of the lama appears,
I mama 'ula 'ia e ka ma'ino	Chewed red by the defacement
E ka malo o 'Umi i kui na huna.[224]	By the malo of 'Umi that strung together the secrets.[224]
I 'ike ai ua ma'awe wai 'olona.	That the thin trickles of 'olona water may be seen.
E makili 'ia nei o Wai-hi-lau	Come to light by Wai-hi-lau
Holo ke olona i pa'a ke kapa, hu'a lepe 'ole ka pa'u.	'Olona cord put through the top of the pa'u, the tapa held in place, the top edge of the pa'u was undirected.
Nani ka ihona, makali'i ka 'ohe.	Beautiful is the descent, very fine is the cord.
Pa'a ka pa'u o Pua-kea i na pali.[225]	Fastened to the "cliffs" is the pa'u of Pua-kea.[225]
I ho'ohou kalena 'ia e ka makani.	Struck stretching by the wind.
I kaomi pohaku 'ia 'e Wai-manu	Weighted down with a stone by Wai-manu
I na 'ala kiolaola, i na 'ala lele, pa'a ia Wai-manu.	The 'ala rocks thrown away one after the other, the flying 'ala held fast by Wai-manu.
O 'oki Wai-pi'o, kau haehae ka 'ohe ia 'Ohe-lau-li'i	Cut off is Wai-pi'o, place the bamboo torn to bits before 'Ohe-lau-li'i
'A'ole 'i 'oki'ia o mo ke kihi.	Not broken and the top cut off.
Malama ka hoaka, ka 'apahu ia Po'e	Take care about the lower edge of the pa'u, conspicious to people
O 'ahiki 'ia la e Maluo, he pola ia no ka pa'u,	Lest hidden parts be fully revealed by Maluo,
I hi'ia mai e Ka-holo-kuaiwa,	Embraced by Ka-holo-kuaiwa,
I 'ume a pa'a; wiliwili ka pa'u[226]	The pa'u is drawn tight and twisted up[226]
Kaupaku hale maluna o Hana-'awili.	House roof above Hana-'awili.
I wili 'ia mai a pa'a, ku ka 'awahia,	Twisted tight, there is harshness,
Ka'a ka 'ope'ope, uwa ka pihe.	Roll the bundles, the shouting is loud.

Ho'okahi kamali'i a hana pilo ka leo i ka nahele i
    ka pa'u e.

The children make a noise and with troublesome voices
    in admiration of the *pa'u*.

Noho no i Puna, he maka ia no ke onaona.

They dwell indeed in Puna, the source of the fragrance.

He inu mahuna 'ia e ka wahine.

A drinking by the god that is to the scaly appearance
    of the skin from *'awa* drinking.

I kanu popo kiele ia e ka wahine.

Planted as a bunch of fragrance by the woman.

I ho'ope 'ia i ka 'ili la'au 'ala o ka nahele

Perfumed with the fragrant bark of the woodland

I 'a'ala i ka hala me ka lehua.

Made sweet with *hala* and *lehua.*

Nono ia pa'u e ho'okakua 'ia nei.

Rosy is the *pa'u* that is here being girded on

Ia Pili, ia Mau, ia Pa'a-e.

To Pili, to Mau, to Pa'a.

Pa'a ka pa'u o Pua-kea i na pali a---

The *pa'u* of Pua-kea is firm on the cliffs (legs).[227]

After the dancers have put on their *pa'u*, they then put on their anklets and wristlets. The following is a prayer said at this time.

'A'ala kupukupu ka uka o Kane-hoa

Fragrant with *kupukupu* fern is the upland of Kane-
    hoa

E hoa!

O bind!

Hoa na lima o ka makani he Wai-koloa,

Bind the hands of the wind, a Wai-koloa,

He Wai-koloa ka makani; anu Li-hu'e

The wind is a Wai-koloa; cold is Li-hu'e!

'Alina lehua i ka uka o Pua

Blighted are the *lehua* flowers in the upland of Pua

Ku'u pu--a--!

My flower!

Ku'u pua 'i'ini e kui a lei

My desired flower let me string into a wreath.

'Ina ia 'oe ke lei 'ia mai la.

Would that it were you put on as a wreath![228]

Just before going to the place where the *hula* will be performed, the dancers put on their leis. This is a prayer said while tying the leis on.

Ke lei mai la o Ka-ula i ke kai, e!

Ka-ula wears the ocean as a wreath;

Ke malamalama o Ni'ihau, ua malie,

Nii-hau shines forth in the calm.

A malie, pa ka Inu-wai;

After the calm blows the wind Inu-wai;

Ke inu mai la na hala o Naue i ke kai.

Naue's palms then drink in the salt.

No Naue, ka hala, no Puna ka wahine,

From the Naue the palm, from Puna the woman,

No ka lua no i Kilauea.

Aye, from the pit Kilauea.[229]

In ancient times the spectators could not enter the area where the performance was to take place before the dancers put on their *pa'u* and anklets. Once the dancers were dressed, a prayer was said and the audience could enter. This particular prayer was used only when the performance was outdoors.[230]

Ho'opuka i kai i ka la inu lau.

Come forth toward the sea on the day of many
    drinkings.

E lulumi 'ana na ale o kauna

The ocean waves are rushing pell-mell

Haki kakala mai 'ana ka makani

The wind is breaking in gusts

Puka ka hala ka lehua o Panaewa

The *hala* and the *lehua* of Pana-'ewa spring up,

Puka hele i kai kulili i kaua

Come forth lushly by the sea Ku-lili-i-ka-ua

Ka papa a Lohi'au apua

The flat place of Lohi'au 'apua.

E lohi mai ana e maukele

Being slowed by those who continually sail

Ka papa o Papa-ka-nene

The flat place of Papa-ka-nene

E puka a ua nei ka makani.

The wind will come forth and bring rain now.[231]

HE KUEHU I NA AKUA: A CALL TO THE GODS

When praying for inspiration in performing the *hula*, some say it is the god Laka[232] that one should approach first. Others say it is Kapo-'ula-kina'u that should receive the first prayer. The first of the following prayers is to Laka; the second calls to Laka as a friend of Kapo (as Kina'u) and includes a call to Lono; the third is to Kapo and calls also to Kane and Kanaloa.

Eia au e Laka
Ke kane a Ha'i-wahine,
Wahine kui pua o ka nahelehele,
Ho'ouluulu lei o Laka.
E Laka e, e Laka e!
E maliu mai!

Here am I o Laka
Husband of Ha'i-wahine,
Woman who makes woodland wreaths,
Building them into altars for you o Laka.
O Laka, oh Laka!
Graciously turn to me![234]

E ho'oulu aku ana au ia 'oe, e Laka, e Ha'i-wahine,
Ha'i pua o ka nahelehele
Hakihana maile 'a'ala o ka wao
O Hii-aka ka ke kua a'ea'e aluna o he kahu noho,

I will cause you to grow, o Laka, o Ha'i-wahine,
Flower picker of the forest
Breaking off sweet *maile* of the upland region
O Hii-aka of the deity with streaks of gray up on the keeper's seat.

E Laka e, e Kapo e, ho'oulu ia.
Ho'oulu mai ana ka o Laka i kona kahu, owau.
Owau no ho'i ke'ia.

O Laka, o Kapo, let there be decoration.
Laka is decorating her honored attendant, me.
It is me indeed.[235]

Noho ana Kapo i ka ulu wehiwehi
Ku ana i Mo'o-helaia
Ka 'ohi'a ku iluna o Mauna Loa.
Aloha mai Kaulana-a-'ula ia'u
'Eia ka 'ula leo la he uku
He uku, he mohai, he alana.
He kanaenae na'u ia 'oe 'e Kapo-ku-lani
E moe hauna iki 'e hea au ia 'oe.
'Aia la na lehua o Ka'ana
Ke kui 'ia mai la 'e na wahine a lawa.
I lei no Kapo.
O Kapo ali'i nui o ia moku,
Ki'eki'e, ha'aha'a ka la o ka 'ike 'e 'ike aku ai
He 'ike kumu, he 'ike lono,
He 'ike pu 'awa hiwa,
He 'ike a ke akua e---
E Kapo ho'i, e ho'i a noho i kou kuahu ho'oulu 'ia

Kapo is sitting in the beautiful grove
Standing on Mo'o-helaia,
The *'ohi'as* that stand up on Mauna Loa.
Kaulana-a-'ula gives love to me.
Here is the voice appeal, a payment
A payment, a sacrifice, an offering.
A chant of affection by me to you, o Kapo-ku-lani.
Let me sleep as a little offering for me to call you.
There are the *lehuas* of Ka'ana
Strung by the woman bountifully
As a wreath for Kapo.
O Kapo, great chiefess of the island,
High and low is the sun of the seeing to see.
A sight of reason, a sight of information,
A sight of black *'awa*,
A sight from the deity.
O Kapo, return and dwell in your altar that is given growth.

'Eia ka wai la, he wai e ola,
E ola nou e.

Here is the water, a water of life,
That there be life for you.[236]

E ho'ouluulu 'ana au ia 'oe Kapo.
Ulu mai o Kane me Kana-loa.
Ulu mai kini o ke akua.

I am offering wreaths to you Kapo.
Kane and Kana-loa make offering.
The multitude of the gods make offering.

Ulu ka 'ohi'a, ka lehua, ke koa	Grows the *'ohi'a*, the *lehua*, the *koa*,
Ulu ka lama ka la'au, ka lama kea,	Grows the *lama* wood, the white *lama*,
Ulu ke kukui, ka la-i, ka 'ohi'a ku makua	Grows the *kukui*, the ti leaf, the *'ohi'a* that stands as a parent,
Ulu ka 'awa-puhi, ka palapalai	Grows the wild ginger, the *palapalai* fern.
A'e mai a ulu a noho i kou kuahu.	Arise and cause growth, and dwell in your altar.
Eia ka wai la, he wai e ola.	Here is the water, a water to give life.
E ola no e---	Have life indeed.[237]

Whether Laka or Kapo receives the first prayer for inspiration, the great gods, the *'aumakua*, the *unihi*, and the other *hula* gods such as Hi'iaka-i-ka-poli-o-Pele and the Maile sisters[238] must not be forgotten. The following is a prayer calling all the gods, great and small, that might have an interest in the dance.

E ulu, e ulu, Kini o ke Akua!	Gather, oh gather, ye hosts of godlings!
Ulu Kane me Kanaloa!	Come Kane with Kanaloa!
Ulu 'Ohi'a-lau-koa, me ka 'Ie-'ie!	Come leafy *Ohi'a* and *I-e*!
A'e mai a noho i kou kuahu!	Possess me and dwell in your altar!
Eia ka wai la, he wai e ola!	Here's water, water of life!
E ola no, e-e!	Life, give us life![239]

PULE HO'ONOA: **PRAYER TO REMOVE TABU**

When a formal *hula* performance is begun, it is placed under a tabu that requires certain respectful behavior of both performer and audience. The following is a prayer to remove this tabu during an intermission.

Pupu weuweu 'e Laka e	A relish of greens for Laka
O kona weuweu e ku ana.	Her greens are standing.
Kaumaha a'e la ia Laka e.	Make an offering to Laka.
O Laka ke kua pule ikaika,[240]	O Laka, deity of powerful prayer,[240]
Ua noa, ua noa ke kahua, ua lulu ka maile.	Free of tabu is the platform, *maile* is the offering.
Noa, noa ia Kaha-'ula[241]	Made free, free by Kaha-'ula[241]
Papalua noa.	Doubly free of tabu.[242]

PULE HO'OPAU: **CLOSING PRAYER**

When the *hula* performance has been completed, it is closed with a prayer. Following are two prayers, one each to Laka and Kapo. These prayers may be used either to close a performance or to remove the tabu at intermission.

Pupu weuweu 'e Laka e!	A bunch of leaves for you, o Laka.
O kona weuweu 'e ku ana	Her greens must be put in an orderly manner.
O Ku-ka-'ohi'a-laka e	Here are Ku, god of the *'ohi'a-laka*
Laua me Ku-pulupulu	He and Ku-pulupulu
Ka lehua me ke koa lau-li'i.	God of the small-leaved *koa*.
O Ka-lama me Moku-hali'i,	Bring the *lama* tree and Moku-hali'i,
Kuikui me ka hala-pepe,	The *kukui* with the *hala-pepe*,
Lakou me Lau-ka-'ie'ie	Not forgetting with these the *'ie'ie*
Ka palai me maile lau-li'i	The fern and the small-leafed *maile*.
Noa, noa i kou kuahu;	Free! The altar is free.
Noa, noa ia 'oe Laka.	Free is your altar, Laka.
Papalua noa.	Completely, doubly free.[243]

Pupu weuweu 'e Kapo e!
O kona weuweu e ku ana.
'E kaumaha 'ia ia Kapo,
A o Kapo e ka pule ikaika.
'E ku ka maile a Kapo a imua
Ua noa ke kahua.
Ua lu ka hua o ka maile.
Noa, noa ia Ka-ha-'ula (Kapo).
Papalua! Noa!

Bunch thy greenery, o Kapo,
Greenery for prayers for special events
To be sacrificed to Kapo,
To Kapo of the powerful prayer.
Place the *maile* of Kapo to the front
The location is free of tabu.
The seed of the *maile* is scattered.
Free, free of tabu by Ka-ha-'ula
Doubly free, free of tabu.[244]

NA MALIHINI: THE GUESTS

Hula dances and *mele* are real property. Etiquette demands that, like personal names, they not be used unless given. Taking a chant composed for another was called *ai hama.*

The following is a prayer to cause trouble for the person who has taken a chant.

E Laka e, ua lawe aku o (inoa) i kekahi o kou mau mele.
E 'olu'olu 'oe, e ho'ou a ho'aa iaia i kona manawa e hoa'o ana e ho'ike aku,
E ho'opoina 'oe iaia e hiki ole ai oia e hoomana'o i na hua'olelo o ke mele.

Oh Laka, (name) has taken one of my *mele.*
Make him stutter and stammer when he tries to use it,
Make his memory fail him so that he would not remember the words.[245]

It might be noted that under some circumstances it was acceptable to rework chants. A few words might be changed, a section added or omitted. Many examples of such reworking, *ho'oili,* survive from the reign of King Kalakaua. Many chants reworked at that time had belonged to King Lunalilo.

NOTES

206. According to N. B. Emerson (n.d.) there were four Lakas: Laka-aloha, the patron of *hula;* Laka-kea and Laka-uli, patrons of the practice of medicine; and "the Laka who was a patron of canoe builders." The first three, females, were said to be the children of Kapo, the sister of Pele. The latter, spoken of as "the king of Kipahulu, Hana, Maui, was said to be the son of Wahieloa and Hina, who was the sister of Kumokuhali'i." (See footnote 232.)

It is interesting to note that Mrs. Pukui (n.d.) has said, "I have not heard of *heiaus* dedicated to Laka, the patron deity of the *hula,* outside of Kauai. The two whose sites were pointed out to me by Keahi Luahine Sylvester were Ka-ulu-o Lono at Wahiawa and Ke-ahu-a-Laka beyond Haena. The plants used on the *kuahu* or altar, the dregs of *'awa* used in daily offerings to Laka, the remains of ceremonial feasts connected with the *hula,* and the skirts and leis worn at graduation were deposited in these *heiaus.* The remains of a ceremonial feast to Laka were never thrown carelessly around lest they become defiled by being walked over or eaten by animals. On the other islands these were cast into the sea or in deep streams."

According to Kuluwaimaka, the stone body of Laka is in the middle of the *hula* altar. The stone is an *ala* stone, that is, dense volcanic stone that has been water-worn. It is about the size of a hen egg. When the greenery for dedicating the altar is brought down from the mountain it is piled on the chosen stone. As part of the decorating, an altar is built of four *lehua* branches. Placed equal distance apart in a square, they are tied together in teepee fashion. The branches are long enough that the place where they are tied is higher than the *kumu's* head with flowers and leaves above the tie. After all the preparations are completed, the stone is placed in the center of the square base.

While Emerson (1965, p. 23) said that a block of *lama* wood was placed on the *hula* altar as a symbol of Laka's presence, Jennie Wilson (Kealiinohomoku 1964, p. 163) said that "the *lama* tree had nothing to do with Laka, but that a branch of the tree was placed on the altar becase of the good meaning of its name, which is 'light'."

The two also differed on the role of the bowl of *'awa* during the training period. Emerson said the bowl of *'awa* on the altar of the *halau hula* was changed daily. Mrs. Wilson said no, that the coconut shell of *'awa* and all the green plants remained the same from the beginning to the end of the training period and were part of the miracle of a successful *hula* school.

According to *kumu hula* John Kaimikaua (1982), Laka taught at Ka'ana, Moloka'i, that a block of *lama* wood was to be used as a resting place for her spirit. *Maile* was placed on the altar to symbolize the umbilical cord. "One end is attached to Laka and the other to this earth or to the person. So you have connection, you have open communications to whom you are praying. From that Hawaiians used it in many other ceremonies, because of the connection." *Lehua* was used because the wood, the tree, is male and the flower is female. "So because those two things are connected, you put them on the altar and it allows male and female to dance." "*Pili* grass was the next to the last thing put on the altar. It was tied in two bundles . . . The tops on one end had to go this way and one end had to go the other way . . . *Pili* means to cling, so that whatever you are taught it shall cling to you and you shall not forget it." The last thing that was put on the altar was *iliahi* or sandalwood, ground to powder and spread all over the altar. The sweet scent was to inspire the dancer to move in such a way as to "inspire and capture the people." He also pointed out that each island has its own special plants and that wherever Laka went, whatever plant captured her fancy she took as her own and used that plant on that island. "So from that time, that's why we have all these differences."

These variations in the rituals and prayers are used by different dancers and in different *halau* reflect how, when in real use, ritual and prayer-like language will change as circumstances change. It might be noted that of the plants commonly associated with the *hula* only ti, *'awa*, *kukui*, breadfruit, and the gingers, *'awa-puhi* and *'olena*, are among those plants brought to Hawaii by man. Others, such as the ferns, *hala pepe*, *'ie'ie*, *lama*, *maile*, *koa*, *pili*, and *'ohi'a*, are native to Hawaii and were adapted to the *hula* ritual in Hawaii.

207. Kewelani is also known as Na-wahine-li'ili'i, Laea, Ulunui, and Laka.
208. *Palai* fern represents Hi'iaka in the *halau hula*; *lama*, enlightenment; *'ohi'a-ku-makua*, mature conduct; and *koa*, boldness. Some *halau*, especially those on the island of Hawaii, have included *Kupaoa* (Peperomia spp., Railliardia spp.) for its sweet scent. They say, "*O ka kupaoa e ho'ope ana i ka 'uhane.*" "*Kupaoa* sweet perfume that softens the spirit." For other symbolism, see the section "Dedication to Lono" in Chapter VII.
209. According to an informant of N. B. Emerson (n.d.), an arrangement was made with only one man who was not a member of the *hula* group to collect the greenery. He went up to the mountains in the day-time to find the greenery, marking it with an adze, then returning home. In the darkness of the following morning, when no dog barked and there were no other disturbing noises, he went into the woodland and collected the greens, observing a strict tabu. Others believe that members of the *hula* troupe accompanied him on the second trip.

According to Kuluwaimaka, the *kumu hula*, or leader, does not go with the group to gather the greens. The *poopua'a* or head student or his assistant, the *paepae*, supervises its gathering.

The required greenery must be removed from the parent plant with respect for the god-form it represents, avoiding unnecessary destruction. In the case of the *'ohi'a*, the greenery was broken off, not cut. (Kuluwaimaka n.d.)

According to Mrs. Pukui (n.d.), the person sent for the greens "must have no fear and under no circumstances should he utter a sound besides the prayers. There were times when the invisible woodland spirits protested against the breaking of their plants and demanded to know what he was going to do with them. To these angry voices he must give no reply and must go about his business as though stone deaf. He went home without a backward glance no matter what he heard."
210. Emerson, N.B. 1965, pp. 18-19.
211. Akoni Mika, n.d.; Kelsey translation.
212. "The altar is built on the east side of the *halau* as an honor to Kane." (Kuluwaimaka n.d.)
213. Kuluwaimaka n.d., Kelsey translation.
214. "Every morning the altar is sprinkled with water to keep the greens fresh. The water is gathered daily. Any water remaining after the sprinkling is thrown either into the ocean or the woodland. The container is left in the middle of the altar. It is a long gourd like a *hokeo*, but smaller. If some of the greens are dry they should be replaced. When the *'ohi'a* or *'ie'ie* dry out all the greens must be replenished." (Kuluwaimaka n.d.)
215. "*'Ohi'a* here does not refer to the male or the water to women or children." (Kuluwaimaka n.d.)
216. "This line does not refer to the amount of water but to the sprinkling. The feast of releasing is a *pupu weu-weu*. When the leaves dry out they are burned." (Kuluwaimaka n.d.) Others say they should be thrown into the sea.
217. "This refers to the water used in sprinkling the altar, the giving of the water of life to the students, not the water for *'awa*. The prayer of the *'awa* is different. The water sprinkled on the chiefs was also different. If there was *'awa* that would do for them. Salt water sprinkling is different." (Kuluwaimaka n.d.)
218. Kekahuna n.d.
219. According to Jennie Wilson (n.d.) *hula* apparel could not be stored with that of ordinary wear.

220. The *imu* refers to the private *(kahi huna,* hidden part) of the woman. (Kuluwaimaka n.d.) The *imu* may refer to the womb. (Kelsey n.d.) The *imu* is the privates of both men and women. (Akoni Mika n.d.)

221. "Ka-wai-kapu refers to the privates of the woman." (Kuluwaimaka n.d.) "The body may represent a beautiful cliff and Ka-wai-kapu, the generative fluid." (Kelsey n.d.)

222. "This refers to the people of Hilo who first fashioned the *pa'u."* (Kuluwaimaka n.d.)

223. *"Manu* pertains to those doing the *hula* as if they flew here and there like birds." (Kuluwaimaka n.d.)

224. "The *malo* of 'Umi was left with his mother by Liloa. It was made out of *wauke.* High chiefs had their own designs as did different *halau hula."* (Kekahuna n.d.)

225. Pa'u Pua-kea, a white *pa'u.* A flower may represent a woman, and a foreign flower a foreign woman. In this case a foreign dancer may be represented. (Akoni Mika)

226. "When the dancer *'ami wiliwili ka pa'u,* the *pa'u* swings up by the head and the privates are exposed. Everyone yells when it comes to that part. You have to be a good dancer to make the *pa'u* come up." (Kekahuna n.d.)

227. Kuluwaimaka n.d.; Kelsey translation.

228. Uncertain source; Kelsey translation.

229. Emerson, N.B. 1965, p. 56.

230. Kuluwaimaka n.d.

231. Kuluwaimaka n.d.; Kelsey translation. This prayer, an allegory, is part of Lo-lale's reminiscing about his wife Kelea, "the surf rider," after she had left him for another man.

232. According to Emerson (n.d.), "This was the same Laka who was the child of Wahie-loa . . . As a canoe-maker this *kupua* was a male but as an *'aumakua* of the *hula* dancers the sex was female . . . Laka himself was not known to us in his own person, but in the shape of many woodland flowers such as the *lehua, ilima, hau,* and *kokio,* all of these and many others not mentioned. In fact, all flowers and leaves of the wildwood were sacred to Laka and were his physical representation. He was personified not only by flowers and leaves but also by the human form at times." Also see footnote 206.

233. Emerson, N.B. 1965, pp. 23-24.

234. Emerson, N.B. n.d.; Kelsey translation.

235. Mika n.d.; Kelsey translation.

236. Emerson, N.B. n.d.; Kelsey translation.

237. Emerson, N.B. n.d.; Kelsey translation.

238. There is some question as to how many Maile sisters there are. According to entries in the Pukui-Elbert dictionary (1971), there are four (p. 393) or five (p. 206). These are Maile-lau-li'i (Small-leaved-*maile),* Maile-ha'i-wale (Brittle-*maile),* Maile-kaluhea (Fragrant-*maile),* Maile-lau-nui (Big-leaf-*maile),* and Maile-pahaka (p. 393) or Maile-pakaha (p. 206).

   According to A. K. Cathcart, one of the Maile sisters is Maile-ka-ulu-hea (Wild-*maile).* Maile-ku-honua, which may be translated as Earth-standing-*maile,* is the name applied to a *maile* seedling before the plant begins to branch.

239. Emerson, N.B. 1965, p. 46.

240. Kuluwaimaka (n.d.) gave this line as *O laka o ka pule ikaika.* However, both Jennie Wilson (n.d.) and Kelsey agreed to the line as given in the text.

241. According to Wilson (n.d.), Kaha-'ula was a god of *hula.* This may be another name of Laka. In one of Emerson's unpublished notebooks he entered in brackets the name (Laka) after Kaha-'ula.

242. Kuluwaimaka n.d.; Kelsey translation.

243. Emerson, N.B. 1965, p. 128; Kelsey translation.

244. Emerson, N.B. n.d.; Kelsey translation.

245. Anonymous (1); Kelsey translation.

XIII KAUA
War

For the men and women[246] who go to war, there are prayers seeking protection and victory. Among others, these prayers are to Ku, Ku-ka'ili-moku (Ku-the-island-snatcher), Ku-ke-olo'ewa (Ku-the-shelf), Ku-nui-akea (Ku-(of)-wide-expanse), Ku'i-a-lua (Ku-lua-fighting-blows), Lono-maka-ihe (Spear-point-Lono), and Kane-poha (ku)-ka'a (Rolling-stone-Kane).

MAMUA O KE KAUA:
BEFORE THE BATTLE

When a battle was in the offing, the ruling chief would consult the appropriate *kahuna* who in turn would seek signs from the gods. If, on the appointed day, the sun rose clear and cloudless and continued so during the forenoon it was a sign the enemy would be victorious and the attack must be postponed. It was also an unfavorable sign if the sun, on rising, was hidden by a cloud which was soon broken up by the wind. However, if the sun was a fiery red and not obscured while rising, and there was a red spot on a dark cloud, the *kahuna* approved the day's battle plans. Services were then held in the *heiau*. The following is one of the prayers said.

94

Ia kini, mano o ke akua,
Ia kini lehu o ke akua,
Ka pa‘a nu‘u iluna,
Ka pa‘a i loko,
E kokua i ka ‘oukou pulapula,
I ku i ka nu‘u,
I ku i ka moku
I ku i ka wohi,[247]
I ku i ka lanakila,
Ho‘auhee i kela ‘ao‘ao
‘A‘ole hope e hele mai,
Ku ‘ia i ka waa mua
O Akea ka inoa,
Ku ‘ia i ka waa hope,
O ‘Iama ka inoa.
Ku ia iluna o ka malau,
A lele ke ka me ka liu
Kulia i ka ihe laumeki
I ke kauila me ka hau
I ka pahoa me ke lei o mano
E ola ia Mano-nui-akea,
E ola i kau pulapula
I kena-mu i kena-wa.
Ka huhu pao ke‘e la‘au
Ua noa, a lele wale.

To the many, the numerous family deities,
To the 40,000 times 400,000 of the family deities,
The solid high place above,
The solid place below,
All of you assist your offspring
That stand in high position
As ruler of the island.
In the position of *wohi*,[247]
Who stood as victor,
Who routed that side (the enemy)
With no backward retreat
Who is stood in the first canoe
Wide was its name.
Who stood in the last canoe
‘Iama was its name.
Who stood above the canoe bait carrier,
And flew the canoe bailer and the bilge
Who stood by the barbed spear
By the *kauila* and *hau* woods
By the short dagger of shark's teeth
Grant life to Mano-nui-akea,
Grant life to thy offspring
To that silence, to that uproar
The wood-boring insect that dubs out crooked wood
Lifted is the tabu, and the prayer flown away.[248]

The following is a chant-prayer said by the ancient chief Kawelo to his war club, whose name was Kuikaa.

A make aku la oe ia Kuikaa,
Ia Hookaa, ia Kaakua, ia Kaaalo,[249]
E ike auanei oe i ka nao hoopai a Malailua,
I ka laau e wali ai ko auwae,
E oki ai o na ka hoola,
E ike auanei oe apopo
I ka moa i hanai ia i ka la,
A puupuu i ka lepo,
A akaakaa ka hulu;
Me he moa kau i ka uwahi,
A eina ka hulu,
Hookahi no pekuna ua a ka moa i mahi la,
Puko–a, puko–a.

There, you are made unconscious by Kuikaa,
By Hookaa, by Kaakua, by Kaaalo.[249]
You will surely see the avenging club of Malailua,
The club that will break your jaws,
For then the avenging club will cease its work.
Tomorrow you shall see
The rooster that is fed of the sun,
Till the crop fills with dirt
And the feathers fall off
Like a rooster that is hung up in the smoke
With its feathers burnt off.
The conquering cock has made but one kick,
They are scattered, they are scattered.[250]

When a warrior fought with sling stones he might say the following prayer.

E Lono e! E Lono e!
Nau ka ala a Oulu,
E lawe oe i ka pololei,
I ka ikaika, i ka maa.
E uli ma o, ma o, e hala,
E nana i ke kahuna,
I ke koa nui o ka hikina,
E ola au! E ola au!
Lele wale! Amama! Ua noa.

O Lono eh! O Lono eh!
Yours is Oulu's stone,
Take you the unerring aim,
The force of the sling stone.
Turn it hither, thither; let it miss.
Have compassion on the priest,
On the great warrior of the east.
Let me live! Let me live!
The prayer is heard! Amen! 'T is released.[251]

This war prayer is to Kiha-nui-lulu-moku, a lizard goddess. It asks for supernatural intervention. When it was used by Waka, the grandmother of Laʻie-i-ka-wai, the Kiha personally helped in the battle.

E Kihanuilulumoku,
Ko makou akua mana,
Nana ia ke kupu,
Ka eu o ka aina nei la,
Pepehi ia a make,
A holo ke olohelohe,
E ao nae oe ia Kalahumoku,
I ka ilio aikanaka a Aiohikupua,
Hemahema oe pau kakou,
Kulia ko ikaika a pau i luna,
Amama, ua noa, lele wale.

Say, Kihanuilulumoku,
Our all-powerful god;
Watch for the enemy,
The mischievous people of the land,
And put them to death
Sparing none.
Be watchful however of Kalahumoku,
The man-eating dog of Aiohikupua.
If you are careless we are lost;
Let all your strength be at your command.
It is ended, the kapu is removed.[252]

MAHOPE O KE KAUA: AFTER THE BATTLE

When the battle is over, the gods are given thanks. In the following prayer thanks is said by alluding to the successful escape of a famous chief.

Ua moku ka iʻa pewa,
He uli ka lani.
Ua moku, na naha ke makaha.[253]
He iʻa kau i ka lewa ʻanuʻu[254]
He nuʻu Kahikinui, Kahiki i lalo o waia
Moku ka iʻa i ka papaku o Wakea.
O Wakea hauli i ka lani,
Hauli i ka papaku o Lono
O Lono, o Lono, e Lono e.
E Lono i ka iʻa nui.
E Lono i ka iʻa iki
ʻAmama, ua noa ia (inoa aliʻi).

Cut off is the fish fin,
The heavens are dark.
The naha[253] were cut off at the sluice gate.
A fish placed on the steps to the heiau[254]
A nuʻu is Kahikinui and Kahiki below
Cut off the fish at the foundation of Wakea.
Wakea blackish in the heavens,
Blackish at the foundation of Lono
O Lono, o Lono, o Lono.
Lono at the big fish
Lono at the little fish.
ʻAmama, it is free of tabu to (chief's name).[255]

LUA: HAND-TO-HAND COMBAT

A select group of men and women, perhaps limited to certain families, was trained in lua. With formalized movements that had the grace of a dance, the practioner of lua could subdue or kill with bone-breaking or sometimes with a touch.

This prayer is "for" the instructor. When it is recited, "rest the body."

Ke kai kuʻi hula, kuʻi momona
Kuʻi e ke kai a Hina-ka-unu-loa
Hina ka ʻohiʻa o papaʻi Wai-mea
Ka ʻohiʻa ou o Leʻa iuka
Ke ne hala ʻole aʻe la Ka-uhi-a-Hiwa
I ke kai mauka o Ke-ʻakuʻi a

The sea of the striking hula, fruitful blow
Striking by the sea of Hina-of-the-thrust-with-wind-force
Hina of the ʻohiʻa trees of Wai-mea's house of games
Your ʻohiʻa, o Leʻa of the upland.
Returns persistently without fail Ka-uhi-a-Hiwa
At the sea upland of Ke-ʻakuʻi.[256]

When in danger, the following brief prayer is quickly said for defense.

Ia ʻoe, Popoki wahine
I ani iluna, i ani ilalo
I ani kuuna,
I ani i ka lawena.

To you, Popoki wahine
That waved above, that waved below,
That waved descendingly,
That waved acquiringly.[257]

The purposes of the following prayers are hidden in references to persons, places, and incidents known only to *lua* initiates.

Ko ke au i Hala-eʻa, punawai Mana,
Wai nana a ke kupa e,
Ka ʻilio nana la, Hae nanahu i ke kai e.
Ka pua o ka ʻiliau,
Ka ʻohai maha pepe.
Aia i Mauoa a Kanaka-loloa e
Hea Ka-welo-hea-la, "Nowai la ke kupa e?"
No Ka-lani-malokuloku pua ehu i ke kai,
Aloha mai nei Hilo, kahi o makou.

The current draws at Hala-eʻa, a spring in Mana,
Water looked at by the native born,
The dog that snarls, barks and growls, bites the sea.
The flower of the *ʻiliau,*
The flat-sided *ʻohai.*
It is at Mauoa, at Kanaka-loloa
Ka-welo-hea calls "Of whom is the native born?"
Of Ka-lani-malokuloku of the spray child in the sea,
Love to Hilo, our place.[258]

Malie Maui ke waiho mai la
O ka ihu ʻakakala i po ia ʻe ke kuʻi
Kai-halulu i ke alo o Ka-ʻuiki
Hiʻi Ka-ʻuiki ia Moki-hana
Hiʻi ka nalu ia Ke-anini
Hiʻi Wai-kolea i Ka-ʻiliʻili
Hoʻea ana i Moki-hana
He waa Hawaiʻi e
O Wai-kaa-hiki ke awa
O Puna-hoa ka wai
Oneone ia Pueo-kahi
Ka-hulili kai uka
Honua ʻula ka kai
Pau Peʻapeʻa o ke ahi
O ka hee palaha.

Peaceful is Maui that lies there
The pink nose thick by the blow.
Ka-halulu at the front of Ka-ʻuiki
Ka-ʻuiki embraces Moki-hana
The waves embrace Ke-anini
Wai-kolea embraces Ka-ʻiliʻili
Arriving at Moki-hana
A canoe is Hawaiʻi
Wai-kaa-hiki is the harbor
Puna-hoa is the water
Pueo-kahi is sandy
Ka-hulili sea upland
Honua-ʻula sea seaward
Peʻapeʻa was ended by fire
The flattened octopus.[259]

The following *pule lua* begins in a similar manner to the foregoing but is longer. Some of the proper names are the names of *lua* holds.

Malie o Maui ke waiho mai nei
O Ka-ihu-a-ka-la kai uka,
Ka-uiki kai kai.
Poʻi e ke kui
Hii Ka-ʻuiki ia Moku-hano
Hii ke one ia Puna-hoa[260]
Hii Wai-koloa i ka-ʻiliʻili
Hii ka nalu ia Ke-anini.
Hoʻea i Moku-mana
He waa Hawaii ke holo mai nei
Wai-kakihi ke awa
O puna hoa ka wai
Oneone ia Ka-pueo-kahi[261]
Honua-ʻula ka i uka
Ka-hulili kai luna
Pau peʻapeʻa i ke ahi
Moku i ka ʻohe.

Calm is Maui that lies there
The nose of the sun is upland
Ka-ʻuiki is by the sea.
Ward off the blow
Ka-ʻuiki embraces Moku-hano
Embraces the sand of Puna-hoa[260]
Wai-koloa embraces Ka-ʻiliʻili
The waves embrace Ke-anini
Arrived at Moku-mana
Hawaii is a canoe that comes
Wai-kakihi the harbor
Puna-hoa is the water
Sandy at Ka-pueo-kahi[261]
Honua-ʻula is upland
Ka-hulili is above
Peʻapeʻa was burned by the fire.
Cut down the bamboo.

Ku ka uahi o Papio
He uwahi puaa, he uwahi ilio
Ma kui a lua e hala ho'i
Ke koe kai pale hewa o ka na, O Ke-ahi-a-loa

Maloko mai, mawaho mai
Maloko kai a ka 'opelu
Mawaho kai a ke aku
I hiki a ka niu kaa
O ka niu kaa
Olelo i ka ipu a ka makani
Moku i ka 'ohe.

Hole Wai-mea i ka ihe a ka makani
Hao mai na ale a ke Ki-puupuu
He laau kala-ihi ia na ke anu
Oo i ka nahele o Mahiki
Ku aku la i ka maka o Ka-wai-o-Uli[262]
Eha ia'u i ka nahele o Wai-ka
Niniau 'eha i ka pua o koai'e
Moku i ka 'che.

Aia la ka ua lehei o Maka-wao
Ke lulumi mai la i ke alo o na kahawai
Auka a'e la ka ihu o ka naulu
I po'i ia e ku'i Piipii ihoiho
Moku i ka 'ohe.

Aia la ka nahele o Oakia la i po'i ia e ke ku'i
Kike ka ala naha ka hala
Pau ka 'i'o o ka 'ai ia
Moku i ka 'ohe.

Aia la ko ki 'awa i lau Ke-alapii-a-ka-'opae

I pii no ka naue la
Ku'i pii ana, hee ana
Moku i ka 'ohe.

Aia la o Ka-lena 'ai a ka wahine[264]
I po'i ia e ke ku'i o Ka-lena haule ilalo
Ia ka hee kuekue, ka hee palaha
O ka hee o kai uli kapae ka 'ala'ala
Moku i ka 'ohe.

Aia la o waiu o Lewa i po'i 'ia e ke ku'i
Lewa ka 'auwae i ka niho 'ole
Make ka 'uku i ke anu
Moku i ka 'ohe.

Aia la Hopoe, he wahine lewa i ke kai
I po'i ia e ke ku'i
He maka'u ka lehua i ke kanaka
I ka maka o Halulu[265]
Moku i ka 'ohe.

Stands the smoke of Papio
A smoked pig, a smoked dog
The two blows that will cause death to be sure
There remains the warder off of wrong of the quitted
    Ke-ahi-loa
From within, from without
Within the gravy of the 'opelu
Outside of the gravy of the aku
Till arrived at the rolling coconut
O the rolling coconut
Say to the gourd of the wind
Break the bamboo.

Wai-mea is rasped by the spear of the wind
A chilly wind and rain at Wai-mea
It is a stick hard by the cold
That pierces in the forest of Mahiki
That stands before the eyes of Ka-wai-o-Uli[262]
It pains me in the forest of Wai-ka
Flowing painfully to the flower of the koai'e
Cut off by the bamboo.

There is the leaping rain of Maka-wao
Crushed in the presence of the streams
Lifted is the nose of the naulu[263]
That is mounded up to strike, lifting and descending
Cutting down the bamboo.

There is the forest of Oakia covered by the punch
The 'ala rock breaks, the hala is broken
The meat is eaten
The bamboo broken.

There is the topmost 'awa that multitudinous be Ke-
    alapii-a-ka-'opae
That the movement be upward
Striking together, flowing together
The bamboo is broken.

There is Ka-lena,[264] food of the woman
Pounced on by the blow of Ka-lena
To the octopus thumping, the octopus flattened
The octopus of the dark blue sea that sets aside its liver
Cut by the bamboo.

There is the breast milk of Lewa
The chin swings because of no teeth
The louse dies in the cold
Cut off the bamboo.

There is Hopoe, a woman that wanders by the sea
Caught by the blow
The lehua is afraid of the man
Before the eyes of Halulu[265]
Cut down the bamboo.

Aia la ka maka o ka ʻopua	There is the presence of the puffy horizon cloud
I poʻi ʻia e ke kuʻi	Caught by the blow
Ke loku mai la ka ua	The rain is in downpour
E hehi ana i ka pua o ka lehua	Treading on the flower of the *lehua*
Nakeke i ka iwi ʻaoʻao	Rattling at the ribs
Moku i ka ʻohe.	Cut down the bamboo.[266]

NOTES

246. Women took full part in the battles of ancient times. They were in the forefront of many attacks, sometimes fighting beside their men, sometimes distracting the opponent.
247. The *wohi* were high chiefs exempt from the prostrating tabu.
248. Emerson, N.B., from Koalii n.d.; Kelsey translation.
249. Kuikaʻa, Hoʻokaʻa, Kaʻakua, and Kaʻaʻalo are all names of strokes used when fighting with a war club and in the hand-to-hand combat called *lua*.
250. Fornander 1918, pp. 26-27, 30-31.
251. Fornander 1918, pp. 456-457.
252. Fornander 1918, pp. 412-413.
253. A *naha* was a chief whose parents were either an uncle and niece or an aunt and nephew both of *niʻaupio* rank.
254. According to N. B. Emerson, n.d., "the *anuu* were the steps up to the floor of the *heiau;* there were six of them, the same as the number of the islands."
255. Emerson, N.B., n.d.; Kelsey translation.
256. Porter n.d.; Kelsey translation.
257. Porter n.d.; Kelsey translation.
258. Kuluwaimaka n.d.; Kelsey translation.
259. Kuluwaimaka n.d.; Kelsey translation.
260. Puna-hoa, a spring made by striking with a stick or club. Kane, when traveling around the islands with Kana-loa, made springs by striking an outcropping of rocks or the ground.
261. Ka-pueo-kahi, port and harbor of Hana.
262. Uli, a goddess of sorcery.
263. Naulu, sudden shower breeze, also the sea breeze at Wai-mea, Kauai.
264. Ka-lena, a *lua* hold.
265. Halulu, a legendary man-eating bird, a demi-god.
266. Anonymous, Kelsey translation.

XIV NĀ PĀʻANI
Sports

Sports and games were, in some form or other, a daily part of the lives of the people of old. Guessing games, riddling, and boasting contests often accompanied routine work. Free time during the day might be filled, on impulse, with swimming, surfing, kite flying, or tug-of-war, while quiet times in the evening might be used for games of skill such as *konane,* juggling, or cats' cradle. A wide range of social games such as *puhenehene, kilu,* or *ʻume* were often the basis for an exchange of sexual favors.[247] During the *makahiki* and on other festive occasions contests such as boxing, spear-throwing, and other sports that required special training were popular.[268]

At some time every sport and every game was the basis for betting. The prize might be an unimportant possession, sexual favors, personal services, or, in extreme cases, one's life. For the casual game the contestant could depend on his own know-how, but if a bet or other special interest depended on the outcome, the participant would call upon the gods, both during the periods of training and practice and when the bets were placed.

The gods shared man's enjoyment of sports, not only as patrons and spectators but at times even joined men in contests or staged contests of their own.[269]

'AU 'ANA: SWIMMING

Swimming was so much a part of the daily life in ancient times that it could hardly be called a sport. However, even today, whenever a person enters the water he calls on the gods to care for him. One way to do this is to take a piece of edible *limu* from along the shore and, breaking it in two, throw one piece up on the shore, offering it to the land gods saying *"Ko uka, no uka no ia."* "Of land for land is this." Then the second piece is tossed out into the water as an offering for the gods of the ocean while saying, *"Ko kai, no kai no ia."* "Of ocean for ocean is this."

PAE I KA NALU: SURFING

Surfing has been one of the most popular sports in Hawaii from ancient times. At times entire villages would leave home and work when hearing the call, *"Ua pi'i mai ka nalu!"* "Surf's up!" On the nights when the tops of the waves shine with a glistening light it is said the gods have joined in the sport.

The lack of waves has never held back a surfer. Whether he felt the urge to body, board, or canoe surf, a call to the god La'a-maomao brings the required waves. The following are versions of a call for waves. Some pray while lashing the waves at the edge of the sea with a length of *pohuehue* vine.[270] Others pray after building a mound of sand and wrapping the *pohuehue* vine around it.

'Alo, 'alo po'i pu
'Iuka i ka pohuehue
Ka ipu nui lawe mai
Ka ipu iki waiho aku.

Come break together,
Run up to the *pohuehue* vines
Bring the big wind calabash
Leave behind the small.[271]

Ku mai! Ku mai!
Ka nalu nui mai Kahiki mai.
'Alo po'i pu!
Ku mai i ka pohuehue
Hu! Kaiko'o loa!

Arise! Arise!
Great surfs from Kahiki.
Waves break together!
Rise with the *pohuehue*
Well up, raging surf![272]

Ku mai, ku mai,
Ka 'ale nui mai Kahiki mai
Ka ipu nui lawe mai
Ka ipu iki waiho aku.
Ho a'e, ho a'e iluna
I ka pohuehue
Ka ipu nui lawe mai
Ka ipu iki waiho aku.

Stand, stand
Waves from Kahiki
Bring the large wind-gourd
Leave the small one.
Go, go up to the beach
Morning glory
Bring the large wind-gourd
Leave the small one.[273]

HO'OLELE LUPE: KITE FLYING

Kite flying, a popular sport in ancient times,[274] is still seasonally popular. It is said that kites were first invented by the demi-god Maui. Made of tapa or fine *lauhala* sail mat, some were as large as six to seven feet wide and fifteen feet long.[275] When wind for kite flying is wanted, it is also to La'a maomao that the petitioner goes to seek the winds of Hilo.[276]

Here are two prayers used to call the winds for kite flying.

Pa mai, pa mai,
Ka makani nui o Hilo!
Ka ipu nui lawe mai,
Ka ipu iki waiho aku!

Blow, blow,
Great wind of Hilo!
Bring the large calabash,
Leave the small calabash![277]

Pa mai, pa mai,
Ka makani nui o Hilo!
O ka ipu iki waiho aku,
O ka ipu nui ki'i mai.

Blow, blow,
Great wind of Hilo!
Leave the small wind calabash,
Bring the big wind calabash.[278]

If a milder breeze is wanted, then the kite flyer will pray,

Pa mai, pa mai
Ka makani nui o Hilo.
Waiho aku ka ipu nui,
Ho mai ka ipu liilii.

Blow, blow
Strong winds of Hilo.
Put away the large wind gourd,
Bring the small wind gourd.[279]

E HOOPAU I KA UA: **TO STOP THE RAIN**

A short, light, misty rain is a sign of the gods' presence, approval, and support. But if the rain seems to be so heavy or lengthy as to interfere with an activity, it is appropriate to ask that the rain stop. This short prayer does that.

Malie,
Malie ka ua i Poha-kea
Makai he ua
Mauka he ua
Kiola,
Kiola, ka ua i kou luawai.

Calm,
Calm is the rain at Poha-kea
Seaward is a rain
Upland is a rain
Throw,
Throw, the rain into your well.[280]

PUKAULA: **A BETTING GAME**

Pukaula, a form of a rope trick, was once a popular game used for gambling. The players, usually experts, used a long, thin, smoothly braided rope. Each end was held by a different man. After the leader made a knot in the middle of the rope, the betters would inspect it from various angles and then make their bets as to whether the knot would hold when pulled. Striking hands, the betters pledged their bets with the oath-prayer, *"Pau Pele, pau mano!"* "Finished by Pele, finished by shark (if I do not keep my oath)." The ends of the rope were then pulled and the winner known.

The patron of this rope game and all activities involving ropes, as well as some sorcery, was Kana.[281] The following is a prayer said when betting on a game of interest to Kana.

E Kana. E Kana.
E mahulu-ku, e kii lalau,
E kuhi a leo, e ka moe,
Ka hanai a Uli.
Kuua mai kou kapa kaula,.
Hoalu mai kou kapa kanaka,
I ka pu a kaua, e Kana.

O Kana. O Kana.
Rough line of *hala* root, or bark of *hau,*
Point and declare as to the sleeper,
The foster child of Uli.
Put on your rope body,
Lay off your human form,
In this trick of yours and mine, O Kana.[282]

NA HEI: STRING FIGURES

Cat's cradle, or string figures, were made by nearly everyone in the ancient times. The figures accompanied chants that told stories whose length varied with the complexity of the plot, which might be a simple riddle, a complex adventure, or a detailed sexual exploit. On occasion, a string figure might accompany a prayer.

The following prayer was used with string figures in one type of medical treatment.

O hana ka uluna.	Make the pillow.
Ka paka a ka ua i ka lani.	The rain is falling from the sky.
Hana no e oki.	Get ready to cut (the sickness).
Ka hana kapu a Lono.	Impose the tapu of Lono.
E Lono e,	Oh Lono,
Eia kou pulapula la, ua maʻi.	Here is your offspring. He is sick.
A e Lono e,	Oh, Lono,
E lawe i ka eha o ka maʻi a pau	Take away all pains of sickness,
I na pilikia o ia nei.	And his troubles.
Kahiki-ku, Kahiki-moe, Kahiki-papaua a Kane,	Gods of the east, of the west, of the pearly shell of Kane (of the sea).
E ola ia Kane-i-ka-wai-ola.	To grant life belongs to Kane of the water of life.
ʻAmama. Ua noa.	ʻAmama. The tabu is lifted.[283]

NOTES

267. Descriptions of these games may be found in "Hawaiian Antiquities" (Malo 1951, pp. 214-218).
268. The sports and games mentioned here are only a small portion of those played in the ancient times. Culin (1899, pp. 246-247) cites nearly ninety games of pre-European origin.
269. On the nights of the moon-month called *po akua*, the gods are said to visit famous sports or surfing sites to stage their own contests or to join man in his contests. The *po akua* are the nights (and days) of the moon month, such as *po Kane, po Lono,* etc., that are dedicated to the gods and on which special religious rituals take place. The names are consistent throughout the islands, but there appears to be some differences as to which nights are *po akua* in different parts of the islands.
270. *Pohuehue* is the beach morning glory.
271. Kukona (Porter) n.d.; Kelsey translation.
272. Kelsey collection and translation.
273. Kelsey collection and translation.
274. Kites were also used ritually. According to Charles Kenn (n.d.), the *kahuna hui* was a *kahuna* who "performed the rite of *lolupe* over the body of a deceased *alii-nui.* He sent a kite *(lolupe)* to search for the spirits of the dead and to bring them before the *kahuna* for identification, interrogation, and judgement. . . . Kapihe was able to recall the spirit of the deceased Kauikeaouli (as an infant) when he saw it against the *uli* (vault of heaven) and caused it to reenter the deceased body." Place names such as Wai-lupe reflect this use of kites. It is also thought that Hilo was "devoted" to the worship of kites. (Emerson, N.B. 1903)

    According to Pukui and Elbert (1965, p. 199) there were four types of kites: *Lupe la,* or sun kite, a round kite; *lupe mahina,* or moon kite, a kite with a tapa covering cut in a crescent shape; *lupe manu,* or kite with wings; and *lupe maoli,* or true kite which was made in a shape similar to European kites. (Culin 1899, p. 229)
275. Campbell 1967, pp. 147-148.
276. It is said that "in Hilo the winds blow from all directions except up and down. When wind was wanted on any of the islands it was the ancient custom to invoke it from the *ipu* at Hilo." (James Iokepa n.d.)
277. Iokepa n.d.; Kelsey translation.
278. Emerson, N.B., n.d.; Kelsey translation.
279. Emerson, J.S. 1921, p. 386.
280. Kaiewe; Kelsey translation.
281. A *kupua,* Kana, was born as a small piece of cord and was "put aside as a thing of no accord" by his parents. However, the goddess Uli recognized his worth and nurtured him until he became a demi-god of great power.
282. Malo 1951, pp. 226-228.
283. Dickey 1928, p. 143.

XV NĀ ALIʻI, KA POʻE, KAʻAINA
The Chiefs, The People, The Land

All the elements of the heavens, the earth, and the seas, including the various classes of men and their gods, are interdependent. Nowhere is this interdependence more visible than in the relationships of the chiefs, the people, and the land.

According to ancient custom, as defined by Kamehameha III, the land "belonged to the chiefs and the people in common."[284] The chiefs were responsible for the supervision of the land and maintaining a reservoir of *mana* for the people as a nation. In turn, the people had the responsibility of supporting the chiefs and working the land which supported both the chiefs and the people.

KE PULE MAI NA ALIʻI:
THE CHIEFS PRAY

As part of their responsibilities, the chiefs often went to the gods seeking abundance for their people. At those times they offered prayers called *pule hoʻoulu* or growth prayers. These prayers might be used for any of the people's general or specific needs. The same prayer might be used to seek an increase in the size of a catch of fish, the size of a family, the growth of plants, or of talent in performing the *hula.*

The first of the two following prayers is a general *pule hoʻoulu,* useable for any need. The second seeks an increase in the productivity of crops in the district.

O Kahiki-ku, o Kahiki-mce, o Kahiki-papaua a Kane,
O Kahiki-'auwae-hina, O Kahiki-'au-lani o-ka-moku,
O ka pae 'aina o Kahiki-moe i Ho-lani la e,
I ka paepae kapu o Nu'u-mea-lani la e.
E ola!
E o 'o Nu'u-mea-lani ka moku!

Ilaila i noho ai o Moana-liha-i-ka-wao-kele,
A me Kiha-nui-lulu-moku.
Noho i ke kapu i ka 'aina kapu o Kahakaha-ka-'ea.
E ola e!
O Kahiki-kau-'ope'a-lani o-ka-moku,
O ka moku nui 'ope'a-ku o ka lani.
Hanau na keiki o Ka'elo-ka-malama,
Puka mai ka pae 'aina o na Kahiki,
I hanau 'ia mai loko mai o Kahiki-nui-'auwae-hina,
Ka pae moku o na Kahiki la e.
E ola!

O Kahiki-ku, o Kahiki-moe, o Kahiki-papaua-of-Kane,
O Kahiki-'auwae-hina, o Kahiki-'au-lani of the island,
The group of lands of Ka-hiki-moe in Ho-lani,
To the tabu house platform of Nu'u-mea-lani.
Live!
Give answer to your name in chant o Nu'u-mea-lani the island.
There lived Moana-liha-i-ka-wao-kele
And Kiha-nui-lulu-moku
Dwelt in the tabu on the tabu land of Kahakaha-ka-'ea
Live!
Ka-hiki of heaven high crisscrossing of the island
The great island of heaven-high crossing.
Born were the children of the month of Ka'elo
The several lands of Ka-hiki issued forth
Given birth from within Kahiki-'auwae-hina
The island groups of the Ka-hikis
Live![285]

E Lono ma ka uli lani,
Eia ka ai, eia ka ia,
He alana, he mohai,
He nuhanuha, he alana ia oe o Lono!
Houlu ia ka ai i keia ahupuaa,
E ulu a maka-ole ke kalo,
E ulu a muaiwa ka uala.
A eia ka puaa,
He puaa kukui nau e Lono.
E kui a ko ahupuaa,
A palahu ka ai i waena
A o kau ola ia e ke akua.
E Lono, nana i kou pulapula!
Amama. Ua noa.

O Lono of the blue firmament,
Here are vegetables, here is meat,
An offering of prayer, a sacrifice,
An offering of fat things to you, O Lono!
Let the crops flourish in this *ahupuaa,*
The taro stays in the ground till its top dies down,
The potato lie in its hill till it cracks.
And here is the pig,
A pig carved in *kukui* wood for you, O Lono.
Let it remain on your district altar
Until the vegetables rot in the fields.
Such is thy blessing, O god.
O Lono, look upon your offspring!
The burden is lifted! Freedom![286]

A service called *ho-'uluulu-ai* was to increase all food production. It might be performed before the beginning of a planting season, at times of famine, or before an anticipated need such as a long voyage or war. The service was performed in a temporary building called a *heiau mao* that was used only by chiefs. The following is a prayer used at such services.

E Kane auloli ka honua!
Honu nee pu ka aina.
Ulu nakaka, kawahawaha ka honua.
Ulu ka ai hapuu, e Lono.
Ohi maloo, kupukupu.
Ohi aa na uala o na pali.
Pali-ku kawahawaha ka ua,
Ka ua haule lani,
He haule lani ka uala.

O Kane, transform the earth!
Let the earth move as one piece.
The land is cracked and fissured.
The edible fern yet grows, O Lono.
Let *kupukupu* cover the dry land.
Gather potatoes as stones on the side-hills.
The rain comes like the side of a *pali,*
The rain falling from heaven.
The potato also falls from heaven.

He aweu ke kalo,	The wild taro is the only taro now,
He lauloa pili kanawao.	The taro of the mountain patches.
O wao-akua ka ai, e Kane!	The only food is that of the wilds, O Kane!
E Kane! e Lono! na akua mahiai,	O, Kane and Lono! Gods of the husbandmen,
Hoola i ka aina!	Give life to the land!
A poho ka ai,	Until the food goes to waste,
A ulu kupukupu,	Until it sprouts in the ground,
A ulu lau poo-ole;	Until the leaves cover the land;
A o ka nui ia o ka ai	And such be the plenty
Au, e Kane a me Lono.	Of you, O Kane and Lono.
Amama. Ua noa.	The burden is lifted. We are free.[287]

If a chief wanted to mingle with the people on equal terms for a time his *kapu* could be set aside. The chief and, according to one authority, those with whom he intended to mingle were shut into a little house where a fire made of *pukiawe* was burning. All were smudged with the smoke and then the following prayer was said.

I Kane ma, laua o Kanaloa,	To Kane and his fellow Kanaloa,
O kahi ka po,	For one night,
O lua ka po,	For two nights,
O kolu ka po,	For three nights,
O ha ka po,	For four nights,
O lima ka po,	For five nights,
O ono ka po,	For six nights,
O hiku ka po,	For seven nights,
O walu ka po,	For eight nights,
O iwa ka po,	For nine nights,
A umi ka po,	For ten nights,
Holo aku oe i kai,	You shall sail out to sea,
Noa aku oe i kai,	And the tabu shall not rest upon you at sea,
Pau kou kapu ia oe, Lono!	My tabu shall be done away with by you, o Lono!
Amama! Ua noa ia Umi!	It is lifted! There is freedom to Umi![288]

KE PULE NEI KANAKA: **THE PEOPLE PRAY**

It is said that the people of old prayed constantly and that "the health of the body was the main thing prayed for by the people of Hawaii." First all the male gods and then the female gods were prayed to. Then, after appeals for their special needs, the people would request "life" for their chiefs. This is a prayer that was said for the health of a good chief. It will always be applicable for a good leader.

O kau ola e ke akua.	Give life, O god.
E nana mai i kau mau pulapula;	Look to your descendants;
E ola a kaniko'o, a haumaka'iole.	(Give me) life until I walk with a staff, and blear-eyed as a rat.
A palalauhala, a kau i ka puaneane;	Yellowed as *hala* leaves, and reach extreme old age;
Alaila, lawe aku oe ia'u i ke alo o Wakea.	Then take me to the presence of Wakea.[289]

The following prayer is for good government and might be said by either chief or commoner. The Kahiko referred to was an ancient chief and Manalu his selfish priest. In time, Manalu's fellow priests "raised heaven and earth" and caused him to be put to death.

Make Kane ia hii,	Kane wearies himself to death with care,
Hii luna i ka lani o Kane.	Care for the government of his own heavenly kingdom.
Hii ka honua ia Kane,	The earth is governed by Kane,
Hii ke ao opulepule,	Kane cares for the mottled cirrus clouds.
Pule ola i Kane e.	Pray to Kane for life.
O Kane ke akua ola.	Kane is the god of life.
Amama Kahiko ia Kane.	Kahiko said *amama* to Kane.
E ola o Kane!	Hail Kane!
Amama. Ua noa.	Amen. it is *noa*.
Noa o Kane, ke akua o ke kupulau,	The freedom of Kane, god of the shooting herb.
Io welo Kahiko o Kane,	Through Kahiko, successor of Kane,
O Kane i o Manaele.	Kane transmitted it to Manaele.
Maeleele ka lani,	Darkened were the heavens.
Ka lani, ka honua, ua kapu no Kane.	The heavens, the earth, are sacred to Kane.
Amama. Ua noa.	Amen. It is *noa*.[290]

HE PULE NO KA UKU 'AUHAU: **TAX PAYING PRAYER**

Taxes in some form have always been considered necessary for the support of the government. In the days of ancient Hawaii, taxes were "a voluntary offering" collected four times a year.[291] If the "tax collectors" were not satisfied with the "offering," they would lower the image of Lono which one of them was carrying. This indicated more was to be given.[292] Other taxes were paid during the year in the form of work days on the lands of the chiefs.

The following is a prayer said after paying taxes. The first part was said by a *kahuna*.

Ou kinoi (kino e) Lono i ka lani,	Your bodies, O Lono, are in the heavens,
He ao loa, he ao poko,	A long cloud, a short cloud,
He ao kiei, he ao halo,	A watchful cloud,
He ao hoo-pua i ka lani;	An overlooking cloud—in the heavens;
Mai Uliuli, mai Melemele,	From Uliuli, from Melemele,
Mai Polapola, mai Haehae,	From Polapola, from Haehae,
Mai Omao-ku-ulu-lu,	From Omao-ku-ulu-lu,
Mai ka aina o Lono i hanau mai ai.	From the land that gave birth to Lono.
Oi hookui aku o Lono ka hoku e mihai ka lani,	Behold, Lono places the stars that sail through the heavens.
Amoamo ke akua laau nui o Lono;	High resplendent is the great image of Lono;
Kuikui papa ka lua mai Kahiki,	The stem of Lono links our dynasties with Kahiki,
Hapaina, kukaa i ka hau miki no Lono!	Has lifted them up, purified them in the ether of Lono!
E ku i ka malo a hiu!	Stand up! Gird yourselves for play!
The people then pray	The people then pray:
Hiu!	Gird yourselves!
Kahuna says	*Kahuna* says:
O Lono—	O Lono—
People respond	People respond:
Ke akua laau!	The image of Lono!
Kahuna says	*Kahuna* says:
Aulu!	Hail!
People respond	People respond:
Aulu, e Lono!	Hail to Lono![293]

KA 'AINA: THE LAND

All the people, chiefs and commoners, share a concern for the land that is shown most often in the prayers of the farmer. At times others, such as those who live on the island of Hawaii, have a special concern for the land.[294] Those are the times that the goddess Pele becomes visible in a volcanic eruption. If the eruption is in one of the numerous caldera it has something of the quality of a friendly visit. However, at other times Pele rampages, spreading *lava* over the land. The following is a prayer that seeks the cessation of her devouring. It is said before eating.

Pele, Pele 'ai la'au la	Pele, Pele, eater of trees
O kau ke ahi iki o 'Ula'ula-ke-ahi[295]	Yours is the small fire, 'Ula'ula-ke-ahi[295]
Pu'u-lena ka makani, he 'awa ko Puna,[296]	Pu'u-lena is the wind,[296] the *'awa'* is of Puna,
'I pili'ia 'e ka hala, 'o ka hala hea la?[297]	That is joined by the *hala,* the *hala* of where?[297]
Ka hala a ke akua i ho'omau ai	The *hala* the god continued
Ia 'oukou ia makou.	For you deities, for us worshipers,
O peke ka 'aina a na ho'ali'i	Lest small be the land of the Pele worshipers
'Ai Pele ka malu, ka ho'ali'i[298]	Pele devoured the peace, the Pele worshipers[298]
He lapa, he uila, e lala ka honua.[299]	Let the lightning flash, warm the earth.[299]
'E ola makou i kou lau kaula la	That we may live, your prophets
'Eli'eli holo iloko o ke kapu,	Profoundly into tabu runs the prayer,
'Eli'eli holo iloko o ka noa.	Profound the lifting of the tabu.
Noa.	The tabu is lifted.

This is the second of the prayers to Pele to cease her devouring. It is recited after eating.

Ua noa ka 'aina a ka puke iki, a ka puke nui,[300]	The land is free by the small attack, by the great attack,[300]
'Ekahi nawa a ka haku,[301]	For the release from the eating (of tabu) of the *haku.*[301]
O ka 'ope'ope, o Kulipe'e noho i ka lua,	O depriver of bundles, o hinder who dwells in the pit turning a deaf ear,
A lele 'e na ho'ali'i,[302]	Till the worshipers of Pele run away,[302]
O Ku-wawa, o Ku-ha'ili'ili-moe,[303]	O Ku-wawa, o Ku ha'ili'ili-moe,[303]
O Ha'iha'i-lau-ahea,	O Ha'iha'i-lau-ahea,
Na wahine i ke ao ma'ukele,	The women in the day, in the rain forest,
O ke kahuna i ka puoko o ke ahi,	The *kahuna* in the hot raging of the fire,
O 'Imi'imi, O Nalo-wale, o Loa'a e.	O 'Imi'imi, o Nalo-wale, o Loa'a.
Loa'a la ho'i ka hala, uku i ka 'oiwi.	When you get the wrong, pay the native son
Na ke aloha i kono aku la,	By love was the invitation given.
Hele mai la 'a—	She comes . . comes . . .
'Eli'eli kapu; 'eli'eli noa.	Profound the tabu; profound the freedom from tabu.[304]

At times devotees of Pele called her to return to the volcano for a visit. The following is one of the prayers used on such occasions. It was said in 1925 when residents of the island of Hawaii sought the return of the goddess to Kilauea. Two translations are given.

O Pele la ko'u akua.	O Pele, thou goddess mine
Miha ka lani, miha ka honua	Heaven and earth in darkness dwell;
E kapu, i kapu kai ka 'awa	A heavenly water, saline water;
Ka 'awa'awa, ka 'awa nui a Hi'iaka	Bring hither Hii's flowing *'awa* bowl,
Ka 'awa, ka 'awa o ola	That I may drink and be satisfied;
I ku ai, ku i Mauli-ola	O thou gallant Mauliola,
E loa ka wai apu	Pour forth sacred water to thine *'awa;*
E Pele-honua-mea, E la!	O Earth's mighty Pele, O Sun!
Eia ka palala, he pule	Here's thy gift, a prayer to thee,

O ka la'e ka o Haumea	Thou art of Haumea's female line,
O ka wahine i Kilauea	Beauteous goddess Kilauea
O ka wahine nana i ai a hohonu ka lua	Who dug a mighty fiery pit
O kahi noho no na wahine mai Porapora mai	Abode for maids of the Summer Seas;
Wahine o ka lani	Lovely woman of heaven,
Wahine lole kohi ahi	Thou maid in fiery apparel aglow,
Eia mai ka 'awa	An 'awa bowl to grace a queenly maid.
Eia mai ka mohai pua'a	Here is the sacrificial pig;
Ka pua'a 'olomea	A lengthwise striped pig;
O ke ola no hoi ia makou pulapula	Save me, thou Pele goddess mine,
'Amama ua noa, ue lele wale aku la.	Amen, 'tis free, fare thee well.[305]

O Pele la ko'u akua.	Pele is my deity.
Miha ka lani, miha ka honua	Silent is the heaven, silent is the earth
E kapu, i kapu kai ka 'awa	Make tabu the 'awa with a ceremonial sea bath
Ka 'awa'awa, ka 'awa nui a Hi'iaka	The bitter 'awa, the great 'awa of Hi'iaka
Ka 'awa, ka 'awa o ola	The 'awa, the 'awa of life
I ku ai, ku i Mauli-ola	That stood, stood at Mauli-ola
E loa ka wai apu	Make long the water in the coconut shell cup.
E Pele-honua-mea, E la!	Pele-honua-mea, arise!
Eia ka palala, he pule	Here is the gift, a prayer
O ka la'e ka o Haumea	The clearing up of the genealogical vine stem of Haumea.
O ka wahine i Kilauea	O woman of Kilauea
O ka wahine nana i ai a hohonu ka lua	The woman who ate the pit until deep,
O kahi noho no na wahine mai Porapora mai	Abode for the women from Porapora.
Wahine o ka lani	Woman of heaven,
Wahine lole kohi ahi	Woman in fiery apparel,
Eia mai ka 'awa	Here is the 'awa.
Eia mai ka mohai pua'a	Here is the sacrificial pig
Ka pua'a 'olomea	The striped pig.
O ke ola no hoi ia makou pulapula	Grant me life, and long life to our descendants
'Amama ua noa, ua lele wale aku la.	'Amama. It is free of tabu. It has simply flown away.[306]

When the earth is shaken by earthquakes or thunder storms, this is a prayer to make it calm.

O'o huli haliu Ka-wai-kini-a-Kane,	Turn with regard Wai-kini-a-Kane,
Hakuko'i ana i ke alo o Wai-kini-a-Kane	Rushing to the front of Wai-kini-a-Kane
O ke kumu 'ie ia o Mauna-iki e...	It is the aerial root of Mauna-iki...
O Mauna-iki huli a'e Kalalea	Mauna-iki that turns toward Kalalea
Ka pa ia Lele-pueo ka'a hihio o Ko'o-lau	The enclosure of Lele-pueo in the path of the Koo-lau wind
He po'o nui ia no Hana-lei-nui-a-moa	It is a great head of Hana-lei-nui-a-moa
Hohe no a Moa, a Moa Hiki-manu	Cowardice of Moa, Moa Hiki-manu
Ua like no laua me me Limu-nui-ke-one-o-Maha-moku	They are like Limu-nui on the sand of Maha-moku
Lu 'ia e 'oe o ka moe,	Scattered by you in sleep
Ha'ule wale ka lu pua pahele hala 'ole	Fell the scattered flowers without ensnaring
He mau la makani ia no Naue e	There are windy days of Naue
He naue i ke kai o Hina i Ma'a'a.	A movement in the sea of Hina in Ma'a'a.[307]

NOTES

284. Kamehameha III, 1840.
285. Kelsey collection.
286. Malo 1951, p. 179.
287. Malo 1951, pp. 158-159.
288. Malo 1951, p. 23.
289. Kamakau 1976, p. 132.
290. Malo 1951, p. 182.
291. Campbell 1967, p. 118.
292. Kamakau 1961, p. 181.
293. Malo 1951, pp. 146-147.
294. Volcanic activity on all the islands except Hawaii and Maui appears to have ceased before human occupation. The last volcanic eruption on Maui is believed to have occurred during the last half of the 18th century.
295. "Ulaula-o-ke-ahi, The-flaming-of-the-fire, is the name of the fire of Pele, not a nickname of Pele." (Kuluwai-maka n.d.)
296. "Puʻu-lena is called the love-snatching wind. It is a plea for Pele to give her *aloha.*" (Kuluwaimaka n.d.)
297. "This is an appeal to Pele for forgiveness of any slight the reciter may have committed." (Kuluwaimaka n.d.)
298. "In this case, *hoʻaliʻi* refers to the Pele worshipers." (Kuluwaimaka n.d.)
299. "Pele overstepped or went above her worshipers when an eruption occurred." (Kuluwaimaka n.d.)
300. *"Puke iki* and *nui* is how Pele flows here and there." (Kekahuna)
301. "Nawa is the release from their eating (tabu)." (Kuluwaimaka n.d.)
302. "Pele gave her followers notice so they can escape." (Kekahuna n.d.)
303. *Kuwa* is to talk loudly, make a din. (Kuluwaimaka n.d.) "If the people offended Pele she might disturb them all the time because of their offense. *Ku-wawa* means Pele was making noise." (Kekahuna n.d.)
304. Emerson, N.B., n.d.; Kelsey translation.
305. Kalaiwa n.d.
306. Keola, 1925.
307. Emerson, N.B., from Keoni Kaulahiwa Keomano, n.d.; Kelsey translation.

XVI NO KA LĀ A ME KĀ ʻIKE
For the Day and Knowledge

The gods, as man's ancestors, share every aspect of his life. They share his greetings to the day, give him the wisdom to live it well, and when needed, the ability to see the happenings in the days to come.

NO KA LA: FOR THE DAY

"Set aside the night, commence the day." For all, the manner in which one begins the day determines the quality of the day. These prayers acknowledge the presence of the gods and using allegory, express hopes for a good day.

E ala ua ao, ua malamalama	Awake, it is day, it is light
Ua hele kanaka aia iluna	Men are abroad
Ua kaio ka hoʻoka ula	The red dawn has shown itself
Ka hoʻoka lei	The bloom of morning
Nau i hoa i kau pu-awa,	You have consecrated the ʻawa root
Pu-awa uli, pu-awa kea	The dark ʻawa, the light ʻawa
Moa kane, moa wahine,	The cock and the hen.
Mahiki na kao, lele i ka lani[308]	*Na kao*[308] have arisen, have climbed the heavens
Owau ka lio-lio e-e, he aka.	I am a ghost, a spirit,
O ke aka no ia mai Kahiki-ku a Kahiki-moe	Now men are awaking from the eastern to the western pillars of heaven
Mai Kahiki-kapakapa ua e Kane	From Kahiki-kapakapa in the rain of Kane
Eia mai ka pule ka wai-oha	Here is a prayer to the water of purification
Kanaenae ia oe, e ke akua	Adoration to you, o god
E ola no e-e.	Give us life we pray.[309]

O Ka-welona a-ka-la ka wahine i ka ulu a ka makani.	The setting of the sun is the woman in the rising of the wind.
O Lau-makani ke kino	Many winds is the body
O Makani-keoe ko mana.	Wind-that-whistles is your spirit power.
O Lau-pouli ko kapa.	Many-darkness is your tapa.
E Uli e, nana ʻia	O Color-of-darkness (Uli) be seen
Nana ʻia i ka hoʻole mana	Let the denial of spirit power be seen
Hoʻole ʻike, hoʻole ola	Denial of knowledge, denial of life
Hoʻole akua e, ʻaʻohe akua	Denial of deity, no deity
Nawai la ka ʻole o ke kua?	Who will deny deity?
O kini i ke kua i Wai-mea	The many gods at Wai-mea
O ka lehu o ke kua iʻo Uli	The 400,000 deities with Uli
O ka mano o ke kua i Hale-mano	The 4,000 deities in Hale-mano
O ka pukuʻi akua ia Kane-a-ka-lau	The assembly of gods by Kane-a-ka-lau
O ka lalani i ke akua ia Ke-ao-lani	The genealogical line of the gods by Ke-ao-lani
O ke akua nunui a Ka-wai-nui	The great god by Ka-wai-nui
O ke akua liʻiliʻi kai a Maka-liʻi	The little deity who is by Maka-liʻi
Kua i Ka-wai-ʻea	Deity at Ka-wai-ʻea
O ke akua loloa kai a Lima-loa, kanaka o Mana	The very long deity who was by Lima-loa, man of Mana,
O ke akua pokopoko ka-i a Ha-makua-poko	The short god who is Ha-makua-poko
O ke akua o ka po ka i Kau-po	The god of the night who is Kau-po,
O ke akua o ke ao ka i ʻIao	The god of the day who is of ʻIao
Pale ka po, puka i ke ao	Set aside the night, commence the day.
O Ka-welona-a-ka-la ka wahine nona ua pule	The Setting-of-the-Sun is the woman of the prayer
Ke walina la	This is the termination.
Walina mai ana hoʻi i ko pule e----	Thy prayer is ended.[310]

PELA E ʻIKE AI KEIA MUA AKU: **TO KNOW THE FUTURE**

The ability to see the future can either reassure man or allow him to prepare for the unavoidable. It may also allow him to change the changeable.

This prayer was said by a *kahuna* named Popolo when he sought to see the future. While praying, he looked into a calabash of water to receive the messages of the gods.

Kanikau aʻe no ka Olopana,	Olopana laments,
Aloha ʻino no ka makua,	Great love has the parent,
E noho i ke ao malama,	To dwell in the light of day,
Aloha ʻino no hoʻi au,	Great love have I,
I hele hoʻokahi mai nei;	Who came here alone;
ʻAʻohe lua ʻaʻohe kolu,	Not two, not three,
ʻAʻohe kanaka e pono ai,	No persons would be suitable,
Lehulehu aku i ke alanui,	They were multitudinous in the road,
Ke ulakahi i pa-ki-wai.	The one way that splashed water.
Ninau na liʻi apau,	All the chiefs questioned,
Nawai keia keiki?	"Whose is this child?"
Na Ha-lulu na Kiwaʻa,	By Ha-lulu, by Kiwaʻa,
Na ka manu eia i ka hulu,	By the bird here at the feather,
Hoʻohonua piele ka,	Firmly established genealogical gourd vine stem,
I noho i kai ʻaeʻa,	Who dwelt in the sea of wandering,
Noho Ulukou i ka hanohano,	Ulukou dwelt in distinction,
Ua lilo mai la ka lani paʻa,	The solid heavens have been gained,
Pau pu me kanawai,	Together with law,
He ʻihi lani la he kalaʻihi,	A sacred heaven high one is a long vine,
O ke ʻano meha la ua pau,	The awesome loneliness is ended,
Ka walania o kuʻu akua,	The torment of my deity,
Haʻawina mai ke aka o Kane,	To give reflection of Kane,
I ku iluna o ka honua ʻaina,	That stood above the earth of the land,
I ke alo oʻu nei la,	In my presence here.
ʻAmama.	ʻAmama.

Then the *kahuna,* still looking in the calabash of water, prayed again as follows.

Hoʻokakaa lani i loli ka honua,	Roll about the heavens to change the earth
Kau mai ka ʻahuʻula ke ewe ka piko o ke akua,	Placed is the feather cape, the kinfolk, the umbilicus of the deity,
Iluna i Halulu ka lani,	Above at Halulu-ka-lani
I ka hale mahina poepoe	At the round moon house
I ka puka haiki pilikia	At the narrow opening of trouble
Puka ki-ke-ke a ke akua	The knocking opening of the deity
Ka wai hiona a Kanaloa	The slanting water of Kanaloa
A ke aka i malu o huʻahuʻakai,	Of the shaded reflection of frothy sea,
O Lono i ka oʻu aliʻi,	Of Lono of the royal supremacy,
O ku ʻioʻio moa,	My peeping chicken,
Owau keia o Pouliuli,	It is I, Pouliuli,
O Powehiwehi,	O Powehiwehi,
O ka popolo ku mai a Kane la.	The *popolo* of Kane that stands here.
Homai ka ʻike i ʻike nui,	Extend here knowledge that I may have much knowledge.
ʻEliʻeli kapu, noa iaʻu, ʻAmama.	Profound the tabu, freedom of tabu to me. ʻAmama.[311]

NO NA ʻAUAO: FOR WISDOM

The skill, wisdom, and power needed for all of man's successful actions can only come from the gods. This prayer asks for those gifts.

E Io e, e Io e,	O Io, o Io,
E ku, e manu e	O stand, o bird
Ke alu aku nei ka pule ia Hakalau	Combine prayers to overcome *haka-lau*

113

Kulia ka lani ia Uli	The heaven-high-one strives to obtain Uli in prayer
Ia namu ia nawe	To mutterings, to pant for breath
Ka nehe i luna, ka nehe i lalo	The rustlings above, the rustlings below
Kaa akau, kaa hema	Roll right, roll left.
Ku makani hai ka lani	The wind that splits the heavens,
Hekili kaakaa i ka lani	Thunder that rolls again and again
Kauila nui Makeha i ka lani	The great lightning that slashes in the heavens
Pane i ka lani e ola ke kanaka	Answer to the heavens, let the man live.
Ho mai ka loea, ka ike, ka mana	Bring cleverness, knowledge, supernatural powers
I ae ka honua la	So that earth may ascend
O waha lau ali'i	By the mouth of many chiefs
O kahi i waiho ai ka hua olelo	The place where words are left.
Elieli kau mai	Profound is the tabu that rests upon it
'Amama. Ua noa.	'Amama. It is free of tabu.[312]

UA PAU

NOTES

309. *Na Kao*. The darts are the belt and sword in the constellation of Orion. The darts are said to be those brought by Paao from Kahiki. (Beckley)
310. Emerson, N.B., n.d.; Kelsey translation.
311. Anonymous (1): Kelsey translation.
312. Anonymous, Kuokoa, March 3, 1922; Kelsey translation.
313. Taylor, A., December 1931, p. 78; Kelsey translation.

NÁ MÁNÁʻO NÁ HUA ʻOLELO
The Meanings of Words

ʻaʻala ula. A seaweed.

ʻaʻalii. SAPINDACEAE *Dodonaea* spp. (1-4). Tree.

ahole. *Kuhlia sandvicensis* fish.

aholehole. Young stage of the *ahole* fish.

ahupuaa. A land division that ideally went from the seashore to the mountain top.

ʻakia. THYMELAEACEAE *Wikstroemia* spp. (20). A plant used to stupify fish.

akua. For lack of a better term, this word is generally translated as god. However, the Polynesian concept of god does not parallel that of the traditional all-powerful, all-present divinity of Western man. The Polynesian "gods" are the personal ancestors of man and share many of his characteristics. They are called upon as family members.

ʻala. Dense, water-worn volcanic stone. Frequently used to hold or call a spirit.

ʻalaʻala heʻe. Liver of a squid or cuttle fish.

ʻalaʻala-wai-nui. Small native succulent of the Peperomia family, sometimes used in a medical treatment.

ʻalaealea. A shellfish.

ʻamaʻama. Mullet fish.

ʻape. ARACEAE *Alocasia mac rahiza*. The leaves of this plant were sharp and biting when placed in the mouth and were used to drive away evil spirits.

ʻauhuhu. LEGUMINOSAE *Papilionoideae Tephrosia purpurea*. This plant was used to stupify fish.

ʻaumakua. Family or personal spiritual guide or "god."

ʻawa. PIPERACEAE *Piper methysticum*. The drink prepared from this plant was part of every offering to the "gods."

ʻawapuhi kuahiwi. ZINGIBERACEAE *Zingiber zerumbet*. This fragrant member of the ginger family was used as a part of some medical treatments.

ʻaweoweo. A red fish frequently used as an offering. *Priacanthus.*

haku. Master, lord, overseer.

hala. PANDANACEAE *Pandanus ordoratissimus*. The leaves from this tree were used to make sails and baskets, and sometimes to thatch houses. The ripe fruit was strung into leis.

hala-pepe. LILIACEAE *Dracaena* spp. (3). One of the plants sacred to the *hula*.

halau. Building used to store canoes, or for instruction such as for *hula* training.

hale. House.

hau. MALVACEAE *Hibiscus tiliaceus*. Flowers and slime from the bark of this plant were used as medicine. Fiber from its bark was used to make rope.

heiau. Place of worship.

hokeo. Long gourd used to hold food, clothing, or fishing gear.

hu. A class of commoners.

huli. To turn, turn over.

ʻieʻie. PANDANACEAE *Freycinetia arborea*. This is one of the plants associated with the *hula*. It was used to make baskets.

ʻiliahi. SANTALACEAE *Santalum* spp. (7). Sandalwood.

iliau. COMPOSITAE *Wilkesia Gymnoxiphium*.

ʻilima. MALVACEAE *Sida* spp. (100+). The yellow flowers from this plant are used to make leis. It is also a medical plant.

imu. Underground oven.

inoa. Name.

ipu. CUCURBITACEAE *Lagenaria siceraria*. Gourd.

kahuna. Priest or expert in any profession.

kaikuaʻana. The older sister or female cousin of a female, or older male sibling of a male.

kala. Surgeonfish.

kalo. Taro. ARACEAE *Coladium esculenta*.

kanaenae. A form of prayer, a prayer chant.

kane. Man.

kapa. Tapa. Fabric made by pounding the bark of certain plants, the most popular being *wauke*.

kapu. Tabu, taboo. That which is forbidden, restricted, or required as well as certain rights.

kauila. RHAMNACEAE *Alphitonia ponderosa*. A hard wood used to make spears and digging sticks.

kauwa. Outcast.

ki. Ti. LILIACEAE *Cordyline terminalis*. The green leaves of this plant were used in all religious rituals. It is said to have the power to shield from evil.

kilu. A game. The player chants as he tosses the *kilu*, a small gourd or coconut shell, towards an object placed in front of a player of the opposite sex. If successful, the prize is a kiss or sexual favor.

kino aka. Spirit, especially of a living person.

koa. LEGUMINOSAE *Acacia koa*. This hardwood tree was used in building canoes.

kokio. MALVACEAE *Hibiscus kokio*.

konane. A game resembling checkers, played with pebbles on either a stone or wooden board.

kukui. EUPHORBIACEAE *Aleurites moluccana*. The nuts from this were used to provide lights and for medicine.

kulipeʻe. To creep along; to stumble awkwardly; to walk as weak-kneed.

kumu. Teacher.

kupua. A demigod.

kupukupu. A fern. DAVALLIACEAE *Nephrolepis* spp. (3).

lama. EBENACEAE *Diosryros ferrea.* The wood from this tree was favored for any buildings in a *heiau.*

lani. Heaven, heavenly. A term frequently applied to chiefs.

lauhala. The leaf of the *hala.*

lehua. See *ohia lehua.*

lei. Wreath made of flowers, leaves, nuts, fruit, feathers.

limu. General name for seaweed.

lu'au. Leaves of *kalo* (taro). Used as a modern term for feast.

maile. APOCYANACEAE *Alyxia olivaeformis.* The leaves of this sweet-smelling vine are used for a popular lei. It is one of the plants associated with the *hula.*

maka'ainana. Commoner.

makahiki. An annual season of about four months during which war was forbidden. It was also a season of special religious and sports activities. Its timing varied from island to island and in different districts.

malo. Loin cloth.

mana. Supernatural power that may be given, inherited, or won through prayers or actions.

manu. Bird.

mele. Song or chant. The term is frequently modified by words such as *inoa* (name) or *pule* (prayer).

mokihana. RUBIACEAE *Pelea barbigera.* The seeds of this tree have a spicy scent that makes them popular as a lei.

naka. A land shell.

ni'aupi'o. Child of a chiefly brother and sister or of a chiefly half-brother and a half-sister.

nu'u. Tower in a *heiau.*

'ohai. LEGUMINOSAE *Samanea saman.*

'ohe. Bamboo.

'ohi'a 'ai. Mountain apple.

'ohi'a lehua. MYRTACEAE *Metrosideros collina* subsp. *polymorpha.* In some *halau hula,* this tree is associated with the *hula.*

'ohi'a ha. *Eugenia sandwicensis.*

'olena. ZINGIBERACEAE *Curcuma domestica.* This member of the ginger family was used in some medical treatments, to scent tapa, and to make a bright yellow dye. Ground and mixed with water, it was used in rituals of purification.

olomea. CELASTRACEAE *Perrottetia sandwicensis.*

olona. URTICACEAE *Touchardia latifolia.* This bushy plant produces what may be the strongest vegetable fiber. It was used to make rope and cordage.

'o'o. Digging stick.

'o'opu. General name for fish in the Eleotridae and Gobidae families.

'opelu. *Decapterus pinnulatus.* Mackerel scad.

paepae. Platform.

paki'i. Various flat fish such as *Bolhus pantherinus,* etc.

palapalai. A fern also known as *palai.* Various ferns in ASPIDIACEAE, ASPLENIACEAE, DENNSTAEDT-TIACEAE, GRAMMITIDACEAE families.

pali. Cliff, steep hill.

pa'u. Wrap-around skirt worn by women, made of tapa.

pili. GRAMINEAE *Heteropogon contortus.* This grass was a favorite when thatching a house.

pi'o. Arch. Mating between chiefly brother and sister or chiefly half-brother and half-sister.

po. The twenty-four-hour period that begins at sunset one day and ends at sunset the next day. Each *po* has a different name which was given for the phase of the moon on that night. There are 30 *po* in each moon-month.

pohuehue. CONVOLVULACEAE *Ipomoea pes-caprae* subsp. *brasiliensis.* A morning glory. This plant was used medically.

poi. Kalo (taro), steamed and pounded soft. A major item in the ancient diet of the Hawaiians.

popolo. SOLANACEAE *Solanum melongena.* A frequently used medicinal plant.

pua. Flower.

puhenehene. A game in which a piece of wood or stone was hidden on the person of a player. Then the other players tried to guess on whom it was hidden.

pu-kiawe. EPACRIDACEAE *Styphelia* spp. (22.).

pule. Prayer.

'uha-loa. STERCULIACEAE *Waltheria americana.* A medically used plant that relieved mild pain.

'ula. Red. Also applied to things sacred, a ghost or spirit.

ulua. A certain species of game fish.

'ume. A sexual game.

'uwi'uwi. A variety of trigger fish, Balistidae.

wahine. Female.

wauke. Paper mulberry. MORACEAE *Broussonelia papyrifera.* The fiber of this plant provided the most popular raw material for making kapa (tapa).

weke. Certain species of surmullets or goat fish, Mullidae.

PAPA KUHIKUHI O NA PUKE
Annotated Bibliography

Amalu, Samuel Crowningburg
n.d. Hawaiian genealogist and writer. Personal conversations with author beginning in 1956.
1976 Honolulu Advertiser, May 6.

Anonymous (1)
n.d. Older male Hawaiian informant to author. Born on the island of Hawaii and said to be descended from a *kahuna* line.

Anonymous (2)
n.d. Older male Hawaiian informant to author. Born on the island of Kauai, his grandparents were from a canoe-building family.

Anonymous (3)
1922 "Makalei, ka Laau Pu Ona a ka Iʻa o Moaula-Nui-Akua I Kaulana," *Kuakoa* March 3.

Ashdown, Inez
n.d. Collection from various Hawaiian informants, largely from the island of Maui. Mrs. Ashdown was born in 1899, and has lived most of her life on that island. She served as Commissioner of Sites for that island as well as Maui County Historian.

Beckely, Fredrick Ka-ha-pula.
n.d. Born May 7, 1874, he was of chiefly descent. Well known for his writings on Hawaiian subjects, he was a professor of the Hawaiian language at the University of Hawaii. He was an informant to Kelsey.

Beckwith, Martha Warren
1917 "Hawaiian Shark Aumakua." *American Anthropologist.*
1970 "Hawaiian Mythology." Honolulu: University of Hawaii Press. Originally published in 1940.

Campbell, Archibald
1957 "A Voyage Round the World." Honolulu: University of Hawaii Press. Reprint of Third American Edition of 1822.

Cathcart, Arthur Kanohi
n.d. Born 1903. He is from the famed Lani-kaula line of Molokai. Informant to the author.

Cook, Tom
n.d. Late surveyor from the island of Hawaii. He was an informant to Kelsey.

Culin, S.
1899 "Hawaiian games." *American Anthropologist.*

Dickey, Lyle A.
1928. "String Figures from Hawaii." Honolulu: Bernice P. Bishop Museum.

Emerson, Joseph Swift
1918 "Selections from a Kahuna's Prayerbook."

Hawaiian Historical Society 26th Annual Report. Honolulu.
1921 "A Kite-flying Invocation from Hawaii." *American Anthropologist.*
1926 "Kahuna and Kahunaism." *Mid-Pacific Magazine.*

Emerson, N. B.
n.d. Unpublished notebooks in the possession of the author.
1903 Records of the Social Science Association of Honolulu.
1915 "Pele and Hiiaka: A Myth from Hawaii." Honolulu.
1965 "Unwritten Literature of Hawaii." Rutland & Tokyo: Charles E. Tuttle Company Inc. Reprint of 1909 edition.

Emerson, Oliver P.
1903. "The Awa Habit of the Hawaiians." *Hawaiian Annual,* Honolulu.

Fornander, Abraham
1917 "Hawaiian Antiquities and Folk-lore." Mem. Bernice P. Bishop Museum, Vol. IV.
1918 "Hawaiian Antiquities and Folk-lore." Mem. Bernice P. Bishop Museum, Vol. V.
1919 "Hawaiian Antiquities and Folk-lore." Mem. Bernice P. Bishop Museum, Vol. VI.

Green, Laura C. and Martha Warren Beckwith
1924 "Hawaiian Customs and Beliefs Relating to Birth and Infancy." *American Anthropologist.*
1926 "Hawaiian Customs and Beliefs Relating to Sickness and Death." *American Anthropologist.*

Gutmanis, June
1977 "Kahuna Laʻau Lapaʻau." Honolulu: Island Heritage Ltd.

Handy, E. S. Craighill
1941 "The Hawaiian Cult of Io." *Journal of the Polynesian Society,* Vol. 50. Wellington.

Handy, E. S. Craighill, and Mary Kawena Pukui
1958 "The Polynesian Family System in Ka-ʻu, Hawaii." Wellington: The Polynesian Society (Incorporated).

Henderson, Rosalie Akana Wong
n.d. Descendant of the high chief Paki, she was born in Lahaina, Maui, and had a lifetime interest in the Hawaiian language and culture.

Hoʻolapa, Daniel Kaʻonohi-lani
n.d. Born in 1864, he lived at Kahaluu, Kona, Hawaii. He was an informant to Kelsey.

Hoyt, Helen
  1976 "Night Marchers." Honolulu: Island Heritage,
      Ltd.
Hukilani, S. K.
  1864 "Na Akua o Koonei Poe I Ka Wa Kahiko" in
      Nupepa Kuokoa letter dated Lahainaluna,
      Maui, October 28, 1964.
Iokepa, James A.
  n.d. Born in 1864, he was a police seargent at Hilo,
      Hawaii. He was a special teacher and inform-
      ant to Kelsey.
Kaelemakule, John
  1929 "Ka moolelo oiaio o ko John Kaelemakule
      ola ana" in *Hoku o Hawaii* during the month
      of May. Born about 1853, Kaelemakule lived
      most of his life in the Kona district on the
      island of Hawaii where he was a storekeeper
      and a recognized authority on the old ways of
      life.
Kaiewe
  n.d. Informant of Kelsey's from island of Hawaii.
Kaimikaua, John
  1982 Quoted in "Views of the Hula." The Hawaiian
      News, October.
Kalaiwaa, Rev. William
  n.d. Born in 1875, Kalaiwaa was a Christian minis-
      ter but he was also called a *kahuna*. On March
      22, 1925, with George Kalama and "Hoohie
      of Kau," he performed rituals on the edge of
      Halemaumau to call Pele to return to the vol-
      cano. Although there was no eruption, when
      the offerings were ready to be cast into the pit
      there was an avalanch on the further wall.
      After the offerings, as an *'awa* root was hurled
      over the observation platform into the pit,
      large clouds of steam gushed into the air.
      Kalaiwaa died November 10, 1949.
Kalama, George P. K.
  n.d. Born at Piliwale, Molokai, in 1829, he was of
      high chiefly stock. An informant to Kelsey, he
      was an expert on the animal hulas. In 1925, at
      the age of 96, he acted as chief *kahuna* in a
      ritual to call Pele to the volcano (see above).
      "Twice before Kalama has wooed Pele and
      both times he has succeeded. Once was many
      years ago when the fire was quite low in the
      pit. Kalama came. . . . Then slowly, it is re-
      ported, the fire rose . . . again, three years ago
      (1922) . . . he was successful. . . ." *Paradise of
      the Pacific.* April 1925, p. 20.
Kalauaokalani, Mrs.
  n.d. Unidentified newspaper clipping believed to
      have been published in Hawaii during the
      early 1920s.

Kalokuokamaile, Z. P.
  n.d. Born in Ka'u, Hawaii, in 1847, he later lived
      at Napoopoo, Kona. He was a writer of many
      articles that appeared in Hawaiian language
      newspapers. He was an informant to Kelsey.
  1923 Articles appearing in the Hawaiian language
      newspaper *Ka Nupepa Kuokoa.*
Kamehameha III
  1840 "(The first) Constitution of Hawaii."
Kamakau, Samuel M.
  1961 "Ruling Chiefs of Hawaii." Honolulu: The
      Kamehameha Press.
  1964 "Ka Po'e Kahiko." Honolulu: The Bishop
      Museum Press.
  1976 "The Works of the People of Old." Honolulu:
      Bishop Museum Press.
Kapepa, Stanley
  1976 "A Canoe for Uncle Kila." Honolulu: Polyne-
      sian Voyaging Society.
Kealiinohomoku, Joann Wheeler
  1964 "A Court Dancer Disagrees with Emerson's
      Classic Book on the Hula." *Ethnomusicology.*
Ke-ahi-nui-o-Kilauea
  n.d. A chanter of note, she was the first wife of
      Kuluwaimaka.
Kekoa, William
  n.d. He was a resident of the island of Hawaii and
      informant to Kelsey.
Kelsey, Theodore
  n.d. Born in 1891, Kelsey seriously began studying
      and collecting Hawaiian language material as a
      young man. By the 1920s he was being called
      "an expert." Material from his work, largely
      from aged informants on the islands of Hawaii
      and Oahu, has appeared in the works of,
      among others, Martha Beckwith, Helen
      Roberts, E.S.C. Handy, and Clarice Taylor. He
      was a frequent contributor to Hawaiian lan-
      guage newspapers. He was also a contributor
      to the *Hawaiian Dictionary* (Pukui 1957). In
      1977 he was designated a "Living Treasure,"
      and in 1980 he was given a "Certificate of Ap-
      preciation" by Alu Like.
      In 1982 Brigham Young University —
      Hawaii Campus gave him the *Na Makua
      Mahalo 'Ia* award.
  1932 "The Prayer of the Gourd of Lono." Hono-
      lulu: *Paradise of the Pacific.*
Kenn, Charles
  n.d. Lecture notes made during the late 1960s.
  1976 (Translator) "Moolelo of Ancient Hawaii."
      Honolulu: Topgallant Publishing Co., Ltd.
      Moolelo Hawaii was originally published in
      1858 in the Hawaiian language.

Keola, James E. K.
1925 "Undertones of Real Belief Back of Volcano Ceremony that Pele Will Heed Wooing," *Honolulu Advertiser*, March 8.

Kepler, Angela Kay
1980 " 'Olona: Hawaii's Remarkable Fiber Plant." *The Maui Sun*, October 1.

Kia'aina
n.d. Of chiefly stock, Kia'aina was born on the island of Kauai in 1817. Later, he moved to Hilo where he lived near Honoli'i on the Hilo side of Wai'a'ea Stream. According to Kelsey, to whom he was an informant, Kia'aina had an *akua* named Mauna-loa, "which he had on a shelf covered with a towel. It was a quadrilateral pyramid a foot or two high, with dark markings on the sides, where Fire Goddess Pele sat is spirit form." The *akua* also "possessed the powers of a Ku'ula, or fisherman's deity, that attracts fishes." Kia'aina also enjoyed a reputation as a *kahuna hana aloha*, praying people in and out of love. He was also the source of many chants, remaining alert until his death in 1922 at age 104.

Koomoa, J. N.
n.d. From Hilo; a Hawaiian informant to Kelsey.

Kuluwaimaka, J. P.
n.d. Palea was the surname used by his family. He was a court chanter of King Kalakaua. Born at Na'alehu, Ka'u, his birth date has variously been reported as 1837 and 1847. It is said that as a young man he traveled with the court of Queen Emma. During the 1930s he worked with Kelsey at the Lalani Hawaiian Village in Waikiki "at the end of the trolley line." There they both lived in grass houses. A broken hip incapacitated him for the last year of his life. During that time, Kelsey cared for him, allowing him to continue living at Lalani in the old style he loved. As a result of his friendship with Kelsey, Kuluwaimaka consented to extensive recording of his chants which Kelsey made, transcribed, reviewed with older Hawaiians, and then translated. He died May 11, 1937.

Kapaiulu
1867 Interviews with Hawaiian medical practitioners on the island of Maui. State of Hawaii Archives.

Kupihea, David Malo
n.d. Born in 1872 at Ka-haka-'aulana, or "Sand Island," Kupihea was related to famed Hawaiian writer David Malo. He was an informant to Kelsey.

Luomala, Katherine
1949 "Maui, His Oceanic and European Biographers." Honolulu: Bernice P. Bishop Museum.

MacCaughey, Vaughan
1918 "The Olona, Hawaii's Unexcelled Fiber Plant." *Science*. September 6.

Makaena, Mrs. Namakahelu
n.d. A noted chanter, she was an informant to Kelsey.

Malo, David
1951 "Hawaiian Antiquities." Honolulu: Bishop Museum (reprint of 1903 edition).

Maunakea, Katherine
n.d. Born on Maui in 1907, Mrs. Maunakea is active in Hawaiian studies and cultural groups. She has written numerous Hawaiian songs, including many for children.
      She also teaches Hawaiian language and *lauhala* weaving. Mrs. Maunakea is an informant to the author.

Mika, Akoni
n.d. Samuel Antone Smith, better known by his Hawaiian name, was born at Kapahukua, Lawai, Kauai, in 1865. A *hula* expert, he moved to Hilo where he lived at Keaukaha. He was an informant to Kelsey, who introduced him to Helen Roberts, who in turn recorded a number of his chants, including several that appeared in her book, "Ancient Hawaiian Music."

Naone, John
1980 Student of Hawaiian culture, whose teachers have been mostly aged Hawaiians. Informant to author.

Porter, Kukona (Mrs. Daniel)
n.d. Aged resident of Hilo, she was an informant to Kelsey during the 1920s.

Pukui, Mary Kawena
n.d. Unpublished notes in possession of author.
n.d. "The Hula." Typescript in possession of the author.

Pukui, Mary Kawena, and Samuel H. Elbert
1965 "Hawaiian Dictionary." Honolulu: University of Hawaii Press.

Pukui, Mary Kawena, E. W. Haertid, and Catherine A. Lee
1972 "Nana I ke Kumu, Volume I." Honolulu: Lili'uokalani Trust.

Remy, Jules
    1868 "Contributions of a Venerable Savage." Boston Social Science Association of Honolulu. 1903. Minutes of the meeting of May 18.

Spencer, Thomas
    1895 "Ka buke lapaau me na mea pili kaulana." Honolulu. All this material was collected by Elisa Helekunihi, but was later published by Spencer.

Taylor, Ahuena
    1931 "The Cult of Iolani." *Paradise of the Pacific,* December.

Taylor, Clarice
    n.d. Miscellaneous clippings taken from the *Honolulu Star Bulletin.*

Thrum, Thomas
    1907 "Heiaus and Heiau Sites Throughout the Hawaiian Islands." *Hawaiian Annual.*

Titcomb, Margaret
    1948 "Kawa in Hawaii." *The Journal of the Polynesian Society.* Wellington.

Wise, John H.
    1911 Partially identified clipping from the newspaper *Ke au Hou.*

PĀPĀ HOʻIKE
Index

It might be noted that this index does not include either the introductory lines to *na pule* or their content.

NĀ ʻŌLELO HOʻOMĀIKAʻI
Acknowledgements

Neither the spirit nor the flesh of this book could have come into being without the help of many people. Some lived generations before I was born, others are still very young. To those who either in past or recent generations shared the knowledge of their ancestors, *Mahalo*. Theirs are the names that appear in both the footnotes and the bibliography. I would like to give a very special thank you to Theodore Kelsey, who in his ninety-second year continues to be an amazing source of information and help.

In alphabetical order I would also like to thank the following:

Sammy Amalu for always being available to try out ideas and whose often humorous comments usually stimulate or challenge;

Arthur K. Cathcart, who has shared many insights on the use and meanings of chants and names;

Bill Char for lots of sharing and hours of waiting;

Jean Dodge, whose amazing patience, imagination, and standard of excellence transformed poor spelling, bad typing, and questionable punctuation into this book;

David Forbes, who can always be depended upon to point a researcher in the right direction for needed information;

Ruth K. Hanner, without whose help this book and many other endeavors would not have been possible;

Sam Kaʻai, who is one of the "parents" of this book because, without his constant searching for information, it would not have been conceived;

Beatrice Krauss, whose frequent encouragement helped keep me at it;

Gary Larsen, who talked the concept over and did the first editing;

Lynette Mallery, who helped supply the thousands of pages of paper that it took to produce the manuscript;

Jan Kahalewai Merryman, who shared the papers of her mother, Rosalie Akana Wong Henderson;

Edith McKinzie and Kiki Mookini, who kept saying, "Do it!";

Marvin Puakea Nogelmeier, who was part of it all, all the way, and then did the proofreading;

Susan Rowe, for her strength in dealing with corrections and revisions;

Lisa Mansfield Vasiloff, who helped in many ways during the early days with typing, reading, and encouraging.

Carol Wilcox for her careful reading and excellent editorial suggestions.